Religion and Political Violence

This book uses the theory of social movements and first-hand interviews to create a new analysis of religiously motivated political violence in the modern world.

Examining the movement to restore Sharia law to a dominant place in the Egyptian government, the movement to make abortion illegal in the United States, and the religious effort to secure territory in Israel, the author contends that religion becomes violent not because of ideology or political context alone, but because of the constantly evolving relationship between them.

The ebb and flow of opportunities for political access ensures that secularization and religion, although polar opposites, depend on each other to define themselves. As a result, while their respective degrees of influence will inevitably undulate over time, both will remain a part of the political process for some time. Thus, a full understanding of both is critical to a meaningful understanding of the political process. Much work has been done to understand secular social movements as part of the political process, and consequentially researchers now know a great deal about the motivations, resources and timing of secular social movements. Considerably less research has been done in the field of religious social movements and this book fills that gap in the literature.

This book will be of great interest to students of political violence, religion, sociology, and Politics and International Relations in general.

Jennifer L. Jefferis is Assistant Professor in the Department of Government, Regent University, USA, and has a PhD in Political Science from Boston University.

Contemporary terrorism studies

Religion and Political Violence

Sacred protest in the modern world

Jennifer L. Jefferis

LONDON AND NEW YORK

First published 2010
by Routledge
2 Park Square, Milton Park, Abingdon, Oxon OX14 4RN

Simultaneously published in the USA and Canada
by Routledge
270 Madison Ave, New York, NY 10016

Routledge is an imprint of the Taylor & Francis Group, an informa business

© 2010 Jennifer L. Jefferis

Typeset in Times by Wearset Ltd, Boldon, Tyne and Wear
Printed and bound in Great Britain by TJI Digital, Padstow, Cornwall

British Library Cataloguing in Publication Data
A catalogue record for this book is available from the British Library

Library of Congress Cataloging in Publication Data
Jefferis, Jennifer L.
Religion and political violence: sacred protest in the modern world/
Jennifer L. Jefferis.
p. cm.
Includes bibliographical references (p.).
1. Religion and politics. 2. Violence–Religious aspects. I. Title.

BL65.P7J44 2009
322′.1–dc22

2009014381

ISBN10: 0-415-55038-6 (hbk)
ISBN10: 0-203-86918-4 (ebk)

ISBN13: 978-0-415-55038-3 (hbk)
ISBN13: 978-0-203-86918-5 (ebk)

To Adam, for always having faith.

Contents

Acknowledgments

When I first explained the concept of this book to a colleague, he rubbed his hands and gleefully exclaimed, "Wow, by the time you're done, everyone you write about will be mad at you! You'll make the religious mad for chronically depicting the advance of secularization and the secularists mad for rationally explaining the rise of the religious violence. How can I help?" In truth, this book could not have been written were it not for the cooperative efforts of people from every sector I've written about. Far from expressing displeasure, members of the religious organizations I wrote about welcomed my efforts to better understand their perspective, and countless "secularists" have devoted time and energy to perfecting this manuscript. I am especially grateful to Ibrahim Hudaiby and other members of the Muslim Brethren for welcoming all my questions and helping me to get even the smallest ones answered. I appreciate Donald Spitz for granting me access to the extensive writings of the Army of God, and to the anti-abortion movement supporters who took the time to talk with me about their cause. I am thankful for the influence Cathie Jo Martin, Emad Shahin and Misagh Parsa had on the early versions of this project. I am indebted to Jessica Medhurst for the hours she spent solving my computer crises. And, of course, I am most grateful of all to my husband for seeing where this could go before I did, and refusing to let me quit.

Introduction

> Those who say religion has nothing to do with politics do not know what religion
> is.
>
> (Mahatma Gandhi)

If a seer is to be judged by the accuracy of his or her prophesy, it may be time to
blot Marx, Freud and Weber from the pages of the social scientists' prophetic
honor roll. At the turn of the twentieth century, these men, among others, heralded the imminence of secularism and, by extension, the demise of religion. Yet
the turn of the twenty-first century has seen not the decline of religion, but rather
its promotion to world-news center stage. While in the 1980s few, if any,
international-terrorist organizations alluded to religion when explaining their
political motivations, the 1990s saw the emergence of religiously motivated
political violence all over the globe. One-third of the international terrorists
groups listed in the St. Andrews Chronology of International Terrorism were
religious in 1994; in 1995 in was 46 percent, and by 1998 more than half were
religious.[1] And this only alludes to the religious organizations promoting violent
action; peaceful religion has flourished as well. In the United States, the 1980s
and 1990s gave birth to the Moral Majority, the Christian Coalition and the
"megachurch." The religious-settlers movement in Israel has demonstrated
remarkable staying power, and one need only to walk down the streets of Cairo
to observe the re-emergence of religious fervor evidenced by men in long white
galabeyyas and women in brightly colored headscarves.

Why, if secularization is as pervasive as sociologists predicted it would be,
are we seeing a rise in religious movements at the end of the twentieth century?
Further, how can we explain the wholly different methods of opposition adopted
by different sectors of the same movement? Were the giants of the twentieth
century wrong? Has secularization been halted in its steps?

This book argues that secularization has unfolded in much the way that Marx,
Freud and Weber predicted it would – but that the advance of secularization has
not entailed the waning of religion. In fact, it is the advance of secularization
that has led to the rise of religiously motivated violence. More specifically, as
religious organizations perceive their access to the political process to become

increasingly limited, they either temper their rhetoric to increase their access, or become more shrill in their condemnation of the process that excludes them. As these organizations become more shrill, they are further excluded from the process, which reinforces the urgency of their cause. As their rhetoric intensifies, they are identified as radicals by the political center, and are limited in the types of organizational structure they can develop. They compensate by developing cell structures that are linked not by the traditional bonds of member ties, but by a frame that ties individuals to God, and emphasizes their moral and religious duty to physically fight secularization.

This book explores three religious opposition movements: the Christian fight against abortion in the United States, the Muslim pursuit of Sharia law in Egypt and the religious-settlers movement in Israel. In each of the three movements, time has produced a fissure between organizations and individuals willing to use violence and organizations and individuals committed to non-violent protest. In each case, the variables of rhetoric, structure and ideology interact to produce unique methods of protest.

A better understanding of the reasons behind the recent rise in religious movements, and a subsequent understanding of their choice of methods, is valuable for a number of reasons.

The ebb and flow of opportunities for political access ensures that secularization and religion, although polar opposites, depend on each other to define themselves. As a result, while their respective degrees of influence will inevitably undulate over time, both will be a part of the political process for the indefinite future. Thus, a full understanding of both is critical to a meaningful understanding of the political process. Much work has been done in past decades to understand secular social movements as part of the political process, and consequentially researchers now know a great deal about the motivations, resources and timing of secular social movements.[2] Considerably less has been done in the field of religious social movements. This book aims to address this dearth.

Second, if religion is likely to be a force within politics for some time to come, it behooves researchers to better understand the methods religious organizations use to achieve their goals. Despite the high level of visibility afforded to violent groups justifying their acts in the name of religion, there is a surprisingly low level of understanding about the conditions enabling this trend to spread.

At present, a chasm exists between the work of those scholars who study violence in religious movements and those who study secular social movements. Scholars of religion often look to religion as a source of violence. In doing so, they fail to consider the importance of the environment in which religious organizations operate as a predictor for their behavior. In contrast, scholars trying to understand contentious protest from a social movements' perspective have traditionally focused entirely on the grievances and motivations of the participants,[3] while often ignoring the underlying belief systems that may have influenced the existence of the grievances or motivations.[4]

While neither perspective is wrong, both are incomplete: it is impossible to understand religion without considering the environment in which it operates, and it is equally impossible to understand the environment without considering the role religion has played in shaping it. The growing prevalence of the religious justification of violence signifies a need for a conceptual bridge that eliminates the gap between two disciplines. This study seeks to help bridge that gap by using theoretical models that can account for both disciplines to better understand the role of religion in the justification of political violence.

Continuing to keep research of religion separate from other social-science research presents a danger of perpetuating inaccurate understandings of the significance of religion. After the attacks of September 11, the term "Islamic Terrorism" became commonplace, and there is a dangerous tendency to see the two terms as causally linked. Indeed, some scholars argue that decisions to use violence rest on beliefs inherent to specific religious texts.[5] Certainly, the cataclysmic events of September 11 brought to the forefront the use of religion and texts thereof to justify violence, but such human-derived justification must not be confused with absolute truth. Rather, it should alert scholars to the importance of understanding such justification as a method for recruitment and further mobilization.

Furthermore, some scholars consider religion as a variable to be as orientalist and out of date as the variable of culture. In fact, scholars of this camp see religion and culture as being very much the same thing. This narrow perspective has limited the understanding of religion in conflict, and consequentially it has ceased to be understood as a significant variable at all. If given credibility at all, religion is seen as a recruitment tool or an element of motivation in conflicts that are not religious at all, but rather economic or political.[6]

On the other hand, several scholars treat religion as an aberration to be solved, rather than a variable capable of assisting in the solution to other puzzles. These scholars seek to understand why religious movements exist at all in otherwise modern societies.[7] The problem with the first school is that it ignores an important aspect of religion – the choice to embrace it. When religion is viewed as something one can be born into, one lacks a central aspect of understanding the passionate devotion of followers and the willful actions that result. In classifying religion as any other variable (i.e. age, sex, ethnicity), one loses the ability to measure the importance of belief and meaning. As long as religion is seen as a refuge for the deviant or isolated members of society, its true significance will remain misunderstood.

Finally, by demystifying the relationship that exists between religion and the use of political violence, society faces a greater likelihood of stemming its existence. When words like "fundamentalists", "evangelicals" and "religious terrorists" are tossed around without careful consideration of their meaning, blame is directed where understanding would be more valuable. When groups such as the Army of God are seen as indistinguishable from the Christian Coalition in the United States, or al Jama'a al Islamiyya from the Muslim Brethren in Egypt, society loses the ability to understand the methods – and, more importantly, the distinctions – of either.

This book will argue that the re-emergence of religion in the political arena is a predictable response to the advent of secularization, and the opportunities available to the religious opposition influence the methods these organizations choose to pursue their goals.

Accordingly, the book is organized into three parts. The first part will argue that the secularization of the political arena has led to the development of religious social movements in efforts to stem that tide. Religious movements develop in response to recognition that opportunities for political access are waning, and organizations develop their rhetoric in response to this understanding.

Chapter 1 of this book will show that, over the last century, the world has undergone dramatic secularization, but that this secularization did not edge out religion as had previously been expected. Instead, religion has emerged as a powerful opposition movement in many areas. Chapters 2 and 3 will examine how the political and social transformations of secularization affected the United States and Egypt in the latter half of the twentieth century. These transformations resulted in the secularization of the political arenas and left religious organizations to act as opposition to secularization. History in both countries will show that doctrinally different organizations and individuals coalesced into definable movements when the cleavage between the power of the secular state and the legitimacy of the religious organizations became too great to ignore.

The second part will explore four religious–political organizations in an effort to understand what leads some organizations to embrace violence. This part will demonstrate that the non-violent Christian Coalition in the United States and the Muslim Brethren[8] in Egypt had similar ideologies to their violent counter-parts (the Army of God and al Jama'a al Islamiyya), but implemented these ideologies in categorically different rhetorical styles. I will show that organizations within movements adopt rhetoric to reflect their understanding of the urgency of their cause. The severity of the religious rhetoric serves to quicken the closing of the window of opportunity, forcing organizations either closer to the mainline secular center or further to the fringe of society.

Chapters 4 and 5 will show that religious organizations are not helpless bystanders watching a window of opportunity close beyond their control. In fact, the rhetoric that an organization adopts influences the degree of access that organization will have to the political process. As will be seen with the Muslim Brethren and the Christian Coalition, when rhetoric is vague enough to support a pluralist ideology, organizations maintain at least limited access to the political sphere. However, as in the case of the Army of God and al Jama'a al Islamiyya, when organizations believe their cause to be so urgent as to make efforts toward pluralism inappropriate, a more rigid and radical rhetoric is developed. While this rhetoric effectively categorizes the strength of their opposition to the current order, it also serves to more quickly sever their access to that order. The consequence is that the window of opportunity closes more quickly which, ironically, reinforces the urgency of the cause, and the rigidity of the rhetoric.

Moreover, location at the fringe of political society limits the structure organizations are able to create and maintain. Chapter 6 of this book will explore the theoretical discussions of organizational structure from two different fields. It will be demonstrated that social-behavior theory indicates violence is more likely to occur in organizations with hierarchal structures because such structures reduce the dissonance individuals may otherwise experience in causing harm to others. The presence of a clear and constant line of authority allows not only for shifts in blame and guilt, but also limits the opportunity for the questioning of the ideological frame that justifies violence.

However, as the case studies will show, there is no evidence of this pattern in any of the four cases. In fact, the Christian Coalition and the Muslim Brethren, the two organizations that have eschewed violence, both have clear hierarchal structures, while the two organizations that have embraced violence do not. Further complicating the puzzle is that social-movement theory comes to a seemingly contradictory conclusion – arguing that hierarchal structure lends itself to greater efficacy and by extension, greater opportunities for success. This chapter will show that the location of radical movements at the fringe of society limits their ability to form hierarchal organizational structures, decreasing their chances for success and increasing their perceptions of isolation from the political process. The consequence is that these organizations see an increased need for drastic change. And therefore, while structure has traditionally been accredited with the most comprehensive explanation for the development of violence, religious belief can act as an intangible alternative to structure when the ideology of the organization frames violence not as a right, but as a responsibility.

Chapter 7 will show that both the Army of God and al Jama'a al Islamiyya have moved from justifying violence to demanding it. Both organizations make clear that the condemnation of violence is a condemnation of God's perfect plan for society. The individual that would issue such a condemnation is not only at odds with the leadership of the organization, but with God Himself. In the Army of God, God is the recognized General. The frame that makes questioning violence equivalent to questioning God, in combination with the omnipresent and omnipotent nature of God, makes Him as effective in policing doubters as any human hierarchy could ever be.

In the last part of the book, we will investigate the religious-settlers movement in Israel in light of the theoretical principles of the first two parts. The settlers movement has many characteristics that mirror those found in the four case studies explored in the previous parts, yet it also exhibits striking differences. Chapter 8 will show that Israel is following a secularization trajectory very similar to Egypt and the United States. Chapter 9 will argue that, while religiously motivated political violence has thus far been kept to a minimum, as this trajectory continues we will see a clear division between groups in the movement that will not use violence, and those that will consider it a religious duty.

A note on methodology

The purpose of this study is to understand, first, the recent advance in religious opposition to the political order, second, the variance in religious groups willing to use violence to further their political interests and, third, its applicability to future cases. It is asserted here that a dual-focus political opportunity process and ideological frameworks will best allow one to focus on these components. Research conducted for this project was based on the assumption that a comparative study of the differing frameworks between violent and non-violent organizations, and different monotheistic religious groups, will illuminate the process that leads religious organizations to use violence to achieve their political ends.

This book has explored religious social movements in three countries, looking specifically at the Muslim Brethren and al Jama'a al Islamiyya in Egypt, and the Christian Coalition and the Army of God in the United States, and Gush Emunim and the broader religious-settlers' movement in Israel. Also considered were each group's methods and actions in pursuit of their particular political goal.

These cases were selected to address a central question for a number of reasons. The majority of studies to date that deal with violent religious social movements at all have focused on exclusively violent[9] or exclusively peaceful cases.[10] While these studies offer valuable insight into these cases, their generalizability to the question of why some groups use violence when others do not is limited.

It is the contention here that by only studying groups that incorporate violence and contrasting them to those that have shunned it can one really draw conclusions about conditions that lead to violent behavior. It is easy to argue that those using violence are suffering from deprivation and isolation, but this conclusion becomes much less powerful when contrasted to similar individuals suffering from nearly identical levels of deprivation and isolation, and yet who still choose *not* to use violence.

Second, while many researchers have argued that religion is inherently violent, few have studied two religions in direct contrast to understand whether the specific type of religion influences the kind of action likely to be undertaken – violent or non-violent. It is assumed here that by studying the ideological frames of three different monotheistic religions, a stronger conclusion will be reached regarding the manner in which ideas of a particular religion influence the structure of an organization and the behavior of its members. Accordingly, it will be demonstrated that the conclusions drawn from the case studies in the first two parts can be used to inform the development of a predicted case in the third part.

However, there are inevitable limits to this type of study. For instance, this book began with the intent of compiling databases of quantifiable (and thus, statistically comparable) information about each group. However, due to the limitations placed on research in Egypt,[11] the available pool of interview sources for this project shrank below that which was originally intended. While greater success was achieved in speaking with supporters of the Army of God, efforts to generate thoroughly objective statistics about the Army and the Christian Coalition were not remarkably successful either. In the case of the Army of God, a number did respond to surveys issued, but the answers on these surveys were not consistent with answers given in one-on-one correspondence via letters or telephone.

While methodological theory would usually suggest that inter-personal inter-action would cause subjects to be more reserved, in reality the opposite proved to be the case. Those surveyed were willing to discuss their use of violence, but they filled out surveys to reflect a more peaceful approach than originally dis-cussed. These limitations have been compensated for by balancing what was learned: through personal interviews and materials published by each group, through past interviews they have done with other academics, and through his-torical accounts of their actions and behaviors.

Hopefully, what this study lacks in statistical generalizability will be balanced out by what it provides in terms of information about these case studies, as well as the theoretical conclusions it draws about the relationship between structure, ideology and action. This study is neither intended nor qualified to be the last word on this complex subject. Rather, it ought to be taken as a modest attempt to justify the value of bringing the study of religion into the study of politics, in an effort to increase the understanding of each.

Part I

Out of the arena

The changing place of religion in politics

1   Changing political landscapes

The National Consortium for the Study of Terrorism and Responses to Terrorism has been tracking incidences of political violence since 1970. Their databases show that in the United States between 1970 and 1979 incidences where religion was the motivating cause for violence occurred only 2.8 percent of the time (when the causes were known). This stands in contrast to the period between 1980–1984 where religious motivations were behind 45.3 percent of the attacks, and 1985–1989 with 96.2 percent, and 1990–1995 with 95.8 percent.[1] This trend is also evident on a global scale. As was discussed earlier, the incidences of religiously motivated terrorism have increased from almost none in 1980 to over half of reported terrorist incidences in 1998.[2]

The introduction to this book described a recent rise in religiously motivated political violence and suggested that such a rise is puzzling in light of the dominance of secularization over most elements of society and the state in the twentieth century. As a discipline, political science has made significant advances toward explaining the development, timing and success of secular social movements, but there is still much left misunderstood about religious movements.

This chapter endeavors to explain the extent of the changes in religiously motivated social movements, the subsequent acts of political violence alluded to in the introduction to this study and the reasons for these changes. This chapter will argue that the advancements in secular social-movement theory can be equally valuable to the understanding of religious social movements, particularly in explaining their recent rise and subsequent methods.

The trend in increasing number of religiously motivated violent incidences is troubling for a number of reasons. In the first place, it is scholastically puzzling in light of the theories that have shaped society's expectations about religion since the turn of the twentieth century. Sociological giants no less than Spencer,[3] Marx,[4] Durkheim,[5] Freud[6] and Weber,[7] and more recently (though no less impressive), Berger,[8] Wilson[9] and Lenski,[10] have all heralded the march of the industrialized world toward secularization and rationalization, the latter by association. Thus, the continued presence (and in some cases, dominance) of religion in political life is in itself a mystery to be solved.

But more disconcerting is the effect these secularization theories have on academia's ability to understand this continuing phenomenon. Indeed, so much time has been spent discounting the future of religion that its surprising increase in importance must be met by a mad scramble to understand its significance. Yet this effort is also hindered by the lingering understanding of religion as aberrational. After all, if the trend toward secularization reflected a move toward rationalization, then does the re-emergence of religion not indicate a regression of some sort? This manner of thinking limits the tools for studying religion to those used to explain irrational or deviant behavior.

In this part of the book, it will be argued that the re-emergence of religion is not a rejection of rationality, but a predictable response to changing political circumstances. Indeed, as will be seen in the following pages, religious movements are currently following the path set by liberal, secular movements decades earlier. In fact, the success of secular liberal movements changed the political landscape such that religious movements were edged out of the political process. These religious movements then turned to opposition tactics in an attempt to reverse this trend.

When seen in this way, there is no reason why the tools that allow for a better understanding of secular organizations cannot be used to facilitate one's understanding of religious movements. The field of social-movements theory began with an assumption that only deviants became involved in protest, but advanced to recognize far more useful indicators of opposition. This same advancement has not occurred in the investigation of religiously motivated movements. In fact, consistent predictions (and empirical evidence) for the secularization of society have resulted in religious movements being viewed as aberrational. The consequence of this is that religious movements are perceived to be different from secular movements, and are most frequently explained using the variables that were limited to the earliest (and least informative) elements of social-movements theory.

The current research into the phenomenon of religious political activism is generally divided between those who study religion and those who study politics, with very little interaction between the two fields. Scholars of religion look primarily to religious texts to predict the behavior of religious adherents. The amount or type of violence within sacred texts is frequently identified as a predictor for violence committed by believers. Scholars of politics, in contrast, are frequently informed by secularization theory, and consequently attempt to explain religion as a front for other conditions. Both the anti-abortion movement in the United States and the Islamist movement in Egypt have frequently been identified as a consequence of unfavorable social and economic circumstances.

Scholars of religion had done much to clarify the theology that drives a movement, but are not able to explain the development, timing and success of religious movements in the political arena. Scholars of politics are frequently so puzzled by the presence of religion in politics at all that they focus on explaining the puzzle of the existence, rather than the elements that religious movements have in common with their secular counterparts. As a result there is little understanding about how the beliefs of a movement interact with the environmental conditions in which the movement operates to influence the political outcome.

This section will argue that the rise in religious movements can be best explained as a reaction to a perceived closing of a window of opportunity. While secularization had been marching across politics for decades, religion had long been afforded a parallel sphere of legitimacy. When decisive events occurred that dramatically challenged the ideology that had protected the separate sphere, religionists – even those of different theological backgrounds – rose up in a movement to prevent it.

Theories of social movements

Social-movements theory was originally predicated on the belief that only deviant individuals sought reform outside the existing political system.[11] The multiple centers of power were perceived to make the political process as a whole extensively permeable and thus open to efforts at reform from any sector, whether generated from the elites or the masses.[12] Social-movement theorists sought to understand the anomalies that produced deviant behavior. Most commonly, a sense of isolation, or other psychological feelings of inadequacy, were believed to prompt individuals to act in ways that undermined the existing structure.[13]

By the mid-1960s, academics began to doubt this interpretation, in part because of the recognition that even liberal democracies were not as permeable as had been previously imagined.[14] Not only does this approach fail to consider the ubiquitous nature of deprivation in the face of less than occasional social uprising, it also ignores the data that proves that most activists were not among the dredges of society. Rather, they are well-educated, economically stable individuals.[15] This forced the realization that it is not only "dysfunctional deviants" that seek political change. In fact, it is most commonly the well-educated, economically stable and politically active elites that headed and organized social movements.

These realizations turned the discussion from movement members to movement resources. Resources are seen as a finite entity, for which groups compete. When one group succeeds in obtaining a resource that was previously uncommitted to any cause, that resource is no longer accessible to other groups. The attainment of that resource can explain the difference between action and inaction.

But this still does not account for the way outside events influence the landscape of the political arena, causing openings to occur at random times. Social groups that are equipped to take advantage of these openings are able to develop into social movements. Kingdon uses the concept of a "policy window" to make the point.[16] This window opens for a short time depending on factors external to political or social institutions.

This phenomenon is evident in the American feminist movement of the 1960s. The women's movement rode into the public consciousness behind the more volatile issues of the day – including anti-war protests and the Civil Rights movement. But between 1965 and 1975, women's issues were catapulted into public awareness, and politicians endeavored to close the newly revealed "gender gap."[17]

Further, movement activists assimilated themselves into other areas of the socio-political arena, establishing a variety of organizations that dealt specifically with women's issues including rape, abuse, gender equality, etc. The development of these organizations served as a breeding ground for later social developments.[18] While it was the political opportunity afforded by the Civil Rights and anti-war movements that facilitated feminists' entry into the arena, it was nonetheless the permeability of the institutions that allowed the changes they advocated to be implemented, as well as the ability of the institution to change which allowed these reforms to be maintained.

We can see a similar principle at work in the decrease in violent acts by nonreligious movements from 1980–1999. This decrease was due in part to the assimilation of the issues for which the secular movements mobilized: the state and social institutions. A more dramatic example of this assimilation process is the case of Bernadine Dorhn and Bill Ayers, former leaders in the Weatherman organization.

Dorhn and Ayers spent most of the 1970s advocating an armed revolution against capitalism in favor of socialism.[19] They were responsible for bombing multiple government buildings including the Capital and the Pentagon in an effort to further their agenda. Dorhn and Ayers turned themselves in to the authorities in 1980, served less than a year in prison, and now both work as professors – Dorhn at the Northwestern University School of Law, and Ayers as a professor of education at the University of Chicago. Dorhn also serves as the director of Northwestern's Children and Family Justice Center.

Ayers and Dorhn have remained committed to their cause, if not their method (although in a 2001 interview Ayers answered that he did not regret his role in the bombings, in fact he "felt we didn't do enough"[20]). And yet, they have been assimilated into society to the point where they are respected members of a relatively elite community. This level of acceptance would not be possible had the structures and norms with which they endeavored to overthrow capitalism not changed in response to their actions.[21] Thus, the social and political revolutions that characterized the 1960s and 1970s succeeded in restructuring the political landscape to reflect their cause. This explains not only society's acceptance of ex-activists, but also ex-activists' acceptance of the new society, which may help to account for the decrease in non-religious violent action.

Limits to the current understanding of religious social movements

Just as the social-movement scholars used to believe that socio-psychological factors provide the impetus for deviant behavior, so do many current scholars seeking to explain forms of religious activism. The structural crises that have developed as a result of dramatic upheavals in the economic, social and political structures of modern society during the height of developmentalism are used to explain the advent of activism.[22]

A number of missing elements that lead to deprivation-motivated protest have been identified. Because religion is more prevalent in agrarian and rural than post-industrialist societies, religion has been tied to the absence of human security. Religion in this context offers the reassurance that although events may prevent an individual from understanding or predicting what lies ahead, there still exists a higher power that not only understands, but a power that even controls such things.[23] Belief reduces the stress individuals feel and allows them to cope with everyday problems as they occur. Furthermore, the lack of predictability in their lives makes individuals crave the rigidity and predictability of religion. This argument is interesting because deprivation is examined on two levels. First, the economic deprivation on a national scale makes a state unable to alleviate challenges to individuals within its borders, and second, this then leads to deprivation of security on an individual scale.

This urbanization and economic-deprivation theory suggests that individuals are most likely to embrace extremism when they face economic hardship and social dislocation. Extremism offers resources, networks and a target – all of which lessen the ramifications of hardship and dislocation. Religion offers an appealingly rigid and predictable set of rules and a persuasive justification of hardship.

Other scholars make a similar argument from a slightly different perspective, suggesting that the legitimation crisis facing many regimes today (in light of the shift from a moral to an economic basis of legitimacy) increases political instability, which exacerbates economic, political and personal unpredictability.[24] And instability need not be relegated to the political realm. As populations shift into more urbanized settings, an individual's susceptibility to the use of violence can rise. These individuals are unaccustomed to the social norms of the metropolis, and become socially isolated. They are then all the more susceptible to the messages being preached of radical Islam, which are a direct tie back to the values they knew from their rural beginnings.[25] Numerous Middle East scholars argue that as Arab states took strides toward Westernization, cleavages developed that left many Arabs feeling isolated.[26] Islam, and Islamic activism, provided these individuals with the means and a justification for seeking change.

Attempts to explain the religious elements of the anti-abortion movement are also almost exclusively limited to explanations of deprivation theory. Movement members are described as being motivated by a fear of modernity[27] and consequential threats to patriarchy, and the anti-abortion movement is argued to be an attempt to bring traditionalism and patriarchy back into social dominance.[28] The same reasoning is used to explain Islamic political violence.

Explanations that look to external variables to explain movement action serve a valuable function in shifting the debate about religious violence outside the constraint of religious exceptionalism. But they are still limited in what they can explain. If violence were limited to those experiencing social, economic or even political deprivation, then we should be able to demographically predict organizational action merely by looking at their membership rosters.

It should be possible to identify members of religious groups employing violence based on their experiences with recent urban migration, economic hardship, social dislocation and low levels of human security. Further, the religious organizations that individuals join should demonstrate an ability to provide counteracting influences to these economic, social and natural disasters.

And there is evidence to support these explanations. Most would agree that Egyptian society has experienced rapid and dramatic urbanization in the twentieth century. However, if this explanation is correct, one should be able to compare the periods of rapid urbanization with periods of high incidences of violence and find a reasonable correlation.

In the case of Al-Ikhwan al-Muslimin, this correlation does tentatively exist. The period between 1947 and 1966 represents the highest level of urbanization from the inception of the organization in 1928 until 1987.[29] It was during this same time period that the Brethren established the Secret Apparatus and frequently employed violence. However, the same is not true of Jama'a al-Islamiyya. Jama'a al-Islamiyya launched the majority of their attacks between 1992 and 1998. During this time, urbanization was measured at an average rate of 1.7 percent each year.[30]

Deprivation theory suggests that groups employ violence when economic conditions are at their worst. Thus, one would expect to see a correlation between low or non-existent levels of economic growth and high levels of incidences of violence. But this is quite the contrary actually. In the period between 1929 and 1973, the years 1959–1964 represented a 6.4 percent increase in Egypt's growth in national income.[31] This, in fact, is the highest growth in income during the entire period by almost double. Yet, this was also the time in which the Muslim Brethren most actively flirted with using violence as a strategic tool. In light of this, one is also forced to consider that, in the case of al Jama'a al Islamiyya, one of their primary targets was, incidentally, the tourism industry. For if they were conducting violent acts as a result of economic deprivation, choosing a major source of income as a target is a rather odd strategy to employ.

The social-alienation theory faces similar challenges. For this explanation to be conclusive, one would expect to see that members of the organizations represented the most isolated members of the newly urbanized society. While there is little question that urbanization stretched the traditional networks that dominated rural societies, evidence does not demonstrate a disintegration of these networks, but rather a reorganization of them.[32] Moreover, research shows that the members of these groups are among the most socially connected members of society.[33] In Egypt, the members of the governing council of the Muslim Brethren are among the best connected members of Egyptian society. Most have graduate degrees, several have PhDs; there are doctors, lawyers and incredibly wealthy individuals quite high up in the organization.[34] A number of members have successfully run for Parliament, and at various times throughout the existence of the organization, they have dominated many of the syndicates that are a significant part of Egyptian civil society. Further, in the United States, at its height, the Christian Coalition was dominated by suburban soccer moms.[35] The anti-abortion movement incorporated these soccer moms with Benedictine monks, Vietnam War protesters and stalwart members of the conservative Republican Party.

Moreover, as will be demonstrated in subsequent chapters of this book, when religious organizations are at odds with the state, they are unable to structure themselves in such a way as to provide the tangible security that the deprivation argument would suggest is imperative. In fact, in both Egypt and the United States, members of violent religious organizations face far greater uncertainty and danger as a result of their antagonism of the state; indicating that pursuit of physical security is insufficient to explain religious extremism.

At a minimum, such evidence indicates there are significant limits to explanations that suggest only deviants engage in religiously motivated social protest. Just as the field of social-movement theory evolved to incorporate a more nuanced understanding of secular movements, those endeavoring to understand religious movements must do the same. As will be explained in the following section, however, the present artificial separation that exists in scholarship of religion, violence and politics has prevented this from happening.

A review of two schools of thought – religion and violence, and religion and politics

Studies abound in the field of American political science testing the impact of religion on politics, or more specifically, the influence of religious institutions on the actions of religious and political constituents. Scholars have probed the links between religious organizations and successful voter mobilization,[36] electoral dominance[37] and civic participation.[38] Other scholars have approached the question of religious influence from another angle – exploring the effect of religious fundamentalism on non-religious voters.[39] Others, still, seek to understand the "puzzle" of religious identification.[40]

While these studies are useful in assessing the impact of individual organizations on political participation and involvement, they fail to articulate whether, and in what way, religious organizations differ from their secular counterparts in terms of their treatment in political science research. In fact, the conclusions drawn in these studies seem to indicate that there is no difference between them at all.

Studies have demonstrated that religious organizations have a greater impact in mobilizing voters than do political parties, but these results can be generalized to incorporate any type of interest group – religious or otherwise.[41] We know that the Christian Right has become more successful in gaining political influence by following the models established by successful secular movements,[42] and that the churches are effective at using community resources to engage citizens in the political process.[43] However, the only studies in the field directly addressing the uniqueness of religion do so under the assumption that support for its existence is an aberration to be solved.[44] The tools used by these researchers in pursuit of their conclusions are valuable: a better understanding of religiously motivated political violence is dependent on the use of the vast array of research methods within political science. Moreover, this understanding is dependent on the realization that the introduction of religion as a variable makes the investigation of religiously motivated action different from secularly motivated action.

In contrast, there are scholars who contend that religion is inherently violent for the emphasis it places on the distinction between the Self and the Other.[45] These authors emphasize the nature of religion itself to identify sources of violence. In other words, violence is understood to be a result of the internal make-up of religion. Just as studies of religion and politics tend to de-emphasize the unique role of religion, these studies of religion and violent protest overemphasize that role. Sociological studies of religion cannot account for the recent rise in religious movements, violent or peaceful. Nor can they explain the development, timing and varied success of such movements. When explanations are centered around the theology or ideology of a particular religion, critical external elements are too frequently overlooked.

Many notable academics provide a valuable set of answers to the question, *Why does religion sometimes lead to violence?*[46] But history is replete with examples of religion affecting dramatic, albeit peaceful, change, and these studies do little to answer the question, *Why does religion in some cases not lead to violence?* When violence is embedded in the context of religion, its absence becomes the puzzle. Indeed, if religion is, as these authors would argue, primarily a means of excluding oneself from the *Other*, then we should expect to see religion pursuing violent change far more often than religion affecting peaceful change, and the historical accounts do not show this to be the case.

This emphasis on internal elements unique to particular movements is an emphasis not placed on any other type of movement. The value of the evolution of social-movement theory was that it allowed for an understanding of movement participants *in relation to* the society in which they operated. Such an investigation of both internal and external movement variables can account for religion as a surprisingly resilient force in light of secularization and as a more predictable presence in the political arena.

An academic remedy

Chapters 2 and 3 of this book will argue that political-process theory has explanatory power in the case of the rise of religious movements in Egypt and the United States in the latter half of the twentieth century. It will be argued that religious movements arose not despite of the increasing pervasiveness of secularization in the nineteenth and twentieth centuries, but because of it.

The argument will begin in Chapter 2 with a discussion of broad changes in the American political landscape in the latter half of the twentieth century and will suggest that such changes account for the rise in religious social movements. Then, there will be a shift in focus to the specific case of the anti-abortion movement in the United States, with consideration of how it reacted to and influenced the changing political landscape. This will be followed with a brief introduction to the history of the specific case of the Christian Coalition.

Then in Chapter 3, the discussion will turn to the development of the Islamist movement in Egypt. Again, the argument will begin with a broad examination of Egyptian political history, with a subsequent focus on the specific development of the Islamist movement of Al-Ikhwan al-Muslimin.

2 Abortion of values or the value of abortion?

Protest movements of the 1960s and 1970s can be grossly categorized as centering on the "liberal" causes of civil rights, women's liberation and sexual liberation. The challenge to more conservative principles spiraled to ultimately shake the foundations on which they were based – leading to a moral revolution of generational proportions. The effects of this dramatic time in history can be measured in two ways, reflecting the two perspectives in political-opportunity theory.

The first measurement is that of public opinion, or public attitude toward current or potential changes in society. To assess this, one can make use of public-opinion surveys conducted over the time period in question. The most reputable and ubiquitous of these, the General Social Survey conducted by the National Opinion Research Center, has been used by a large number of researchers to show changing trends in public opinion. Over time, these surveys demonstrate a dramatic change in American's attitudes toward each of the three broad categories of issues that dominated the decades in question.[1]

For instance, in 1963, when asked to react to the statement that "Whites have a right to keep blacks out of their neighborhoods," 60 percent of those surveyed agreed. In 1976, 40 percent agreed, and by 1996, the number had dropped to 13 percent. One prominent realignment expert suggests that if American society had not undergone such a revolution of rights, Republicans would have held on to the presidency without fail through 1996.[2] In other words, the political views of enough of the populace changed so dramatically as to see a consequential change in the type of candidate elected into public office, thereby ensuring that changes would not be relegated to the social landscape, but the political process.

Evidence can also be seen of a complimentary shift in views of Americans on the role of women in society and the workforce.[3] During the late 1970s and continuing through the 1980s, support for the traditional belief that a woman's place was in the home decreased significantly. In 1977, 36.8 percent of women (and 31 percent of men) disagreed with this statement: *It is much better for everyone if the man is the achiever and the woman takes care of the home and family*. Yet by 1985, 53.4 percent of women and 49.3 percent of men disagreed with that same statement. This change in attitude has been paralleled with a constant increase in the number of women in the workforce.[4] Over the course of less than a decade, the United States has seen a sweeping redefinition of gender norms.

Moreover, similar changes occurred in the sexual revolution of the 1960s, with important changes in perceptions of sexuality of both genders. A survey of college females reveals that the percentage of college females that engaged in premarital sexual activity increased by 28.4 percent between 1965 and 1975 – compared to increases of only 9.6 percent between 1965–1969 and 18.8 percent between 1970–1975.[5] This was accompanied by a shift in the perception of the morality of premarital sexual activity. For, in 1965, 70 percent of the college females surveyed believed premarital sexual activity was wrong. By 1970, this number decreased dramatically to just 34 percent, and only a mere 20 percent by 1975.[6]

Further (albeit slightly later), one can also observe evidence of a change in perception of homosexuality, or at least the entitlement of homosexuals to the same civil rights afforded to heterosexuals. GSS data demonstrates a small but statistically significant increase in the acceptance of the morality of homosexuality between 1973 and 1977, and in 1977, 56 percent of Americans agreed with the statement that "homosexuals should have equal rights in terms of job opportunities"[7] in contrast to a much larger 83 percent who agreed in 1996.[8] In fact, the willingness of Americans to restrict the civil liberties of homosexuals has declined consistently since 1973.[9]

And what of the second element of political-opportunity theory? For it has been demonstrated here that a clear shift in public attitudes during the decades in question did in fact take place, thus changing the political landscape in which social movements were operating. But was there necessarily a concurrent change to the political institutions themselves?

The passing of the civil rights legislation of the 1960s, and other "rights-oriented" legislation of the 1970s indicates there was such a change. There is a relatively clear, if delayed, link between changes in attitudes and opinions and subsequent changes in institutional structures. While there is some discussion about whether Congressmen and Senators themselves actually increased their support of civil, gender or sexual rights, their actions reflected their understanding of a change in their constituency,[10] and the result was a new set of laws (structure) that would define the new political landscape.

But the relationship between attitude and institution is not exclusively uni-directional. Because, in reality, changes to the institutional structure can herald the development of new advances in social attitude just as changes in social attitude lead to changes in institutional structures. This symbiotic relationship can be seen in the changes that occurred after the Civil Rights movement reached its peak.

The Civil Rights movement resulted in an increased public awareness (and later public support) of civil liberties for all members of society, but with a particular emphasis on minorities. This resulted in legislation changes that institutionalized the new public sentiment. But in the years following this legislative change, new movements began using the vernacular made popular by the success of the Civil Rights movement to generate support for their own causes.

In 1975, the U.S. Commission on Civil Rights issued a report embodying this development. The report urged the rejection of any anti-abortion legislation on the grounds that such legislation was a threat to the civil rights guaranteed in the Ninth and Fourteenth Amendments, and it ran the risk of beginning a process which would weaken the civil-rights foundation of the Constitution.[11] Further, the report argued that efforts to outlaw abortion because of religious sentiment could be seen as an attack on the First Amendment.[12] Thus, one can see that the institutional changes that resulted from the success of the Civil Rights movement were later used to justify new applications of the issue.

By 1973, 68 percent of Americans supported the legalization of abortion. But what is particularly interesting is that this figure is correlated with a commitment to civil liberties.[13] The parallel correlation found in opponents of abortion is a commitment to religious values and the belief that the fetus is a child. So, while religious values and civil liberties are not at odds with each other as innocuous ideas – in that religion could well demand the support for civil liberties, and support for civil liberties in no way undermines support for religion – they have come to represent two competing hierarchies of values. Civil-liberty supporters champion the values of equality and liberty, while religious adherents may value God-given life and God-prescribed norms as more important. As a result of this spectrum of development, a zero-sum game simultaneously developed in that an advance for civil liberties is often perceived as a loss for religious values and vice versa.

At the same time that these political changes were taking place, Americans were undergoing a transformation of their religious beliefs as well. In 1972, 94 percent of Americans identified a particular religious affiliation. Yet, by 1998, 14 percent, when asked the same question, indicated they had no preference.[14] Of those who had no preference, only 12 percent attended church services of some sort more than once a year. Some 64 percent never attended at all. This is in contrast to the 67 percent of those with a preference who attended several times a year or more.[15]

How does this all relate to the current study? Returning to the idea that while grievance may be constant, types of grievance can change in response to changes in the social or political fabric of a community, we can conclude that the social and political changes that began in the 1960s and have continued to the present time have left the American landscape more favorable to the groups that mobilized in support of the liberalization of society. This can explain the decrease in violent non-religious attacks since the end of the 1970s.

But the argument need not stop there. For, as the landscape has become more favorable to non-religious movements, and because of the divergence of the two hierarchies of values discussed earlier, it can be argued that the landscape has inevitably also become less favorable to religious movements. This shift is epitomized in the abortion debate. While civil liberties are certainly not antithetical to religious values (or vice versa), the frame and consequence of non-religious social movements in the 1960s emphasized one over the other, and the emerging religious movements in the 1980s and 1990s have done the same.

Wilson defines this secularization as "the process whereby religious thinking, practice and institutions lose social significance."[16] And while America is frequently identified as an exception to the secularization thesis, one can certainly see evidence of this definition during the period in question. It would be easy at this point to conclude that the advances made in civil rights during the 1960s and 1970s were morally right and necessary, and thus render the debate about whether secularism preceded or succeeded the changes irrelevant. However, not only is it possible to applaud the advances in civil rights while still questioning the consequences of secularization, it is necessary.

Religion is a social agreement about that which is sacred.[17] Symbols, rituals (and, arguably, legislation) are a means of communicating this shared understanding of the things that the community regards as valuable. Religion fosters increased social interaction by highlighting bonds of shared meaning between individuals and their communities.[18] When religion is rejected by society, these bonds are no longer present. When there is no longer a social agreement about that which is sacred, it is the equivalent of a political window of opportunity slamming shut. Because, while the structure of the arena has not changed dramatically, the value system that gave flesh to its bones has. Those still clinging to those values find themselves for the first time on the outside looking in.

Supporters of conservative values can view themselves as being under attack from the progressive protesters (and later, institutionalized reforms) advocating secular civil liberties. Moreover, the shift in the dominant public perception of religious versus civil values has resulted in a trend toward the increase in toleration of sentiments that were, prior to the 1960s, considered deviant (atheism, communism, homosexuality, etc.), and a decrease in tolerance toward the now passé sentiments of the far right, including white-supremacy and militancy.[19]

Yale law professor Stephen Carter argues that religion has come to be perceived as a hobby for adherents, rather than as a legitimate and independent source of moral authority. He indicates that religion is tolerated so long as no one attempts to use it to interfere with society and social behavior.[20]

And, in many ways, this process is self-perpetuating. As society becomes more secularized, many churches are devoting themselves to evolving with the times in order to be relevant to a rapidly changing population. Emphasis is placed on the "feel-good" elements of religion, and the more controversial elements of faith are de-emphasized. But the efforts to reach a secularized society further marginalized those already bemoaning the ebb of shared religious values in the public sphere.[21] And deviance, then, becomes a self-fulfilling prophesy.

It has long been acknowledged in the field of social-movement research that perception is equally (if not more) important than reality. This is why Ted Gurr's explanation of relative grievance was so powerful: it crystalizes the importance not of deficiency for its own sake, but of deficiency in relation to abundance.[22] The same principle is at work in the increase in religiously motivated political violence. For instance, many supporters and leaders of the Christian Right lament the fall of the United States from grace – that is, their definition of grace as the utopist period of the nation's founding. Similarly, political Muslims lament the absence of Sharia law in Arab nations today in contrast to their blessed status at the time of Muhammad.

Therefore, this book will, for the purposes of analysis, take these perceptions at face value, not out of an implicit wholehearted acceptance of their validity, but out of an interest in identifying what grieves some religious individuals so much as to inspire them to commit acts of violence. Gurr argues that violence is most common following a gradual rise and then a decrease in opportunity. The shift in previous decades from a dominance of Christian values in American politics to a sidelined position mimics the rise and fall of which Gurr speaks. Accordingly, it does much to explain the shift being observed in incidences of violence.

As will be seen in later chapters, the Christian Right has not gone quietly from a political arena that no longer welcomes their values with unerring faith, but ironically, this also may serve to exacerbate the problem. The frequency of the term "Religious Right" in the news media accelerated from an average of 14 times per year from 1980–1984 to 578 times per year from 1994–1996.[23]

Jerry Falwell, Pat Robertson, Ralph Reed, and many others, have demonstrated remarkable competency at keeping the religious agenda only slightly off-center of a more and more secular stage. But, to do so, they have had to emphasize the seriousness of the plight of the religious population. Later, it will be discussed how Reed likened the situation to a war – rhetorically urging Christians to paint their faces, camouflage their activities and put their enemies in body-bags. While, for Reed, this was simply a clever metaphor, for others, when coupled with the readily recognizable changes in the values that shape society, it became a call to arms.

Hence, where the intention may be to get apathetic suburban Christians to reverse troubling trends in local polls, the reality is that the war cry serves to emphasize declining values and exaggerate the dangerous morass of an immoral society – while simultaneously causing more moderate individuals, otherwise sharing the same religious views, to run from the extremism of that position. Consequently, the gap between the religious and the secular grows ever wider.

In this chapter we will explore the development of the anti-abortion movement in the United States. The rise of this movement highlights the change that has occurred in the American political landscape and its effect on a particular movement. It will be argued that abortion has been controversial throughout all of American history, but became a cohesive movement only when activists perceived the threat to their access to the political process to be imminent.

The development of the anti-abortion movement

Charles Tilly famously characterized modern politics as "status politics with a vengeance,"[24] and identified the political arena as a forum in which individuals and groups routinely struggle for identity.[25] The idea behind Tilly's argument is that at the heart of such struggles is a desire on the part of social movements to be recognized by the state, and by extension accepted by society. The anti-abortion movement in American politics is a clear example of this struggle for identity and state and social recognition.

As will be demonstrated in the pages that follow, researchers are unable to agree on the nature of the change movement members seek. Some contend that the opinions and beliefs of movement operators are based on efforts to resolve disjunctions that have evolved as society has modernized in the face of unchanging values,[26] while others have suggested the movement is motivated by anti-feminist interests[27] and that "the primary goal of the movement is to keep women in their place and in particular, make them suffer for sexual libertinism."[28] Movement members themselves consistently contend it is neither of these, but that they are motivated by a moral concern for the life of the child in the womb.

Contradictions are not limited to the interactions of one argument and another. In fact, there are striking contradictions within arguments as well. The dominant paradigm explaining the development of the anti-abortion movement centers on an understanding of the movement as anti-modern, or traditionalist. Blanchard defines this position as

> Cultural fundamentalism: a protest against cultural change: against the rising status of women; against the greater acceptance of deviant lifestyles such as homosexuality; against the loss of prayer and bible reading in schools; and against the increase of sexual openness and freedom.[29]

In this paradigm, abortion is symbolic of the end of an age of innocence, to which anti-abortionists would give anything to return. This paradigm firmly rejects the rhetoric that anti-abortionists themselves use, that of moral altruism. Blanchard and Cuneo argue that of those who rhetorically justify their protest in the terms of fetal life, only a small sect of activists actually believe the rhetoric they use. Cuneo says that only those who view the anti-abortion crusade in terms of civil rights could even potentially be considered altruistic.[30] And Cuneo carefully notes that these individuals do not come at the argument from a religious perspective – indeed they are "embarrassed by the activities of the religious activists."[31] According to Cuneo and Blanchard, beyond the relatively small group that fits into the aforementioned category, all others using the rhetoric of fetal rights are more appropriately recognized as being "religious seekers; sexual therapeutics, plagued by guilt and fear of female sexual power; and punitive puritans who want to punish women for sexual transgressions."[32] Blanchard uses Cuneo's findings to conclude that "The majority, but by no means all, of those involved in the movement act out of self interest, particularly out of defense of the cultural fundamentalist position."[33] Taking this argument further, Luker suggests that the anti-abortion movement has provided low-status homemakers with an opportunity to achieve state (and by extension, societal) recognition of their motherhood.[34] Each of these "self-interested" motivations is framed in the broader picture of a call to the return of traditional values, under assault from secularism and an amoral society. As Cavanaugh explains:

> The claim gains appeal if the audience is prepared to believe the story that individuals and societies have been well regulated by traditions (say from

450 BC to 1900 AD) but that modern ideas have recently shaken social stability and moral order. As anyone who has ever taught sociology will know, this orienting myth of a recent "fall from grace" is alive and well as part of the structure of ordinary common sense.[35]

The explanatory themes of the anti-abortion movement will be echoed later in the next chapter, but it is interesting to note that in both cases, the arguments are very similar to those made in the early stages of the development of social-movement theory, when opposition activists were identified as deviants acting against a grievance. Just as secular social-movement theory has developed to account for a more nuanced understanding of protest and its motivations, this book seeks to advocate a more nuanced understanding of religious social protest.

The quickening of a movement

Nearly every book on the anti-abortion movement begins with some reference to the historical place of abortion in American history, and some go back even further to its role in Christian Europe. Most of these sources argue that the absence of any legal restrictions on abortion prior to the second half of the nineteenth century indicate its acceptance as a practice.[36] According to these authors, the woman's prerogative to terminate early pregnancy was recognized in early common-law tradition.[37]

Most historical accounts suggest that even in places where abortion was legally limited, any limitations that did exist were not in place out of a respect for fetal life. In fact, until the end of the nineteenth century, there was limited understanding about the reproductive process beyond Aristotle's linking of quickening and ensoulement.[38] Accordingly, many authors view efforts to suggest a long history of a "value for human rights" with skepticism because the fetus was not recognized as human until much later in pregnancy.[39]

Further, between 1450 and 1750 the Church accepted abortion as a practice before quickening and in cases where the woman's life was in jeopardy.[40] And where it did not (for a period under Pope Pius IX in 1854, the Church underwent a focus on the Immaculate Conception, and the elevated status of motherhood. During this time, Pius made abortion punishable by excommunication), scholars consistently deny the significance.[41] It is commonly cited that the first laws to be passed concerning abortion did not come into existence until around 1821 in Connecticut and 1845 in Massachusetts.[42]

Were these the only sources on the subject, it would be possible to conclude that anti-abortionist rhetoric, where it is understood by researchers to support "traditionalism," is founded on inaccurate history. Demographics demonstrate that often members of the anti-abortion movement are less educated than other activists, and so faulty historical analysis would be less surprising. But these are not the only sources on the subject.

In fact, scholar Marvin Olasky challenges the entire premise of the faulty-history argument.[43] The aforementioned argument is based on the reasoning that there is little historical documentation of legal condemnation for abortion, and therefore there must have been widespread acceptance of the practice. Olasky argues the opposite – that there is little historical documentation of legal condemnation for abortion because the dominant mindset firmly against the practice made it almost non-existent. Using first-hand documents recording such events, Olasky identifies cases in 1629, 1648, 1662, 1656, 1663, 1665, 1681 and 1719 in which individuals were tried for the murder of an unborn child. While eight cases in 90 years is not many, it is enough to cast doubt on the argument that, prior to 1821, women could abort their children without fear of legal recrimination. Olasky argues that formal laws were not instituted until well into the twentieth century because the American state was a minimalist legal system up until much later. In other words, laws were not passed unless they addressed problems of significant proportions, and the social structure of local communities made abortion an uncommon issue until the mid-nineteenth century. Prior to this time, communities were largely stagnant, with individual behavior closely moderated by the community norms. When individuals engaged in extra-marital sex and women became pregnant out of wedlock, colonial records consistently show that the cases were taken to court and, more often than not, the man was instructed to marry the woman and give the child a legitimate family name. In instances where the man refused, he was still required to pay child support until the child reached apprenticing age (usually around 13).[44]

Despite the sharp contrast in the historical records presented by Blanchard, Cavanaugh, Mohr and Olaksy, there is a consensus that abortion began to become more common place in the second half of the nineteenth century, and it was around this time that official legislation limiting its practice began to develop.

There are a variety of explanations for the increase in abortion leading up to the legislative changes. Olasky identifies the changes as being a consequence of a change in social structure, brought on by the birth of more mobile societies. Blanchard points to the more measurable (but not necessarily conflicting) changes brought about by the industrial and urban revolutions.[45] When America was primarily agriculturally based, children were a source of free labor and contributed to the families' economic well-being. As society became industrialized, many Americans moved from farms into cities and more children meant less space and more stomachs – without a corresponding rise in productivity. Birth rates reflect the changes that occurred between 1810 and 1890; they had declined by half.[46]

Most accounts of anti-abortion history put the emerging American Medical Association at the center of every discussion of nineteenth-century legislation.[47] Abortion provided the opportunity for doctors to separate themselves from "quacks," by arguing that abortion was murder, and only a trained physician could determine when such an act was necessary.[48] But again, Olasky paints a different picture, suggesting that abortion rose so quickly to legislative significance in the later 1800s because for the first time reputable doctors were being approached by middle-class ladies asking for abortions. Physicians prior to this time had no need to pursue legislation against a practice that was largely requested by prostitutes and, as result, of a lower caliber of medical professionals.[49]

Blanchard has argued that the anti-abortion crusade of the nineteenth century was an issue of medical liability, not morality. But, at the same time, Sauer has studied the shift in public and elite attitudes toward abortion in the United States and notes that while there is evidence to suggest that abortions were practiced in the early days of the nation, there are no cases in which doctors actually condoned the practice.[50] Further, there are references to an understanding of abortion as a means to reduce the consequence of non-marital sex, thereby threatening the moral fabric of society. And during the nineteenth, and even well into the twentieth, century doctors were some of the most vocal critics of the practice. Moreover, literature of the time equally condemned the practice as "ante-natal infanticide," and the *New York Times* described abortion in the nineteenth century as murder.[51]

Whatever the motivation, the American Medical Association succeeded in getting laws limiting abortion on the records of all the states by 1910. And while most types of abortion were now illegal in all states, the conditions of urbanization and industrialization that had led to its rise at the end of the nineteenth century continued to dominate the social landscape. Urban living conditions for industrial workers were squalid, with large families squeezing into single-roomed apartments. Under the justification of the newly popular ideas of Charles Darwin, little was being done to alleviate the challenges facing the downtrodden.

Religion on trial

In an ever-secularizing society, Christians of all denominations struggled to find their role. Fundamentalism and the Social Gospel were two such attempts. During this time, the inerrancy of the Bible came under attack, and between 1910 and 1917, a group of Christians published a series of pamphlets they called "The Fundamentals." The leaflets identified the core bedrock elements of the Christian faith, and at its heart was a Bible that was the revealed word of God.

During the same period, another group of Christians rose to challenge the Darwinian philosophy that suggested hardship and poverty were useful tools for ensuring only the strong would survive by campaigning for political reform that would curtail the abuses of the Industrial Revolution. William Jennings Bryan was a leader in this movement, and used the ideas as the basis of his three presidential campaigns. Bryan, perhaps unwittingly, brought elements of Fundamentalism and the Social Gospel together when he began actively campaigning against the teaching of Darwin's theory in public schools. He succeeded in getting a number of laws passed to this effect, to the frustration of many teachers. One of these teachers, John Scopes, agreed to challenge the law and was arrested for violating it. Jennings Bryan was asked to serve as the prosecutor in Scopes case.

The media latched on to the case, taking a mocking view of Bryan's "out-of-date" perspective. The trial became so huge that it was held in tents in front of the courthouse so spectators could attend. The seminal moment in the trial came when ACLU lawyer Clarence Darrow questioned Bryan, and cast doubt on what Bryan himself purported to believe about the inerrancy of the Bible. The courts struck down the law and, at least politically, Darwinism triumphed.

The trial was an influential moment in the lifetime of the burgeoning fundamentalist movement. Already skeptical of the idea of the Social Gospel, the Fundamentalists saw Bryan's downfall as a rejection of Christianity by a now thoroughly secular society, and vowed to remove themselves from its influence. The idea behind the separation was pre-millennial dispensationalism – a theology that interpreted the biblical book of Revelation to mean that when Jesus returned to earth, believers would be taken to heaven by way of the rapture, and God, Satan and the remaining unbelievers would embark on Armageddon. This theology supported separatism because it suggested that, except for the elected few, humanity was condemned to an eternity of hell, and thus political efforts to ease suffering on earth were at best short-sighted, and at worst a waste of time.

The rise of a secular state

The next several decades of American history were as tumultuous as they were transformative: World War I marked the end of American isolationism; the Great Depression led to the election of Franklin Roosevelt and the development of government involvement in the alleviation of poverty; World War II thrust America into the foreign spotlight and its end resulted in a bi-polar world with nuclear weapons; at the same time, World War II saw the large-scale entrance of women into the workforce, which led to questions about the traditional role of the woman, and her place in the home; the Cold War inspired some questionable foreign entanglements, perhaps the most momentous of which was America's involvement in Vietnam; protests against war in Vietnam developed into a culture of protest wherein social movements began to actively pursue civil rights and full-scale equality for women.

Through all of this, divorce rates increased and birth control became a widely accepted practice (although the Catholic Church continued to denounce its use). The consequence was that women began to view their roles differently. If it was acceptable to limit pregnancy by taking a pill, then it was not a big step to correct mistakes in one method (getting pregnant while on the pill) by using another (abortion).[52]

Against this backdrop, challenges were issued against the restrictions on abortions. In the 1940s, there are records of a few attempts to make inroads against the existing laws, but for the most part these attempts at reform were undertaken by doctors who the courts generally ruled against because none were seeking abortions for themselves. Most attempts to legalize abortion during the 1960s were focused on changes at the state level. By the late 1960s, laws in 14 states had been revised so as to permit abortion when the woman's health was at risk, or when the fetus was believed to be deformed. In Hawaii, Alaska, New York and Washington, there were no restrictions against abortion in the first trimester.[53]

The discovery of the effects of a particular drug on fetal development thrust abortion to the front of the political scene once again in 1962, when it was widely published that women who took thalidomide during pregnancy ran a substantial risk of damaging the fetus. American Sherri Chessen Finkbine had unknowingly been taking high doses of thalidomide during her pregnancy. When she contacted her doctor, he advised aborting the fetus. Finkbine was so distraught by her experience that while waiting for approval for the abortion, she called a local newspaper to warn more people about the drug. The phone call resulted in a front-page headline the following day, and a call from Finkbine's doctor saying her request had been denied. In Arizona in 1962, abortion was only permitted to save the life of the mother. Finkbine's story set off a firestorm and brought the issue to the public consciousness, paving the way for later reform.

As the women's liberation movement of the 1960s gained ground, abortion reform became a bigger part of social consciousness. In the late 1960s, abortion was transformed into a feminist cause, with the National Organization for Women (NOW) endorsing calls for reform. In 1969, NOW formed a coalition called the National Association for the Repeal of Abortion Laws to initiate efforts for broad change.[54]

As the women's rights movement moved forward, there was an accompanying realization that woman could not support high fertility rates and corporate gender equality at the same time. In 1965, 87 percent of women approved of abortion when the mother's life was in danger, 50 percent when the child was suspected of having deformities, 52 percent when the pregnancy resulted from rape, but only 8 percent approved of abortion for any reason.[55]

Another poll in 1969 showed 40 percent of adults to support abortion (for any reason) during the first trimester and, in 1972, the number jumped to 46 percent. By the 1970s, there were Protestant groups advocating abortion rights, and the American Medical Association began calling for the repeal of restrictive laws. Hawaii, Alaska and New York were the first states to permit abortion on request, followed by the 1973 national decision by the Supreme Court that no state had the right to prohibit any woman from obtaining an abortion in the first six months of pregnancy.

Through the changing legislation, evangelical Protestants were relatively quiet, the separatist notions of fundamentalism still limiting their political involvement. The Catholic Church, in contrast, had no qualms about clearly identifying its position on abortion, with Pope John XXIII issuing a statement that called abortion a "supreme dishonor to the Creator."[56] Eunice Shriver, sister to John and Robert Kennedy, helped to push abortion into Catholic prominence with a 1967 conference sponsored by the Kennedy Foundation and Harvard Divinity School. Shriver's political pedigree and the publication of a book against abortion called *The Terrible Choice* gave the issue a respectable level of prominence. While there were a few sit-ins and public protests prior to the 1973 court decision, they were quite small and generated little press. Risen and Thomas suggest that mainstream Catholics were appalled by even the idea of using illegal actions to achieve political objectives. And because the movement was still dominated by Catholics and suburban moms, the movement could not take off.[57]

Social revolution

All this changed on January 22, 1973, as a result of what has been called the fastest social revolution in American history. On this day, the Supreme Court ruled in the case of *Roe* v. *Wade* that states could not restrict a woman's decision to have an abortion in the first trimester of her pregnancy, and that in the second trimester, the state could only intervene to protect the health of the mother. States were entitled to regulate third-trimester abortions, but explicit legislation had to be in place justifying such an act. The decision stunned advocates on both sides of the debate because the change the Court instigated was so sweeping as to find no more than four states in compliance with the new interpretation at its issuance.

Initially, opposition to the decision was largely in the form of the Catholic Church members writing to their Congressional Representatives to protest and to plead for a legislative challenge. But there was a strain of Catholics who believed anti-abortion activism could not be a hobby, but must be a full-time undertaking.[58] Unlike the Protestant fundamentalism that had spawned a separatist movement that removed evangelicals from political life, the Catholic Charismatic Renewal Movement called believers to action. Against the backdrop of the late 1960s and early 1970s, action took the form of civil protest, and the initial opposition response to *Roe* v. *Wade* was composed of peaceful sit-ins.

Absolute non-violence was a condition of these protests, with leaders of the movement urging the emulation of the civil protest models established by Martin Luther King and Mahatmas Gandhi. Just as these men had achieved reform by highlighting the peaceful justice of their cause in contrast to the ugly violence of the state they challenged, anti-abortion leaders sought to emphasize the violence of abortion by contrasting it with the peaceful nature of their approach. The method was slow to take off – in part because the mainstream Catholics abhorred even the idea of civil disobedience. This forestalled any hope of a united front, as the more active Catholics derided what they considered to be ineffective letter writing. As a result, the few sit-ins that were organized were small and ultimately ineffective.

One of the leaders of this burgeoning movement, John O'Keefe, endeavored to widen the appeal of the group by reaching out to members of other protest movements, including the anti-war and anti-nuclear movements. For O'Keefe, the partnership was a logical one, as he viewed abortion as murder, and war and nuclear weapons were murder on a large scale. However, the relationship did not develop because abortion rights had, in the 1960s, come to be synonymous with feminism – a cause the anti-war and anti-nuclear groups saw as more similar to their own.

The movement was in danger of never really taking off when Joseph Scheidler entered the fray. Scheidler had at one time intended to become a Benedictine monk, but ultimately found himself working as a public relations manager. When *Roe* v. *Wade* was announced, Scheidler was horrified, and as months passed and no significant protests were launched, he began to get angry. Scheidler quit his job and began full-time protest work, using his knowledge of public relations to bring media attention to the protests he organized.

Scheidler was quite different from either previous brand of Catholic activists, as he thought polite sit-ins were not enough in a war for America's children. He went after abortion-providers, urging activists to call their homes, harass their wives, get them to quit, if they wouldn't convert. Scheidler was famous for the bull-horn he seemed to carry with him everywhere and for the national media attention he generated. Thanks to such attention, Scheidler successful turned abortion back into a national issue, and consequently generated support for his movement across the country. Scheidler could arguably be identified as the seed of violent protest that would grow to murderous proportions in future decades. While Scheidler himself had a fear of being arrested, and was consequentially careful to choose his words judiciously, he made no secret of his approval of militant tactics, and his indirect support of violent efforts.[59]

Under Scheidler's tutelage, Randal Terry launched Operation Rescue, and began using Scheidler's methods on a huge scale. Terry, like Scheidler, was careful in what he said about the use of force, but his comments are interesting for their pragmatism: "I believe in the use of force. But I think to destroy abortion facilities at this time is counterproductive because the American people has an adverse reaction to what it sees as violence."[60]

The impact of Francis Schaeffer

But even for all the press Scheidler and Terry were getting, it took the re-emergence of Christian fundamentalists to launch the anti-abortion movement to the next level. And theologian and activist Francis Schaeffer was happy to oblige. Schaeffer was a Presbyterian Evangelist, and in his three seminal works, *How Shall We Then Live?*, *A Christian Manifesto* and *Whatever Happened to the Human Race?*, Schaeffer revolutionized fundamentalist America. Schaeffer woke fundamentalists from their separatist existence by introducing them to the enemy of humanism. This enemy could be identified as any truth not clearly rooted in scripture, and any act separated from God. Because of Christians' twentieth-century slumber, the enemy had taken hold of society and politics, and evidence of this was most clearly seen in the tragedy that was abortion.

Perhaps Schaeffer's most significant contribution to the development of a Christian movement in American politics was his definitive explanation of the difference between humanism and a Judeo-Christian worldview. Schaeffer strongly condemned those who argued that Christians could live obediently to

God in a morally declining society. He adamantly states that "Christians should be inalterably opposed to the false and destructive humanism which is false to the Bible and equally false to what Man is."[61] Schaeffer believed that this opposition was dependent on the understanding that the two worldviews had nothing in common, and that efforts to synthesize them were a perversion of God's purpose.

Schaeffer was particularly concerned with the immediacy of the crisis – an immediacy born of the belief that events reflected a dramatic change in the political landscape. He says:

> Until recently, in our own century, with some notable and sorry exceptions, human beings have generally been regarded as special, unique and nonexpendable. But in one short generation we have moved from a generally high view of life, to a very low one. Why has our society changed? The answer is clear: The consensus of our society no longer rests on a Judeo Christian base, but rather on a humanistic one.[62]

Schaeffer alludes to the intermediate period in which Christian values had not yet been wholly rejected by the state, but were no longer being actively practiced. During this time, he perceived Christian ethics as still being dominant, but out of "sheer inertia" rather than a genuine commitment to their value.[63]

He condemns the state for its abrogation of the moral responsibility to protect human life in a manner that is later mimicked by the Army of God in their justification of the use of force:

> The civil government, as all of life, stands under the law of God. In this fallen world God has given us certain offices to protect us from the chaos which is the natural result of that fallenness. But when any office commands that which is contrary to the word of God, those who hold that office abrogate their authority and they are not to be obeyed. And that includes the state.... God has ordained the state as a delegated authority; it is not autonomous. The state is an agent of justice, to restrain evil by punishing the wrongdoer, and to protect the good in society. When it does the reverse, it has no proper authority. It is then a usurped authority, and as such it becomes lawless and is a tyranny.... The bottom line is that at a certain point, there is not only the right, but the duty to disobey the state.[64]

Having primed his followers to feel frustrated over an immoral shift to a society that had been formed on Christian values, and let down by a state that had violated its citizens' collective trust, Schaeffer identifies the time of his writing as a unique period in history, in which political action was the duty of all believers:

> The reason that we are writing this book is that we feel strongly that we stand today on the edge of a great abyss. At this crucial moment, choices are being made and thrust on us that will for many years to come affect the way

people are treated. We want to try to help tip the scales on the side of those who believe individuals are unique and special and have great dignity.[65]

And he explicitly calls for Christians to rise up against the erosion of values in politics:

We implore those of you who are Christians to exert all your influence to fight against the increasing loss of humaneness through legislation, social action, and other means at your disposal, both privately and publicly, individually and collectively, in all areas of your lives.[66]

He went on to ensure there be no further question of fundamentalists claiming immunity from social responsibility: "The danger in regard to the rise of authoritarian government is that Christians will be still as long as their own religious activities, evangelism and life-styles are not disturbed."[67] He later goes so far as to question the sincerity of belief that would exempt a believer from action:

If, in this last part of the twentieth century, the Christian Community does not take a prolonged and vocal stand for the dignity of the individual and each person's right to life – for the right of each individual to be treated as created in the image of God, rather than as a collection of molecules with no unique value – we feel that as Christians we have failed the greatest moral test to be put before us in this century. Further generations will look back, and many will either scoff or believe in Christ on the basis of whether we Christians of today took a sacrificial stand in our various walks of life on these overwhelmingly important issues. If we do not take a stand here and now, we certainly cannot lay claim to being the salt of the earth in our generation.[68]

Schaeffer himself was cagey on the use of force. He referred to violence against abortion providers as "unfortunate" but in the same breath (a breath he took while writing a supportive preface to confrontational anti-abortionist Joseph Scheidler's how-to protest manual *Closed: 99 Ways to Stop Abortion*), he implies the fault of violence must be laid at the feet of those who are performing abortions:

From time to time we have seen some unfortunate episodes of violence against the abortion industry. However, the case can be made that this violence has often been instigated by the abortion industry itself, because the very violence of abortion, the cruel dismembering piece by piece of unborn children, sparks a violent antagonism which though not excusable, is understandable. The abortion industry and organizations such as Planned Parenthood create a feeling of tremendous frustration with many pro-life activist groups by the systematic attempt to strip pro-life activists of their constitutional rights for free assembly and free speech. In case after case abortion clinics are bringing lawsuits against pro-life activists in an attempt to intimidate them into silence. Court injunctions by pro-abortion judges against pro-life demonstrations strip pro-life activists of the peaceable means of protest.[69]

While technically Schaeffer is not condoning violence, for someone so committed to recognizing the fine line between right and wrong, he walks a less than linear path with this statement.

Schaeffer is a figure critical to the emergence of Christian activism in the United States. Virtually every book and a majority of the essays written in support of Christian activism by the leaders of both violent and non-violent movements cites Schaeffer at least once. One author says, "In Francis Schaeffer, eager young religionists like Randal Terry, who sensed that a new day was coming, had found their philosopher king."[70]

Indeed, Schaeffer's work inspired Randal Terry in the creation of Operation Rescue, an organization committed to stopping abortion by physically preventing its occurrence. Schaeffer's influence is evident in Terry's call to arms:

What will the Lord Jesus say when He looks at our lives? How will your children and your grandchildren view your response to this current holocaust? Will they see your example of courage, sacrifice and love for your neighbor? Will you be remembered as the one who helped end abortion and turn America back to God? Or will you be just another face in a sea of self-centered Christians who stood by while millions of children were killed and our nation collapsed into hell?[71]

Just as Schaeffer could be identified as the pivotal link between the fundamentalists of the earlier half of the century who rejected political activism in any form and those of the latter half who saw activism as a responsibility of the sincere believer, Terry could be identified as the conceptual bridge between O'Keefe's peaceful protest and the later acts of physical violence perpetrated by the Army of God. Operation Rescue was far from peaceful, but also managed to be pragmatically removed from destructive violence. Members were taught to crawl past police barricades outside clinics, to physically attach themselves to clinics, and to resist arrest as much as possible without actually causing harm.

While Schaeffer saw abortion as the defining moment of the twentieth century, he was concerned about the erosion of Christian influence in all areas of politics. Schaeffer saw an opportunity to put his concerns into action in the person of Jerry Falwell, an evangelical Baptist minister interested in joining the fight against abortion. Schaeffer urged Falwell to do what no evangelical had done up to that point, and build a coalition of multi-denominational Christians.

Four men in particular moved to capitalize on this unique moment in political history: Richard Vinguerie, Paul Weyrich, Howard Phillips and Terry Dolan were united in their belief that liberals were running America to the ground, and embarked on a joint campaign to stop them.

These four men approached Falwell to solicit his help in forming a political organization that would force Republicans to once again take up the mantle of ideological conservatism on social and economic issues. Weyrich said to Schaefer, "There is in America a moral majority that agrees about the basic issues. But they aren't organized. They don't have a platform. The media ignores them. Somebody's got to get that moral majority together."[72] Prodded by Schaefer, Falwell agreed, and the Moral Majority was born. The purpose of the Majority was to undermine the boundaries that separated secular Republicans, Fundamentalists, ordinary Protestants and Catholics by tying them all together under the banner of a commitment to "pro-family" values.

The organization focused on training pastors to use scripture to inform politics and, in turn, use politics to achieve Christian objectives.[73] But the foundling movement needed an issue around which all its disparate members could rally, and abortion was the perfect cause.[74] By making abortion an issue of family values, it would force a cleavage between traditional Democrat-voting Catholics and the Democratic Party.[75]

The new coalition had its first test in the 1980 presidential elections, in which Weyrich urged movement leaders to "Frame issues in such a way that there is no mistaking who is on the right side and who is on the wrong side. Ultimately, everything can be reduced to right and wrong."[76] John Buchanan, running for re-election in Alabama, lost his campaign due to his low "moral rating." He says of the organization, "They did a rather thorough job of beating my brains out with Christian love."[77]

The Moral Majority was successful in seeing Ronald Reagan and many other conservatives elected. But their success in actually making inroads against abortion was not so clear. Although Reagan had filled anti-abortionists with optimism during his campaign, his time in office was a different story. Activists had expected drastic change, and instead Reagan elected to chip away at abortion one small action at a time. Senator Orrin Hatch sponsored a law that would return abortion to state control, but the law was defeated in the Senate, and Reagan used this to justify his inactivity, saying that even if he did push for reform, Congress would override him. He angered activists further by putting first Sandra Day O'Connor, and then Anthony Kennedy on the Supreme Court, actions that caused many activists to bitterly denounce "gradualism" as a method.[78]

Others, however, dug in for the long fight, comparing their task to that of civil rights and themselves to the NAACP.[79] But for those who saw abortion not as a political cause, but a moral one, gradualism was a terrible strategy. If one-and-a-half-million children were being killed every year, a minor court case is not a victory.

A coalition launched

It was into this mix that Pat Robertson jumped when he founded the Christian Coalition. Beginning with a television ministry and quickly expanding into many other business/ministry opportunities, the end of the Reagan administration and the Schaeffer revolution found Robertson weighing a run for the presidency. In his memoirs, Robertson is adamant that he never *wanted* to run for president. He recalls years of fervent prayer seeking to understand God's will in what his followers had asked him to do. He remembers distinctly words coming to him over and over: "You will not want to do this, but you should do it,"[80] and Robertson cites many signs from God that confirmed the "rightness" of his candidacy.[81]

Although Robertson believed he had God's confirmation of his candidacy, he wanted the assurance of the people before he made it official. To this end, on September 17, 1986, Robertson gave a speech lamenting the atrophy of morality in America, calling on his supporters to fight the disease of immorality. He explained that he had been asked to run for president and that he knew God's will for the decision, but he would not run unless he could collect the signatures of three million supporters willing to pray and work toward his election.

Robertson later explained that he figured that it took six million votes to secure the Party's nomination for President: if he could obtain three million signatures in one year, then all he had to do to get the nomination was to have each of those three million convince one other person, and he would be on his way to the presidency. Eventually, Robertson did get the signatures, resigned as president of CBN, and declared his candidacy for President of the United States.

Robertson performed well in the early caucuses and primaries. He shocked the nation when he came in second in the important Iowa caucus. Although Bob Dole won the event, newspaper headlines trumpeted "Robertson Beats Bush." But in New Hampshire, Robertson tied for last place and performed miserably in the important southern states. Robertson attributes his loss not to an absence of support, but to poor planning and journalistic bias. This conclusion led Robertson to realize that he had a vast resource at his fingertips – a huge number of individuals that shared his ideals, and his passion for seeing them implemented into policy.

Further, the relative success of the campaign inspired thousands of Christians with no previous political interest to become involved with the political process. In fact, studies show that while Robertson did not get the nomination, he did nonetheless hugely impact the direction of the campaign and the Republican platform.[82]

Determined not to allow the political capital he had acquired during his campaign to go to waste, Robertson used what remained of his campaign networks and resources to launch the Christian Coalition. Robertson's political experience, national exposure and personal charisma ensured that his image (and beliefs) would dominate the Coalition even years after he stepped down as its head.

A hostage on the right?

While the Christian Coalition was established in 1988, the date of the founding of the Army of God is not so clearly identifiable. The Memorial Institute for the Prevention of Terrorism identifies nine leaders of the Army. What the leaders know about each other is not clear. *The Army of God Manual* (a handbook for would-be and existing soldiers detailing methods of violent action) explains that it is the very non-connected nature of the organization that makes it so hard for federal officials to track. The manual identifies the Army as "a real Army, with God as the Commander in Chief."[83] Vicki Saporta, president of the National Abortion Federation (NAF), contends that the group is more organized than this, saying, "The Army of God is a small group of extremists who believe that it's justifiable to murder abortion providers," she explains. "They actively recruit and train people to commit these acts of violence."[84]

The soldiers communicate primarily through the Internet, which is also a vast source of information about the organization. The Army sponsors its own website with lists of members, their important deeds, and in many cases, valid contact information. The group was first identified in 1982 in conjunction with the kidnapping of Dr. Hector Zevallos and his wife, Rosalee Jean.[85]

Dr. Zevallos owned the Hope Clinic in Granite City, Illinois. One evening in January 1982, Zevallos and his wife were kidnapped at gunpoint. The pair were held handcuffed and blindfolded for eight days, while their captors urged them to record a tape demanding that President Reagan issue a firm statement against abortion. The kidnappers informed the Zevalloses that they were members of a group called the Army of God and that God had called them to fight abortion "to the death." The kidnappers also explained to the couple that they would continue to do any kind of violence to accomplish their objective.[86]

In the end, three men were later convicted of the kidnapping: Don Benny Anderson and Wayne and Matthew Moore. The same men confessed to setting fire to two Florida abortion clinics, and bombing a clinic in Virginia. At his sentencing, Anderson thanked God for the opportunity to do what he had done.[87]

Anderson's arrest did not stop the Army of God from continuing their fight. In 1984, a clinic in Norfolk VA was firebombed, and the letters "AOG" were found written on the wall; also in 1984, an individual claiming to be a member of the Army sent a letter to Supreme Court Justice Harry Blackmun, challenging his decision in *Roe* v. *Wade*.[88] Eventually (these acts will be explored in more detail in later chapters) members of the Army graduated from arson to murder.

How should we then understand?

The United States anti-abortion movement rose out of a shared belief that the fetus is a human being – a belief that is reflective of a broad spectrum of religious doctrine. While many Christians exited the political arena after the Scopes Monkey trial, they did so with the expectation that the government, while increasingly secular, would not act in direct violation of religious values. In this way, the government was still afforded some legitimacy from the religious sector, even as it moved farther and farther from their ideological position. But the decision of *Roe* v. *Wade* was a gross violation of the perceived understanding between government and religion. The religious community viewed *Roe* v. *Wade* as a total disregard for the values that made government legitimate. If life itself was not to be regarded as valuable, then what could be? *Roe* v. *Wade* was a clear indication of a window of opportunity closing quickly.

As different sectors of religious society came to recognize this waning opportunity, efforts toward opposition were undertaken. However, it wasn't until Francis Schaeffer used his unique multi-denominational background to form a rhetoric that defined the enemy of humanism and called for a new practice of co-belligerency that the opposition coalesced into a powerful movement. Robertson recognized this movement as his for the taking, and together with Ralph Reed created an organization that pragmatically (if not always gracefully) traversed many of the lines that had traditionally separated sects of religious opposition.

However, while the rise of the anti-abortion movement demonstrated an affinity for cross-denominational cooperation, its failure to achieve its objectives despite the election of a conservative president emphasized the continued closing window of opportunity. Some movement participants reacted to this with an increased urgency, while others perceived it as an admonition for greater subtlety of method.

In the next chapter we will see a similar principle at work in the cases of the Muslim Brethren and al Jama'a al Islamiyya.

3   Allah's place in Egyptian politics

Interestingly, both the rise of the Islamist movement in Egypt and the academic treatment of this rise have in many ways mirrored their American counterpart. While, for the anti-abortion movement in the United States, the defining moment around which religious opposition coalesced was the decision of *Roe* v. *Wade*, for the Egyptian movement it was the combination of the 1952 Free Officers Revolution (and the failed expectations for Nasser's commitment to religious legitimacy) and Sadat's historic trip to Jerusalem in 1977. Both of these events represented an end to the tentative balance that had existed between political power and religious legitimacy, and led to a movement that lasts to the present day. The next section will first examine the traditional academic explanations for the rise of the Egyptian Islamic movement, and will then provide a historical account of the changing political landscape.

The changing landscape of Egyptian political society and the consequential rise of the Islamist movement

Just as researchers frequently question the sincerity of anti-abortion activists' concern for the fetus in light of the pragmatic strategy that has characterized their movement, many researchers are challenged to see the quest for the implementation of Sharia law in Egyptian politics as a genuine religious interest. Many other explanations are offered instead, with the most dominant sharing common themes with those used to explain the American anti-abortion movement. Often the Islamist movement is perceived to be a reaction against modernity, ushered in by colonialism, industrialization and urbanization. Islam is viewed as an obvious aberrant problem, and the task of the researcher becomes to find the "real" reason for its resurgence.

Studies are peppered with references to high rates of illiteracy among the population, continuous and pervasive poverty, limited political awareness,[1] and political and social alienation.[2] And while the term is not used, these arguments are reminiscent of Ted Gurr's theory of "relative deprivation," in that they imply that the Islamic resurgence in the 1970s was born out of discontent and frustration in light of previous promises of prosperity.

While strands of these arguments are seen throughout the literature explaining all sorts of religious resurgence, in the rise of the Islamic movement in Egypt, empirical evidence cannot support this claim. The demographics of the Islamist groups are not only similar to each other (there is no clear socioeconomic difference between violent and non-violent organizations) but to other secular organizations in society. When President Sadat moved to consolidate his legitimacy in the 1970s, he courted the religious right, and the organizations rose as competition to the socialist groups that had previously dominated the university campuses. The Islamists drew from the same member pool as the socialists, resulting in a demographic that is virtually indistinguishable. Further, the leadership in the Muslim Brethren is, if anything, unrepresentative of the greater society because of the wealth of its members, not the deprivation.[3]

In an interview with the author, current Brotherhood member Ibrahim Hudaiby made a statement that hinted at a solution to this puzzle. He was speaking about the value of a government founded on Islamic law when he pointed out:

> The Law [Sharia] has been around for 13 centuries. It is only in the last 50 years that this has changed. Our support of the Law has not changed; the absence of the state's reliance on the Law is what has changed.[4]

The arguments of Vakitosis[5] and Safran[6] touch on a similar point, as they, in different ways, articulate the difference between the legitimacy afforded by power and the legitimacy afforded by religion. In the pages that follow, it will be argued that up until the twentieth century, Egyptian politics had reflected a careful balance of political power and religious legitimacy. Islam had receded from the forefront of the political arena, based on a careful balance that afforded power to the state based on the understanding that the state would not interfere with the citizens' opportunity to practice their religion. But the decline of the Ottoman Empire, the resulting foreign dependence, and the eventual Free Officers revolt combined to upset this balance and put physical power in opposition to religious legitimacy, and the Islamist movement coalesced around a shared understanding of a rapidly closing window of political opportunity.

The difference between this argument and many others is that it views the Islamic movement as something that has always existed, but that it was catapulted into public awareness in the 1970s. Essentially, the rise of the Islamist movement illustrates political-opportunity theory at its finest. In this chapter, we will see that Islam emerged as a single (although not monolithic) religious–political system, but over time changes in international relations led to a division between the religious and political elements of the system. The Egyptian state never really addressed the division: leaders continued to rhetorically recognize a singular entity, while pragmatically they acted according to dualism. For several generations this split was feasible because the public acceptance of political power did not require the denial of religious legitimacy (even though they were found in two different places). But when it became clear that the acceptance of one meant the rejection of the other, public sentiment was primed to launch a sustainable Islamic movement.

The changing landscape of Egyptian society

It is ironic to realize that had political science been a dominant field in the seventh century, it is likely that Muhammad would have been identified as a religious radical against the onset of modernity. Seven-hundred years after the life of Christ, Muhammad looked with disapproval at the corrupted state of Christianity, and concluded it was not what God had intended it to be. He received visions which were later transcribed as the Qur'an.

Islam developed not as an alternative to Christianity, but as the completion of it.[7] Islamic history is similar to Jewish and Christian history, in that time can be broken down by the series of prophets that God sent to guide his people in accordance with His will and purpose. The prophets began with Adam, included Abraham, Noah and Jesus (among several others), and Muhammad is believed by Muslims to be the final prophet. After Muhammad died, God's revelation to humanity was complete.

The Qur'an offered corrections to errors that had crept into the Bible. One of the more significant of these corrections is the belief that Jesus was not the son of God, but merely a human (if great) prophet. It is believed that at the time that Judas betrayed Jesus, God supernaturally intervened and put another man in Jesus' place. It was this man that was beaten and crucified, while Jesus hid. The difference between the two accounts is fascinating for a number of reasons.

The entire Christian faith is predicated on the belief that humanity is sinful, God is perfect, and the only way for a relationship to exist between the two must come from atonement. In the Old Testament, atonement took the form of ritual animal sacrifice, all the while pointing toward the time when a Messiah would come to permanently tear down the wall between God and Man. Jesus, the Son of God, came to serve as the final atonement. Although he lived as a man, he lived an entire life without sin, and thus served as the perfect sacrifice, and in so doing opened the opportunity for an uninhibited relationship between God and His creation.

The theme underlying this series of events is the desire that God has for a relationship with humanity. He was willing to endure the pain of sacrificing his son in order to have this personal relationship.

The message God gave Muhammad differed on several points. The Qur'an does not suggest that humanity is inherently sinful, but is inherently good. Sin is something people, not something that they invariably are; sin is not transferred from one generation to the next. Accordingly, there was no need for God to sacrifice his prophet. God's supernatural intervention to prevent the humiliation that Christians believe Jesus suffered for them is indicative of a different function of God. Where Christian theology places much emphasis on God's willingness to be vulnerable, Islam emphasizes the power of God to avoid vulnerability.

Evangelical Christianity places great emphasis on God's relationship with the individual ("Jesus died for *me*"). While the individual is not neglected by any means in Islam, the Qur'an that God revealed to Muhammad placed a greater emphasis on God's purpose for humanity. At the risk of making a gross general-ization, it can be carefully said that the Christian focus on the crucifixion empha-sizes God's desire to reach humanity. In contrast, the Islamic focus on God's power and humanity's ability emphasizes His desire for humanity to reach Him. This subtle difference is relevant to the political discussion at hand for several reasons.

In recent years, much emphasis has been placed on Sharia law and its poten-tial incompatibility with democracy in Middle Eastern states. Frequently this assumed incompatibility is explained as a result of the inability of Islam to sepa-rate religion from politics. Whereas Jesus urged his followers to "render unto Caesar what is Caesar's," Muslims have a set of laws established by the Qur'an that ensure that Caesar has no separate sphere. While, in a strict sense, this is accurate, it is not a complete representation of the relationship between Islam and politics.

The Western idea of the state rests on the idea of the social contract – individ-uals cede elements of personal autonomy for assurances of stability. From this perspective, the state exists to enable the citizen to live as he or she chooses, and pursue his or her own wishes. If an individual wishes to pursue religion, he or she may do so, provided his or her pursuit does not infringe on anyone else's security. The state is essentially valueless, or amoral. Morality is left to the indi-vidual according to his or her interests.

In Islam, the purpose of the state is different. The state exists to promote life according to the will of God, by the precepts He determined and defined in Sharia. As a result, political legitimacy is not conferred on the state's ability to protect a person's ability to pursue his or her own interest, but on the fulfillment of its responsibility to provide people a forum for obedient living. Muhammad enforced this vision of the state during his lifetime, but upon his death there was some ambiguity about how to proceed. The eventual split between Sunni and Shi'ia was a result of this ambiguity, with the former electing the next leader based on some standard of merit, and the latter advocating an inherited form of leadership.[8] The Caliphate was established, and the Caliph was entrusted with the responsibility of enforcing Sharia law.

What the crucifixion did for Christians, Sharia does for Muslims. Sharia is God's provision for humanity to be able to live in harmony with Him. In the words of Safran, "In short it should be emphasized that historically Sharia did not provide for the political self-fulfillment of the Muslim as it did for the real-ization of his moral potentialities."[9] Thus the purpose of the state is to provide the opportunity to live in obedience to God.

In the first centuries following Muhammad's death, the Caliphate held both political power and religious legitimacy. Over time, however, military conquest led to the development of institutions of power separate from the Caliphate. Sunni ideology accepted this development, reasoning that all power came from God, and thus His authority rested with those who had power. While this was a departure from Muhammad's embodiment of political power and religious legitimacy, the new arrangement was accepted in part because the political powers did not threaten the religious legitimacy of the Caliphate. In other words, the Caliphate was left to enforce Sharia, while the political leaders concerned themselves with other matters.

The arrangement was a state structure that superficially operated like the European feudal system – with a single authority overseeing several smaller autonomous territories. The difference between this system and Europe was that the "feudal lords" did not serve any function except to collect revenue from the land they owned. All other functions were overseen by religious sheikhs, and the operation of schools, medical services etc. were supported by private endowments. Political power had virtually no influence in social or religious life; not because it rejected religious rule, but because it embraced it as a fully complementary function to political rule.

But, over time, the structure of the international system changed, interaction between kingdoms increased, and rulers began to take a more active role in the societies they oversaw. Napoleon's short foray into Egyptian territory was the first step in this direction. For the first time in centuries, Muslims in Egypt were subject to the same taxes as Christians and Jews – despite the Qur'anic injunction for a separate type of tax for the latter. The Egyptian revolts at the very end of the eighteenth century were markedly Islamic in flavor, with slogans emphasizing the religious nature of the conflict: "May God grant victory to the Muslims" and "O Muslims, the jihad is incumbent upon you. How can you free men agree to pay the poll tax to the unbelievers? Have you no pride? Has not the call reached you?"[10] One of the most famous Egyptian leaders of this time was Muhammad Ali, and his rule came to characterize the end of the tentative balance that had existed between political power and religious legitimacy since the time of the first Muhammad. Determined to hang onto a power the Ottoman Empire preferred he not have, Muhammad Ali embarked on a series of massive reforms to build the Egyptian state. Muhammad Ali dismantled the feudal system and redistributed land ownership. He took a detailed interest in most forms of production, bringing many forms of craftsmanship under the control of the state. Further, he introduced Egyptian cotton to the international market and joined Egypt's economic health with that of the international economy. Muhammad Ali ended the right of private endowments to sponsor education, and made the appointment of the leadership of Al Azhar (Egypt's pre-eminent religious institution) a prerogative of his office.

Muhammad Ali the visionary was encumbered by the persistence of detail, and Egypt soon found itself unable to support the economic and social system he had created. Serious debts led to Muhammad Ali seeking outside assistance, and Egypt soon found itself dominated by foreign powers. Whatever legitimacy Muhammad Ali had retained by the sheer audacity of his reforms was lost when his immediate successor was forced to declare bankruptcy in 1876. At this point, Egypt came entirely under the control of foreign powers.

These powers were not interested in past arrangements between political power and religious legitimacy, and consequentially political power came to dominate all elements of Egyptian life, with little regard for Islamic doctrine. In the cases in which Sharia was referred to, it was as a tool to solidify support of political power. This shift reversed the functional relationship that had existed between Islam and politics since the conception of Islam.

Foreign domination was not just a political occurrence, it was perceived as an attempt by Christianity to dominate, or perhaps even eradicate, Islam. With this danger in mind, Egyptians began to call for a return to self-rule.

The end of World War I also marked the end of the Ottoman Caliphate and a weakening in Britain's ability to sustain its empire. Repeated insurrections in Egypt led to the 1919 revolution, and by extension the 1922 constitution. Although the Constitution recognized Islam as the "religion of the state," there was a concerted effort to avoid detailing precisely what this entailed. The Constitution was decidedly liberal in character, with clear similarities to the Western style of a social contract. The document emphasized individual freedom and sovereignty, two entities accorded in Sharia to reside only with God. Further, the Constitution declared all Egyptians to be equal, without regard for race, language or religion. This made official the lack of distinction Napoleon had made between Muslims and non-Muslims years earlier. Additionally, the Constitution ensured the right to a "freedom of conscience," while Islam (and Sharia) called for death for apostates.[11]

The years following the establishment of the Constitution resembled a political dance between three adversarial allies: the British (who had retained a significant amount of political control despite the declaration of independence), King Fuad (appointed by the British) and the Wafd Party (represented by Sa'ad Zhaglul). King Fuad hoped to secure his power base by assuming the Caliphate after the Ottoman Empire fell, but Zhaglul and the nationalists did not want Fuad (whom they viewed as a British puppet) to gain this type of religious legitimacy. The British were content to play Fuad and the nationalists against one another depending on their current interest.

It was into this uneasy mix that the Muslim Brethren made its entrance in 1928. The Brotherhood was appealing to many Egyptians because it assimilated many of the contentious issues that had been plaguing the Egyptian political scene. The organization was fundamentally Muslim and diametrically opposed to the creeping Westernization of society. The movement gave citizens the ability to protest Western imperialism and embrace their Islamic culture, where the nationalist movement before them had offered a choice of one or the other.

Brotherhood founder Hassan al-Banna was born in 1906 to a watch-repairman who was also the local imam. Al-Banna's propensity toward activism began at a young age, and while still a young student, he became involved with a variety of Islamic groups that promoted devout living and total commitment to the faith. Al-Banna was impressed with Sufism as a student, and this religious order played a large role in shaping his views throughout his life.[12] By 1927, al-Banna had established himself as a dedicated, charismatic man, and a persuasive leader. He was appointed to be a government schoolteacher and began to work with the parents of his students, laborers in the Suez Canal Company.[13]

Eventually, al-Banna became involved with the Young Muslim Men's Association in Isma'iliyya. The organization was newly formed, but al-Banna quickly became impatient with flaws he saw in the system. Al-Banna had long been dissatisfied with the lack of commitment in society to Muslim education. He believed that the Young Muslim Men's Association was in a perfect position to promote better education for Muslim youth and had the potential to bridge what he saw as the vast gulf between Islamic theology and Muslim living.[14] The failure of the Young Muslim Men's Association to take advantage of their unique position left al-Banna ripe for a request that came a short time later.

The Muslim Brethren was formed when six members of the labor force came to visit al-Banna and expressed their frustration with their lack of knowledge on how to pursue the right way to live out their Muslim faith. Richard Mitchell writes that the laborers articulated their desires as follows:

> We are unable to perceive the road to action as you perceive it, or to know that path to the service of the fatherland, the religion and the nation as you know it. All that we desire now is to present you with all that we possess, to be acquitted by God of the responsibility, and for you to be responsible before him for us and for what we must do. If a group contracts with God sincerely that it live for his religion and die in his service, seeking only his satisfaction, then its worthiness will assure its success however small its numbers or weak its means.[15]

The Brotherhood was not explicitly political in its earliest years, although it was not specifically apolitical either. Rather, al-Banna's concern was in educating the Egyptian populace regarding the encompassing nature of Islam. While it is not evident he himself aimed for political office (although he did run for parliament in later years), there is little question that he expected the effective education of the public would ultimately result in a popular insistence on a return to a religiously legitimate government.

Al-Banna's concern with Islamic education made this a primary focus of the organization. He believed that Muslim youth falsely associated progress with Westernization and strove to demonstrate the all-encompassing potential of Islam for progress and development. He saw the Muslim Brethren as "staunch defenders of an embattled identity in the face of the onslaught of modernism."[16]

The organization was also unique in its ability to excite young Muslim men about the faith in a way that had been lacking for some time. Al-Banna had truly reached his goal of providing a bridge between the traditional and the modern by demonstrating the development potential of Islam.

And yet, the 1940s were tumultuous in Egypt. Tensions were high as more and more of the Egyptian populace began to actively oppose the presence of the British in their state and the acceptance of their presence that the monarchy consistently displayed. Times were turbulent within the Brotherhood as well; in 1946, two top Brotherhood officials resigned over disagreements with al-Banna. These resignations led to a crisis of morale among the remaining organization administrators. The man that was chosen to replace the two officials was Salih Ashmawi. Not long after his appointment, Ashmawi became the first head of the controversial and mysterious Secret Apparatus of the Brotherhood.

This apparatus ultimately caused much divisiveness within the organization. Sources suggest this element of the Brotherhood was established between 1942 and 1943 – although the idea had been in existence for much longer.[17] Al-Banna's support for this element of the organization is not clear. Al-Banna is on record as saying that secrecy was a necessity if the organization was to survive, and he structured the membership of his organization to include a group of members he called "mujahid," or the strugglers.[18]

However, several years later, when alleged members of the Brotherhood began bombing areas in Cairo in an effort to protest the political order, al-Banna issued a communiqué denying that the perpetrators of such acts could be members of the Brotherhood, or even Muslims at all.[19] He also pleaded directly with the perpetrators, saying that he would view any further acts of violence committed by individuals associated with the Brotherhood as directed at him – and that he would accept full legal responsibility.[20]

At the same time that Egypt was facing an uncertain political future, the Palestinian people were facing an uncertain geographic one. Many members of the Brotherhood took an active role in the Palestinian War of 1948, and many others assisted by collecting arms and coordinating information. The Secret Apparatus played a significant part in the war, and al-Banna would later lament his loss of control over this group of the Society.

The years between 1945 and 1950 were violent ones for Egypt. In 1945, an unsuccessful attempt was made on the life of Nahhas Pasha; then in 1946 and 1947, bombs were set off in Cairo, and by the end of 1947, paramilitary sections of a number of opposition groups including the National Party, the Wafd and the Young Muslim Men's Association staged armed demonstrations in Cairo, boasting their arsenals that had been compiled for the Palestinian conflict.[21]

In 1948, the Egyptian government arrested members of the Muslim Brethren when they found 165 bombs and cases of arms. The men were soon released when they revealed they had been collecting the arms for the Palestinians. In February of the same year, a coup took place in Yemen, and correspondence between al-Banna and the Yemenis surfaced, and the government's interest in and fear of the Brotherhood also intensified.

On March 22, a judge was assassinated on his way to work. The judge had sentenced a Brother to prison for attacking a British soldier. Al-Banna was arrested along with two members of the Brotherhood who had actually perpetrated the crime. The two Brothers were sentenced to life in prison, and al-Banna was released for a lack of evidence. Al-Banna was apparently quite troubled by the judge's assassination, as he viewed it as further evidence that he no longer influenced the actions of the Secret Apparatus.

Then, a series of arrests in October made public for the first time the existence of the Secret Apparatus. This, combined with the judge's assassination, the weapons that were still being uncovered and the general unrest in the region, served as the foundation of the case that would soon be built against the Society. A riot at Cairo University in December resulted in more Egyptian deaths, and while no conclusive evidence existed to prove their involvement, the Muslim Brethren was the group officially accused. The group's newspaper was ordered to close, and the inevitable began closing in.

Al-Banna fought to defend the existence of the Society, but the government pressed its case. Al-Banna vehemently denied all the accusations against the Muslim Brethren in a pamphlet that he distributed clandestinely. Al-Banna was not arrested, but instead was shot in the street outside the building for the Young Muslim Men's Association in February of 1949.

Uncertainty, instability and violence

After al-Banna's execution, the government cracked down even harder on the Society, arresting and sentencing over 4000 members. The Brotherhood believed that relief would come in the form of the Free Officers revolution in 1952. However, the officers that came to power, and eventually the authoritarian regime of Nasser, quickly made clear that the revolutionary alliance had been born out of expediency rather than ideological sympathy. Indeed, Nasser's government struggled to maintain legitimacy in any form – often relying on little more than Nasser's own charisma for success. Cooper argues that the new regime was just strong enough to overthrow the unpopular monarchy, but not nearly strong enough to establish its own identity.[22]

The absence of a clear ideology in the 1952 revolution only served to exacerbate the differences between religious legitimacy and political power that had been fermenting over the last century. The Free Officers revolution of 1952 took place with the support of Al-Ikhwan al-Muslimin, based on an understanding between the officers and the Brotherhood about the role of Islam in the new state. The Brotherhood had issued both public and private announcements throughout the process of reform about the importance of establishing a state based on the precepts of Islam. Events suggested the revolutionary government supported these pronouncements. While the new government was struggling to find its footing, it did not hesitate to use repression when it was deemed necessary, but in the nascent years, the Brotherhood was demonstrably safe from these measures.

In January 1953, the government ordered the dismantlement of all political parties and organizations – except for Al-Ikhwan al-Muslimin. Three members of the organization were invited to sit on the Cabinet; another member was designated as a liaison between the organization and the government's "director of religious guidance,"[23] and there was talk of renaming an Alexandrian street after the founder of the Brotherhood, Hassan al-Banna.

But as early as late 1953/early 1954, fissures began developing between al-Ikhwan al-Muslimin and the state. In January 1954, a confrontation broke out at a university between members of the Brotherhood and members of the government-sponsored Liberation Rally and Youth Formations. While the Brothers were holding a rally to commemorate university martyrs, members of the government-sponsored organization pulled up in an Army jeep and began delivering nationalist speeches over a loudspeaker. Requests for them to leave were denied, and fights broke out, which resulted in injuries to several and the burning of the jeep.[24]

The next day, the Egyptian cabinet declared the Muslim Brethren to be a political party, and thus in violation of the 1953 law that had abolished all political parties. At 12:45 a.m. on January 13, the government accused the Brotherhood of "planning to overthrow the present form of government under the cover of religion,"[25] and all schools, hospitals and clinics established and run by al-Ikhwan al-Muslimin had to change their names or cease to operate. This opened a fissure between the Islamists generally, and the Brotherhood specifically, and the state that continues to this day.

In 1954, a member of the Brotherhood attempted to assassinate Nasir. Nasir came down quickly and harshly against the organization. And again, thousands of Brethren were sentenced to prison. Among these members was Said Qutb. While in prison, Qutb and the other Brothers experienced horrific suffering at the hands of their Egyptian captors, and this time in captivity had a huge impact on the future of Al-Ikhwan al-Muslimin.

In 1961, the Socialist Laws were passed, dramatically changing the social and political landscape of the country. Where the Islamists would have pursued the demarcation of this heritage by returning to the Islamic history of their nation, Nassir's regime turned instead to a Soviet model. In December 1961, Nassir delivered an address in which he stated:

> The cultural revolution puts itself at the service of the political and social revolution. We are on the way to building a society based on self-sufficiency and justice. We must have a cultural revolution which will be hostile to imperialism, hostile to reaction, hostile to feudalism, hostile to the domination and dictatorship of capitalism, hostile to all forms of exploitation.[26]

Nassir expected this to be accomplished by emphasizing the good of the nation over the good of the individual, and under this umbrella he justified the continued limitation of political parties, opposition, etc.[27] He undertook extensive reforms of the state and private sector, and undermined the traditional influence of the Ulama by reforming the historic Al Azhar University. For the first time, university professors could be selected from sources other than the religious Ulama.

Because the officers had come to power without a genuine prescribed power base, they used the mechanisms of the state to buy such a base through the establishment of networks of distributive rewards. The result was the co-option of large groups that would otherwise been unlikely to support the new regime.

Nasser built the Egyptian state into a hybrid system combining elements of socialism with strategic opportunities for private ownership. He generated support among the middle class by guaranteeing a job with the state to all

university graduates, and earned the loyalty of the lowest classes by subsidizing
the most basic goods. He brought the majority of production under the control of
the state, including the distribution of field crops. However, he left larger land
owners to sell their grocery crops as they saw fit, enabling them to build personal
wealth – and in so doing ensured their loyalty to his state.[28]

But the ad-hoc system Nasser established was expensive – both politically
and economically. The economy could not stand up to the strain Nasser's semi-
capitalist, quasi-corporatist state was placing on it, but Nasser could not politically afford to make any changes. He had built his power based on his ability to
feed his people, and any change to the system would be dangerous to his political power.

Although (or perhaps because?) Nasser likely knew the economic model he
had created was not destined for long-term success, he endeavored to gain legitimacy in other elements of his leadership. Nasser was responsible for the relatively short-lived efforts at Arab nationalism, and the foreign policy feats he
accomplished dancing on a tightrope between two superpowers during the Cold
War were little short of spectacular. Nasser had undeniable charisma, and this
unquestionably contributed to his popularity. However, it did little to build a
legitimate state, as all legitimacy was based on the person of Nasser, rather than
the institutions he founded.

Nasser addressed the issue of Islam inconsistently at best. He repressed the
Brotherhood severely if sporadically, but out of fear of the threat they constituted to his political power. In the years between 1962 and 1965, most of the
Brothers had been released from prison, but the Brotherhood, although physically together, was ideologically divided as to how to implement its mission.
Many members of the group were plotting to undermine the regime, but the
group was so fragmented that it is unlikely these plots could have amounted to
anything. However, Nasir was facing domestic and foreign conflicts and sought
to exert control where he could. The floundering Society, as well as the blatant
Qutb manifesto, provided an inspiring target.

Then, in July 1965, Qutb and his brother Muhammad were arrested, along
with several other Brethren. One young militant revealed some of the plans of
the organization, and the entire organization was summarily arrested. The government then instigated an impressive campaign against the Brethren, linking
them to foreign governments, accusing them of being spies for the United States,
and calling them terrorists and religious fanatics. The imprisoned Brothers were
again viciously tortured, with many breaking under the pressure and "confess-
ing" to the deeds of which the government had accused them. Qutb himself was
hanged on August 26, 1966.

Nasser made little effort to address the crisis of legitimacy such persecution
evoked. To some extent, the severity of the crisis was averted by his promotion
of Arab nationalism, as Arabism was often understood to be predicated on Islam.
However, even as secular powers began to override religious legitimacy, a
Western-style dualism ensured the problem was at best ignored, and at worst
exacerbated rather than resolved. Islam was technically the religion of the state,

but the constitution guaranteed rights not guaranteed in Islam: "The transcendent referent for authority and political power remained partly divine, and not purely secular."[29]

When Nasser died unexpectedly of a heart attack in 1970, his legacy was an economic system on the verge of collapse, and a vacuum in the state structure that had been filled by the sheer force of his personality. None of the remaining leaders could hope to fill that vacuum. Legally, Anwar Sadat was next in line for the presidency, but few expected that he would maintain power for long. This is to some degree a testament to the shaky legal power of the state, and also a comment on Sadat's own absence of personal charisma. But Sadat demonstrated a political cunning that belied his lack of charisma. Whether he did so because he recognized he could never rival Nasser's personal popularity, or because he knew the socialist system was on the verge of collapse, or because he recognized the political potential in the repressed Islamic movement, Sadat never even attempted to generate support from Nasser's nationalist/socialist base. Instead he immediately moved to consolidate his power around a religious reformation of sorts by releasing a majority of the jailed members of al-Ikhwan al-Muslimin, establishing religious camps for youths, and counteracting the strength of the socialists by creating incentives for religious organizations on university campuses.

In May 1971, Sadat initiated the "Rectification Revolution,"[30] which most sources identify as little more than an effort to purge the Egyptian government of Nasir cronies.[31] As many of these purged individuals had been supporters of Nasser's Soviet plan, the Egyptian Left became suspicious that Sadat would soon purge them of influence as well.

When Sadat returned from the Camp David Accords in 1979, a verbal war broke out between the regime and the Islamists. Sadat condemned the Islamists, accusing them of cloaking their contrary political aspirations in the mantel of religion.[32] The Islamists, in turn, condemned his efforts toward peace with Israel and challenged his reputation as the "pious president."

Sadat did not limit his changes to the universities. He also made structural changes to the state by appointing new governors, re-organizing the Cabinet, purging the intelligence and military community, dismantling the party system, and revising the constitution. Cooper identifies it as "both a masterly lesson of how to proceed from quasi importance toward supreme power, and a lesson in how to head off a coup."[33] Sadat's methods had the potential to remedy the gap between religious legitimacy and political power, but he ultimately fell prey to the same issue that had troubled Nasser – how to garner religious legitimacy without ceding power to religious leaders. Sadat was responsible for the growth of the Islamists, but he allowed them to grow to such an extent that he could no longer control them except by utilizing the monopoly of force that accompanied his power.

Often, historical accounts of the rise of Islamist groups in the 1970s attempt to portray their development as surprising or puzzling, but in reality this is not the case. Again, although the political power had become secularized, Egyptians more generally had maintained religious values.

Surveys conducted prior to and after Nasser's regime, intended to measure the "emancipation of Egypt," showed that religious values had changed scarcely at all, and that youths in 1976 were actually more conservative than those in the time of Nasser.[34] In fact, a 1972 study showed that

> High percentages [of youths] opted for the family stock as the first criterion in choosing a spouse. Eighty three percent of the young males supported the attitude that, given that a man and women are equal in every respect, the man should be considered superior. The majority of young males agreed that "the treatment of a girl in the family should be stricter than that of a boy." And over fifty percent supported the idea the natural place for the woman was in the home. Finally eighty seven percent of the youths surveyed said that the morality crisis (lack of public modesty) was the main problem disturbing them, and seventy five percent believed that the application of sharia would right these wrongs.[35]

Sa'ad Ibrahim explains:

> The extremists are not coming from Mars.... They don't hail from the margins of society, but from its very heart. Let's ask ourselves, who of us does not have a friend or relative, or a son of a relative or a son of a friend in the religious organization? Who of us does not have a relative who has taken the hijab in recent years?[36]

Now, since the early 1970s, the Muslim Brethren (and Islam more generally) has made something of a comeback in Egyptian society. However, with the exception of the early years of Sadat's regime, the state remained largely secular and consistently repressive against Islamic opposition movements. Most of the countries in the Arab world are governed by authoritarian regimes, and so the means by which the exclusion has occurred is different from the American experience in that most of the transitions toward secularism have been instituted from the top down, rather than the bottom up. However, a secular authoritarian regime has the power and means to dramatically shift the political landscape into a secular field, and indiscriminate repression against religious opposition is one way of accomplishing this.

Conclusions on the landscape

It has been demonstrated that secularization has changed the American and Egyptian political landscapes, and that incidences of violent, religiously motivated political protest have risen at a concurrent rate. This section has shown that secularization edged religion out of the political arena, but until recently still allowed for a parallel sphere of religious legitimacy. Critical events (the social revolution of the 1960s and the culminating decision of *Roe* v. *Wade* in the United States and the reneging of promises made to the religious movements by both Nasser and Sadat in Egypt) symbolized the erosion of that parallel sphere and resulted in a furious rise of religious opposition. It was the threat of a closing of the system in which religious supporters had traditionally operated that spurred the rise of the religious Right in both countries. In order to incite religious supporters to engage in protest, movement leaders developed a rhetoric that emphasized the urgency of the crisis.

The advancement of theories of secularization carried with it the assumption that the rise of secularization meant the decline of religion. In reality, in both Egypt and the United States, religion did not deliquesce; rather, it was merely dispersed into different arenas. The dispersal was motivated by an understanding that government was still constrained by its dependence on religion for legitimacy. While religion had retreated from an active role in the political arena, the state was still expected to legislate within the values and norms of religion. In describing the power of the Egyptian government, Muslim Brother General Guide Hudaiby said, "No government has the right to prohibit what is specifically ordained, or allow what is prohibited. It has the right, however, to legislate other matters for the public good."[37] When members of the religious communities in both countries perceived this arrangement to have been violated, religious social movements were born.

While most other efforts to explain religious movements in light of the advancement of secularism have focused on classical social-movement theory (and sought to explain the movements by focusing on grievance born of an aversion to modernization), this account has shown that when state power was understood by religious adherents to have violated its relationship to religious legitimacy, religious forces bonded together to form an opposition movement.

This part of the book has shown that, as the political landscape has become more secular, in both the United States and Egypt, religious movements have developed in response to a recognition that political opportunities for their participation are waning. Fear of such an occurrence leads to alliances between organizations that may not otherwise have existed. The next part will turn to the effects of movement rhetoric on the window of opportunity. After looking at the development of each of the four examples of this study, it will be argued that as rhetoric becomes more shrill in denouncing the secularization of society, the window of opportunity begins to close more quickly, forcing movement supporters to move in one of two directions: out of the movement into the political mainstream; or further to the fringes of the political arena.

Part II

Definition, development and consequence

Opposition movements in the United States and Egypt

4 A discussion of rhetoric

The previous part of this book explored the puzzle of the continued advancement of religion in the United States and Egypt, despite the prevalence of secularization in the political arenas of both states. It was argued that the rise of religious social movements can be explained using a political-process approach to understand the impact of secularization on the twentieth-century political process in both Egypt and the United States, and that religious social movements developed in response to this continued secularization. While this argument is useful in predicting where and when religious movements might be likely to arise, it does not explain why organizations pursue the methods they do. In other words, if all religious organizations are reacting to the same threat of secularism, why do some organizations use violence while others do not?

Previous efforts to answer this question center around two categories of variables: external influences on organizational behavior; and elements unique to the internal make up of the organization's ideology. This chapter will begin with a discussion of these approaches and recognition of their explanatory limitations in light of the American and Egyptian cases. Specifically, we will discover that while variables in both categories are useful indicators of the timing of political violence, they are unable to explain how organizations with similar ideologies and objectives come to endorse such variant methods of action. To better explain this phenomenon, we will look at the ways in which an organization's rhetoric changes the political process.

This chapter aims to show that the religious rhetoric used to mobilize supporters serves to quicken the closing of the window of opportunity available to them, forcing religious movements to either move closer to the political center to preserve their waning influence, or further out to the fringes of the political arena to preserve the purity of their cause. This will be explored in light of the Christian Coalition and the Army of God in the first portion, and the Muslim Brethren and al Jama'a al Islamiyya in the second. It will become evident that the Christian Coalition, the Army of God, the Muslim Brethren and al Jama'a al Isamiyya are motivated by similar ideological interests. It will also be demonstrated that the Coalition and the Brotherhood both moved closer to the center of the political process by adopting rhetoric that allowed for a varied political base. By developing a rhetoric that was more encompassing than clear, they successfully found themselves in positions to influence the future development of that process. However, in so doing, they were forced to give up some of the demands that had inspired their movement to begin with. In contrast, the Army of God and al Jama'a al Islamiyya maintained a rhetoric that emphasized the urgency of their cause and, in so doing, faced a window of opportunity closing more quickly, and as a result were thrust to the fringe of the political process.

Internal variables

Many scholars of religious violence attribute its existence to the nature of religion itself.[1] In fact, many Christian hymns sing of violent images, while others promote the idea of the Christian as a soldier, "marching as to war." The Qur'an and the Bible are filled with stories of blood, sacrifice, martyrs and enemies to be conquered.

Regina Schwartz argues that violence is a result of identity formation and indeed, that identity formation is the "most frequent and fundamental act of violence we commit." Identity is formed when individuals discover who they are. And this, most often, is a composite of who they are *not*. When identity is formed in such a way, its maintenance depends on the "perpetual policing of its fragile borders." For it is in the name of identity (religion, ethnicity, race, nationality and gender etc.) that some of the most horrific acts of violence have been committed.

For example, the Bible begins with the murderous rivalry between Cain and Abel, and emphasizes the relationship of a jealous God that declared Israel His chosen people. Schwartz argues that the Bible is a book of repeated efforts to form identity, based on exclusion from something else. Cain was not Abel, Israel not Canaan: the Bible is full of what Schwartz calls "efforts to strengthen the precariousness of collective identity." Further, the Bible is based on monotheism, which is the ultimate form of "other exclusion." Schwartz argues that it is in the pursuit of this identity that so much violence was, and continues to be, committed[2].

Not only will a better understanding of the religious undercurrents of Western society be beneficial for its own sake, but recognition of the very nature of religion as an exercise in boundary creation between one entity and its "Other" will remedy the mystery that plagues the relationship between religion and political violence.

While Schwartz focuses exclusively on the Bible as the source for violence, others point to the Qur'an as the source. Mark Gabriel, former Imam and professor at Al Azhar University, argues that while there are verses in the Qur'an that promote peace, love and forgiveness, the principle of *naskh*[3] limits their relevance. Gabriel argues that there are 114 verses in the Qur'an that promote peace and forgiveness, but each of these is overridden by subsequent verses promoting forceful conversion, war and violent jihad.[4]

These studies are valuable when answering the question: *Why does religion sometimes lead to violence?* But, interestingly, they do little to answer the question, *Why does religion, in some cases, not lead to violence?* When violence is seen to be embedded in the context of religion, its absence becomes the puzzle. Indeed, if religion is, as these authors would argue, primarily a means of excluding oneself from the "other," then the lingering question is not why does religion sometimes lead to violence, but rather, why sometimes does it not? And this is the limitation that researchers find themselves up against when they consider religious ideology as the only, or even primary, causal variable in outbreaks of religiously motivated violence. If belief alone were predictive of violence, then our case studies should convincingly demonstrate a clear difference in belief among those who would use violence and those who would not. However, as the investigation in the following pages will show, no such clear distinctions exist. In both the American and the Egyptian cases, the violent and non-violent cases share remarkably similar ideology, venerate identical ideological heroes of the faith and call for the same political objective.

This chapter will proceed by looking comparatively at the ideological similarities between the Christian Coalition and the Army of God, and the Muslim Brethren and al Jama'a al Islamiyya. It will be demonstrated that, while the consequence of their ideologies differ dramatically, the fundamental beliefs of the organizations in both cases do not differ as much as one might expect. In the next chapter, the discussion will then turn to an examination of the different ways this ideology is manifested in the rhetoric of each organization, and then, finally, how this rhetoric influences the political opportunities available.

Ideological similarities in the Christian Coalition and the Army of God

Taken collectively, we can learn much about the ideology of the Christian Coalition from the views of Pat Robertson's supporters in the 1988 presidential campaign. The ideology of Robertson supporters focuses more intently on social issues (abortion being one of the most important) than does the ideology of more mainstream Republicans:[5] "For example, a quarter of Reagan activists and nearly half other candidate donors accept abortion on demand, compared to 3 percent of Robertson supporters."[6] Another survey showed 81.3 percent of Robertson supporters to strongly favor an anti-abortion amendment, in contrast to 32.8 percent of other Republicans.[7] Further, future Christian Coalition members were demonstrated to be

> more likely to accept a literal interpretation of the Bible, believe in an afterlife, consider religion important to their lives and regularly attend church services in conservative denominations.... In addition they exhibit greater support for civil religion, believing that God has blessed America above other nations and that religion should play an important role in politics.[8]

Of supporters surveyed, 91 percent identified themselves as born-again Christians (in contrast to 27.2 percent of other Republicans), and 42.4 percent were involved in some type of anti-abortion group.[9]

As may be fitting given its conservative outlook, the Christian Coalition looks with suspicion on instances in which it believes the state is overstepping the limitations the founders intended for it. Robertson has been particularly vocal about his concerns over the judicial branch of the American government. He argues that the judiciary has a history of trying to exude more power than it is intended to hold – and he considers abortion to be one of the most tragic consequences of this effect. Robertson is adamant that abortion would never have been legalized were it not for the Supreme Court's desire to legislate from the bench. He frequently quotes Thomas Jefferson's warning that if the judiciary is left as the final arbiters of all constitutional questions, Americans would find themselves under the "despotism of an oligarchy."[10] Robertson went even further in November 1999 when he "described the nation's highest legal court as a 'dictatorship that's been imposed upon us,' and encouraged followers to 'throw off their shackles' and ignore court decisions they found to be contrary to their religion."[11]

This data allows us to reasonably conclude that members of the Christian Coalition differ in fundamental ways from the mainstream Republican Party. But while interesting, this does not get us closer to answering our question, because the Coalition, for all their differences, has never used or endorsed the use of force in the implementation of their beliefs. So it is necessary, then, to turn our attention to the beliefs of an organization that has used force, to determine what, if any, differences there are.

The Memorial Institute for the Prevention of Terrorism identifies nine leaders of the Army of God. What the leaders know about each other is not clear. The *Army of God Manual* (a handbook for would-be and existing soldiers which details methods of violent action) explains that it is the very non-connected nature of the organization that makes it so hard for federal officials to track. The manual identifies the Army as "a real Army, with God as the Commander in Chief."[12] The soldiers communicate primarily through the Internet, and indeed the Internet is a vast source of information about the organization. The Army sponsors its own website with lists of members, their important deeds and, in many cases, valid contact information. Members are quite prolific in their writing. In the course of this research, I spoke with a number of individuals in the Army, and received answers to survey questions from others. The organization is very small (at most, two-dozen active members), and extremely secretive and suspicious of inquiries into their beliefs and activities. As a result, percentages (like those used to gauge the beliefs of the Christian Coalition) are limited in their applicability, as one or two individuals can affect a survey by over 10 percent. With those restrictions in mind, it is nonetheless interesting to note that seven out of ten believe the Bible to be literally true, and nine out of ten attend church at least once a week. All of those surveyed agreed with the statement that "abortion is murder."

Much like Robertson condoned the "throwing off of the shackles" of government when laws were created that contradicted an individual's religion, the Army of God sees the illegitimacy of the government to be directly tied to its decision to legalize abortion. Army member John Brockhoeft says:

No government can pass a law or issue a decree making it legally possible for anyone to take your life away. If such a "law" were enacted, the "law" itself would be illegal; and since there can be no such thing as an illegal law, the thing wouldn't be a law at all. It wouldn't just be a bad law – it wouldn't be a law at all. As Thomas Aquinas wrote long ago, when man-made laws deviate from the laws of nature they are "no longer law but a perversion of law" and "are acts of violence rather than laws ... because an unjust law is no law at all." At the very moment a legislative body would pretend to enact such a thing, or the very moment a judicial body would issue such a decree (such as *Roe* v. *Wade*) two things would happen:

1   The law itself would become null and void
2   The "government" that pretended to pass it would be come illegal.[13]

There are ideological similarities between the Muslim Brethren and al Jama'a al Islamiyya as well. One of the most recent controversial Islamic philosophers is Sayyid Qutb. Qutb was attracted to the Brotherhood because the organization appeared to combine Islamic thought with practice, a principle that Qutb advocates in all of his works. He was made a member of the Brotherhood in 1952 and was given responsibility for the publishing wing of the organization. Qutb revealed certain perspectives on Islamic government in his writings that grew more extreme over time, and these writings came to serve as the splinter that would wedge itself between the violent and non-violent Islamist movements.

Qutb believed that the purpose of politics was to establish harmony in the world by restructuring society to reflect the parameters of absolute truth:

Politics is, therefore, about the achievement of a community of uniformity, placing worldly power in the service of divine harmony. Politics should be about maintaining the community, and the maintenance of the community requires unanimity among men in conformity with the will of God. Political activity must, therefore, be directed towards ascertaining the will of God, putting it into practice and ensuring that dissenting practice does not rupture the harmony thereby established.[14]

From politics and society to arts and the sciences, Qutb identified all aspects of life as under the authority of God – and thus required to be in alignment with God's governance. Thus, says Qutb,

Man should not cut himself off from this authority to develop a separate system and a separate scheme of life. The growth of a human being, his conditions of health and disease, and his life and death are under the scheme of those natural laws which come from God.... Man cannot change the practice of God in the laws prevailing in the universe. It is therefore desirable that he should also follow Islam in those aspects of his life in which he is given a choice and should make the Divine law the arbiter in all matters of life so that there may be harmony between man and the rest of the universe."[15]

In this, Qutb and the Muslim Brethren were in full agreement. Both agree that when Islam is recognized as a fully integrated religious doctrine and comprehensive political system, there is no need for laws made by humanity. Indeed, government should never be more than the humble servant of Allah – fully recognizing that leaders are no more privileged than those they govern.

The significance of Qutb's work was not so much in the theology he promulgated – many Islamists fully supported his promotion of Sharia law and a government that respected Islamic principles. Indeed, in 1964, the first Hudaiby "declared that the book vindicated all the hopes he had placed in Sayid Qutb, who now embodied the future of the Muslim mission."[16] Forty-two years later, in an interview with the author, Ibrahim Hudaiby (great-grandson of Hassan Hudaiby) praised Qutb as a courageous hero, even as he condemned the violence that ultimately resulted from Qutb's position. What ultimately resulted in major controversy was the method Qutb advocated to advance his ideology.

In 1969, Hudaiby published "Missionaries, Not Judges," an essay wherein he reversed his initial endorsement of Qutb, now rejecting "the practice of takfir, thereby rejecting the rational for active revolution and stressed Egyptians need only be educated in matters of Islam."[17]

As scholar Saad Eddin Ibrahim explains,

[The Muslim Brethren's] remaining leaders had made the strategic decision to discard violence. The decision preceded heated debates among the membership inside and outside Nasir's prisons. Some younger members never accepted the new strategy of non-violence, and became the founders of the new jama'at and jam'iyat as well as a number of relatively apolitical Islamic reform groups.[18]

But the thing that is most interesting (and most frequently overlooked by policy-makers) is that these members had to split because the Brotherhood was committed to not using violence. Despite indiscriminate repression against Brotherhood members and supporters, the organization emerged from prison committed to a non-violent method. The Brothers, still hoping that they would soon be given the right to operate openly, expressed their desire to see Sharia as the only source for Egyptian law; but, nonetheless, they still displayed a willingness to work within the current system.

This change was reiterated in the Brotherhood's choice for the new Supreme Guide in 1973. Umar al-Tilmisani had been a member of the Brotherhood since the 1930s, but he made it clear when he came to power that he did so as an advocate of moderation. Tilmisani argued that the broadly sketched goals of the Brotherhood had not changed. They still sought the "building of a new generation of believers who will support the call and become a model for others, such that ultimately the Islamic nation will be liberated from foreign domination and a free Islamic state will be established."[19]

Tilmisani was careful to point out that the purpose of establishing this type of state was not to empower the Society. He and other leaders of the Society stressed that their ideal Islamic state did not have to be governed by a Brother, but simply one who upheld Islamic precepts. Tilmisani wrote:

> The first level of power is the power of creed and belief. The second is the power of unity and belonging. And third comes the power of weapons and strength. If the power of creed and belief is lost and there is no unity, reliance upon weapons results in destruction. The Brethren do not consider revolution, nor do they depend on it, nor do they believe in its utility or is outcome. As for rule, the Brethren do not request it for themselves. If they find among the nation one who can handle this burdensome responsibility ... who can rule following Islamic and Qur'anic mores, the Brethren will be his soldiers, his supporters and his assistants.[20]

There is little question (and this issue was raised in the course of several interviews) that members of both the Christian Coalition and the Army of God would insist that their respective organizations differ ideologically. And members of the Muslim Brethren are quick to differentiate between themselves and members of al Jama'a al Islamiyya. But, if we define ideology as Merriam–Webster does, as simply being "a systematic body of concepts especially about human life or culture," then we are forced to recognize that the organizations are not ideologically all that different. Certainly, the manner in which they attempt to implement their ideology is different, but the beliefs that drive their goals are quite similar. This is all to suggest that belief alone is not sufficient to explain the action it may or may not lead to.

External variables

If the impetus for a particular type of action cannot be said to be internal to religious organizations, then it is sensible to look next at external elements that act on the organization to stimulate action. A common explanation for the use of violence by social movements comes from measuring the violence meted out by the ruling elite. Former General Guide of Al-Ikhwan al-Muslimin, Omar al-Tilmisani, has frequently remarked that "violence invites violent counter reaction" and has repeatedly referred to the period of Nasir's rule as the "inquisition era."[21]

As pioneers in the application of social-movement theory to Islamic activism, Hafez and Wiktorowicz favor a similar understanding.[22] According to their theory, the actions of activists are very closely linked to the actions of the ruling power. Activists employ violence as a tool depending on the timing and targeting of violence used by the regime.

While Hafez and Wiktorowicz's argument provides a refreshing rational-choice perspective in a field largely paralyzed by arguments about religious exceptionalism, it does not fully answer the question driving this study. For Hafez and Wiktorowicz's argument to be effective in solving the puzzle of this book, there would have to be evidence of clear distinction on the part of the regime between violent and non-violent groups.[23] In other words, we would expect to see that al Jama'a al Islamiyya was subject to indiscriminate repression prior to their use of violence *and* that the Muslim Brethren were not. In reality, this is not the case. In fact, the tumultuous history of the Muslim Brethren shows that every regime under which they operated has repressed the organization at one time or another. Moreover, the Army of God and the Christian Coalition both operated in a non-repressive state system, and yet reacted in polar-opposite ways. So the question that Hafez and Wiktorowicz ultimately answer is not why some groups use violence as a tool for social activism and why others do not, but instead, when groups already willing to use violence will consistently employ it.

What is missing from the discussion on both sides (internal *and* external) is some manner of assimilating the two. In other words, exclusive focus on either internal or external variables limits the explanatory power of both. What is missing from the study of religiously motivated political violence is a comprehensive look at elements that act in and upon religious organizations.

This study accepts the premise that religious organizations operate in a political system, and that system influences them as much, if not more, than they influence it. However this study also recognizes that, in the four case studies chosen for investigation, there was not a clear difference in levels of state repression before two of the four organizations turned to violence. As was demonstrated in the first part of the book, all four organizations within their respective movements found themselves on the outside of an increasingly secularized political process. Moreover, this study argues that one is best served in combining the internal and external approaches by acknowledging that belief matters, but primarily when it interacts with a changing external political situation.

It is in light of this assumption that the discussion of rhetoric in the next chapter is undertaken. Rhetoric is understood to be reflective of ideology, but also influenced by (and influential on) political circumstance. The following pages discuss the development of rhetoric in each of the groups. In fact, as the case studies will show, the rhetoric organizations use reflects their understanding of the urgency of their cause: the more urgent they perceive the cause to be, the more radical the rhetoric an organization is willing to use. However, as their rhetoric becomes more radical, the more quickly their opportunity for political access diminishes; and, consequentially, the greater the urgency of their cause.

5 The consequence of rhetoric

Chapter 4 argued that existing explanations, whether they look to variables internal or external to opposition organizations, are unable to account for why some organizations will use violence and others won't, despite similar ideological understandings of the political process and similar exposure to regime-sponsored repression. This chapter will argue that part of the explanation centers around an understanding of the way in which organizations articulate their ideology and, further, that an organization's rhetoric acts on the political process so as to influence the political opportunities available to the organizations in question. By comparing the rhetoric first of the Christian Coalition and the Army of God, and then the Muslim Brethren and al Jama'a al Islamiyya, it will be shown that rhetoric affects an organization's place in the political process, thereby reducing or increasing the urgency of the cause for which they fight.

Coalition rhetoric

Interviewing Pat Robertson was a little like looking behind the curtain to discover the Wizard of Oz was a regular man. His answers to questions about his understanding of the role of government and the problems that plague American politics were consistent with those he had written in his many books. And yet the answers did not reflect the esoteric philosophy one would expect from such a large-scale religious leader. Robertson defines the purpose of government in light of God's plan for humanity:

> Government must insure peace and freedom so that each of its citizens may freely work out on earth the special plan of God. Restraint should only come to prevent one citizen from hindering another citizen from enjoying life, liberty and the pursuit of happiness.[1]

Additionally, Robertson draws this purpose for government from his interpretation of several verses from Isaiah: "Before I formed you in the womb, I knew you. Before you were born I sanctified you and ordained you to be a prophet to the nations."[2] From this, Robertson identifies a God-given plan for the life of every person. Thus, the purpose of government is to ensure individuals have the freedom to pursue that plan.

At the same time, Robertson is vague on details. When this author asked him to identify his greatest political adversary, he said, "The liberal left ... whoever they are."[3] Robertson refers to the establishment of the Coalition as a defensive, not offensive, plan. He noted that the "cherished beliefs" of Christians of all backgrounds were under attack, and that the Coalition provided a vehicle for them to fight against those who would threaten their values.[4]

Robertson has been largely consistent in his condemnation of abortion. He frequently refers to the act as murder, and commonly invokes the struggle as one of spiritual warfare – where abortion is a tool of Satan to gain a hand in the world. He says,

> In my opinion, abortion is murder. Once you begin to understand that the taking of an innocent life is murder, then that raises the bar from a "constitutional right" to something that needs to be stopped.... Abortion is murder. Whenever Satan is at work in the world, people's lives aren't safe. One of the things we must protect from the moment of conception to the moment of natural death is the life of people.[5]

But even as Robertson's rhetoric clearly defines abortion as murder, he refrains from using the language which would put the emphasis on the lives of the babies being lost. Instead he focuses on what he might call the bigger picture – the spiritual struggle that continues between God and Satan.

In the interview with the author, Robertson had an interesting explanation for his decision to pursue political expediency over more confrontational efforts to protect unborn children. Robertson was asked, "If you believe that abortion is murder, and is condemned by God, then what stops you (and members of the Coalition) from using force to end its occurrence?" He responded that, while he considered Randal Terry (founder of Operation Rescue) a friend, he also saw him as an embarrassment, because he "kept on getting arrested." Robertson emphasized his interest in efficient action and says, "If efficient action means standing before a firing squad, by all means do so," but went on to point out that it was his organization, the American Center for Law and Justice, that "had to rescue their hides after they got arrested."[6] He called the more confrontational tactics that resulted in arrests "self-perpetuating ego-trips," and said that such efforts were not the face he wanted for the Christian Coalition.

And yet, struggles within the organization suggested that political pragmatism could be taken too far. Every policy platform that the organization has distributed has dealt with the issue in no uncertain terms. In 1996, an inter-group struggle erupted when executive director Ralph Reed suggested changing the organization's support of the Republican Party platform's wording on abortion. Reed suggested going from "We believe the unborn child has a fundamental individual right to life which cannot be infringed. We therefore reaffirm our support for a Human Life Amendment" to:

We are a party that respects the sanctity of innocent human life as the basis of all civil rights. We will seek by all legal and constitutional means to protect the right to life for the elderly, the infirm, the unborn and the disabled.[7]

In an interview, Reed had indicated he might support legislation that allowed for abortion in the case of rape or incest, but other Christian Coalition members were outraged, suggesting that Reed was betraying his duty to protect the rights of the unborn. Reed quickly hopped back on board the Coalition bandwagon and denied that he would ever threaten the firm anti-abortion platform of the group.

The Christian Coalition was built in a time when the majority of political organizations were single-issue advocacy groups based on impersonal direct mailings to raise support for controversial issues. Reed developed an organization that reverted back to a different model of political activism in which a standing support system was in place to mobilize quickly and effectively. To this end, Reed sought to build the organizations first in churches, then precincts, then counties and then states etc. Reed's focus was less on religion, and more on political success.

Accordingly, members were trained in political methods, rather than just mobilized by issues. In active precincts, members were invited to attend satellite meetings every third Tuesday of the month. Reed would spend an hour offering instructions via satellite on how to organize campaigns, mobilize voters, create persuasive literature and the like. Then, a list of law-makers would be distributed, and members were encouraged to call to make their views known.[8]

Ralph Reed began to aim the vernacular of the Christian Coalition at capturing the hearts and minds of a different demographic. A survey conducted during the Robertson presidential campaign defined two primary demographics within Robertson supporters:

1   Individuals over 50 who identify themselves as concerned by the decline of morality in society since the 1960s.
2   Young couples with children.[9]

When Reed discovered the results of this survey, he salivated over the untouched potential of the second group – and prepared to structure the Coalition in such a way as to bring these individuals into its fold. Reed conceded that not all members of the second demographic agreed with the politics or religion of the Coalition, but saw that as secondary to the influence a larger voting bloc could attain. Reed made a concerted effort to frame the issues of the Coalition in the language of these sought-after suburbanites, and this strategy was distinctly different from that of organizations that came before the Coalition. While the Moral Majority and others like it had targeted fundamentalist Christians with a narrow political message, Reed broadened the appeal of the Coalition simply by changing the vocabulary used to promote it.

He says:

> You say, "We're concerned about children, we're trying to strengthen the
> family, we're trying to reverse the coarsening of culture, we believe that
> faith has a role in civic discourse." You see, that's totally different than
> saying, "We're evangelicals and we're here to take over." … You don't
> need a Christian Coalition in a Bible Belt town that has blue laws. I mean,
> you've sort of already won.[10,11]

Later he elaborated, saying:

> I became convinced that we had spoken sometimes … in the evangelical
> vernacular that the secular ear could not comprehend. And it really was self-
> indulgent…. You don't just show up at the meeting and speak Hebrew if
> they speak Greek. You have to speak in their language. We weren't doing
> that – not because there was any philosophical or theological objection to it.
> We were just selfish.[12]

Reed's point is fascinating in light of his evident awareness of the political process.
He understood, perhaps far better than Robertson ever could, that issues do not
immediately translate into action – rather, issues must be framed into rhetoric,
which informs the opportunities for action. His comment that "you don't need a
Christian Coalition in a Bible Belt town that has blue laws. I mean, you've sort of
already won" perfectly articulates his understanding of the Coalition as a vehicle for
political access. It was not that issues did not matter, but rather that issues could
best be addressed once supporters were in places of authority to address them.[13]

Thus it is evident in the case of the Christian Coalition that the organization
built a political platform very similar to the mainstream arguments of Francis
Schaeffer. Like Schaeffer, the organization frequently defended their right as
evangelicals to be a part of the political process. Also like Schaeffer, they justify
the necessity of their existence in terms of the changing political culture of the
last 50 years. As Robertson said, they are playing defensive, not offensive, politics. Yet, the presence of Ralph Reed assured that idealism rarely entirely out-
weighed pragmatism – and ensured that the Coalition maintained political
access, even if it meant sacrificing ideological clarity.

This is seen to the opposite effect in the development of the Army of God.

Toward the use of force

In 1993, Shelly Shannon was arrested for shooting abortion doctor George Tiller.
Shannon indicated that her actions had been influenced by a guidebook, which
she called the *Army of God Manual.*[14] A copy of the manual was found hidden in
Shannon's backyard.[15] The manual is over 100 pages long and encourages a
wide range of illegal activities, including the assassination of abortion personnel.
In one chilling passage, the manual explains:

The use of force is woefully inadequate against mass murder, unless that force is directed against the perpetrator of the crime. Imagine an investigator discovering a killer. He knows where the crimes are committed. He knows the building contains all the instruments of torture that this criminal will be using. So the investigator goes out in the middle of the night and destroys the murder weapons, and even the structure where the killer did his crimes. So the psychopathic mass murderer packs up, moves down the street, reinvests in more instruments of torture, and continues killing. Our Most Dread Sovereign Lord requires that whoever sheds a man's blood, by man his blood will be shed. We are forced to take arms against you. You shall not be tortured by our hands. Vengeance belongs to God only. However, execution is rarely gentle.[16]

Shannon describes her decision to use force as a gradual one,[17] influenced by her correspondence with the men and women listed as "Prisoners of Christ" on the Army of God website. Shannon began her involvement in stopping abortion in 1988, participating in 35 different protests led by Operation Rescue, resulting in 98 days of jail time. But, in 1991, Shannon began to wonder whether what she was doing was enough. She says:

The biggest hurdle was being willing to even consider that God could indeed require this work of anyone. Christians don't do that sort of thing, do they? But prayer and God cleared that up. Then I realized I needed to stop the killing too.[18]

Shannon began by starting fires in buildings where abortions were performed. Her attempts were not always successful (including one instance wherein she set fire to the California Board of Chiropractic Examiners building by mistake), but Shannon was continually encouraged by other members of the Army. She wrote to Army Chaplain Michael Bray after one failed attempt, "Was so sure it was God's how, when and where. Why no results?" Bray responded, "Little oaks fell mighty oaks."[19] Shannon also used foul-smelling butyric acid to shut clinic doors, using syringes to inject the liquid into building walls.

Around the same time that Shannon made her transformation from protestor to vandal, Michael Griffin shot and killed Dr. David Gunn, a doctor who frequently performed abortions for women. Shannon wrote in her diary that "[h]e didn't shoot Mother Teresa, he shot a mass murderer such as Saddam Hussein or Hitler. I don't even think it is accurately termed as murder."[20]

Shelley's rhetoric reflects the continued transformation going on inside her at this time:

Sometimes I felt like a failure when I stood with a sign and didn't do everything I could to save babies' lives. I let them kill babies! Allowing many babies to be killed day after day may not even be "pro-choice". It may actually be pro-abortion. Think about it. I was allowing the choice of abortion, but didn't really stop it. I didn't give the babies any choice.... Claiming it's only pro-life to want all people alive, including the abortionist, is deception. If the abortionist remains alive, many babies die. Keeping Hitler alive as long as his men did was not pro-life, and neither is the death of thousands of innocent babies rather than one guilty murderer. That "choice" is abortion. Those who killed abortionists chose "life" for all the innocent babies he would have killed, and did our country a great service.[21]

On August 19, 1993, Shannon decided to put her beliefs into practice. She borrowed a gun from a friend and taught herself how to shoot. She went to an abortion clinic in Wichita, Kansas, and stood around with other protesters until the doctor left the clinic at 7:00 p.m. Shannon attempted to shoot the doctor, but succeeded only in wounding him slightly. Shannon fled the scene but was taken into police custody somewhere between Wichita and Oklahoma City. Shannon, who has remained in prison since the shooting, says of the act, "It was the most holy, most righteous thing I've ever done."[22]

Shannon was not the only one to be profoundly impacted by Griffin's action. So also was Paul Hill, a regular (and vocal) protestor at a Pensacola, Florida, abortion clinic. Women seeking abortions were frequently subject to Hill's presence outside the clinic, and once inside, could still here him calling to them, "Mommy, Mommy, please don't kill me!"

Hill appeared on Donahue after the Gunn killing, and defended Michael Griffin's actions as justified, but he was careful to refrain from identifying the act as "wise," as this was not something he had yet resolved in his own mind. However, as weeks passed, Hill came to believe that

> [u]sing force necessary to defend the unborn gives credibility, urgency, and direction to the pro-life movement. These are the traits that it has lacked, and that it needs to prevail.... Thus it is not unwise or unspiritual to use the means God has appointed for keeping his commandments, rather, it is presumptuous to neglect these means and expect Him to work apart from them.[23]

The idea to kill Pensacola doctor James Britton occurred to Paul Hill barely a week before he implemented his idea. He identifies the idea for the attack as coming into his mind on a Thursday evening. He went to protest outside the clinic on Friday, and in the course of the visit, he accumulated essential information about the comings and goings of Dr. Britton.

Interestingly, Hill says of his emotions the day of the shooting that "I was fully determined to act, but my usual zest, and the zeal I expected to feel were missing. The lower half of my body was gripped with a gnawing emptiness."[24] Despite his uneasiness, Hill went through with his task, shooting and killing both Dr. John Britton and his security escort James Britton. After the men were dead, Hill set the shotgun on the ground and walked away from the bodies, as he describes it, "waiting for arrest."

The introduction of a moral duty

While in prison, Hill wrote a book, *Mix My Blood with the Blood of the Unborn*, which has since become the theological cornerstone of the Army of God. In his work, Hill argues that God condones murder when it is done to protect innocent babies from being aborted. The whole tract is centered around Hill's understanding of what he calls the "Moral Law" and what he sees as his (and other's) responsibility to uphold it in the face of a changing and sinful society. He says:

> The duty to defend the innocent with the means necessary is an essential aspect of the Moral Law that is found in both the Old and New Testaments, and has been recognized and implemented throughout history. Neither the overwhelming majority of citizens, nor the government, questions the duty to defend the innocent. Not everyone agrees on the degree of force that is appropriate, but the obligation to defend the innocent people with the means necessary is such a clear and compelling aspect of Moral Law that it can scarcely be denied. Not only does the Moral Law require the means necessary for defending the innocent, this duty comes directly from God and cannot be removed by any human government. The duty to defend your own or your neighbor's child, thus, is inalienable. When the government forbids this defense, the people, "must obey God rather than men" (Acts 5:29 b)…. As a consequence you do not need the state's permission before defending your (or your neighbor's) unborn child.[25]

When interviewed days before his scheduled execution, Hill stated,

> I don't feel any remorse because I think it was a good thing, and instead of being shocked, more people should do what I did. I think more people should act as I acted. I didn't seek the death penalty. The state's seeking the death penalty, but I'm willing and I feel very honored that they are most likely going to kill me for what I did. I'm certainly, to be quite honest, I'm expecting a great reward in heaven for my obedience.[26]

Paul Hill was finally executed by the state of Florida on September 3, 2003.

Similarly, in 1996, Eric Rudolph bombed an abortion clinic, as well as Atlanta's Olympic Park, and for five years police were unable to locate Rudolph to make an arrest. In 2001, Clayton Wagner sent 550 anthrax letters to abortion clinics around the country and was later sentenced to 30 years in prison.[27] In 2003, North Carolina nurse Brenda Phillips turned herself in for firing shots at an abortion clinic. She was later accused of harboring then-fugitive Eric Rudolph.

The Army of God website lists many such "anti-abortion heroes of the faith," as well as soldiers incarcerated for the cause. Uniting each of these individuals is a belief that God condones murder in defense of the unborn, as well as a firm conviction that peaceful resolution to the abortion question is unacceptable.

Michael Bray, commonly identified as the chaplain of the Army of God, argues that groups like the Christian Coalition who condemn abortion as murder, but fail to actively, and if necessary, violently stop its occurrence, have made themselves into hypocrites. He says:

> By condemning themselves to defensive action, they belie themselves and nullify all their pro-life proclamations.... Rather than advance the effort to contend for justice for the womb children in our land, these anti-violence dupes, with their irrational rhetoric, continue to turn the movement backward.[28]

Bray is not alone in characterizing the non-violent anti-abortion organizations as aimless in their purpose. Army of God supporter Dave Leach criticizes the Christian Coalition in particular as an organization operating without "a vision."[29] In an interview with the author, Leach recounted a story about Randall Terry, saying that prior to the existence of the Army of God, Terry (director of Operation Rescue) regularly cited Proverbs 24:10–12 as justification for his aggressive protest strategies. The verse reads:

> If you falter in times of trouble, how small is your strength! Rescue those who are being led away to death, hold back those staggering towards slaughter. If you say, "But we knew nothing about this," does not he who weighs the hearts perceive it? Does not he who guards your life know it? Will he not repay each person according to what he has done?[30]

According to Leach, when the Army of God burst onto the scene, they also used this verse to justify their actions. In fact, Army member Paul Hill quoted it to justify killing David Britton, and in so doing challenged Terry's "real" commitment to its meaning. After this comparison was made in the media, Terry never again cited the verse.

Bray, a father of 11 children, authored the book *A Time to Kill* in which he defends the moral right to use force to prevent abortion. One of the chapters of this book is dedicated to contrasting the "heroes" of the movement with those who "have decried the use of force in its various forms and degrees."[31] In this chapter, Bray names several leading Christian politicians including Jerry Falwell, Pat Buchanan and Chuck Colson, and highlights their "double-mindedness" as they lament abortion, but condemn those committed to forcefully stopping it. Bray spent four years in prison in the 1980s for his connection to the destruction of several abortion clinics in the D.C. area.

As of February 2007, addresses for 16 "Prisoners of Christ" are listed on the website. An additional six names and addresses are listed in a second list; however, they are distinguished from members of the first list as being

> supportive of stopping the murder of unborn children, but are incarcerated for things unrelated to abortion. These prisoners have taken the initiative to

contact us to let us know of their support and agreement to stop the slaughter of the unborn children. Be advised, we are not vouching for anyone on this list. [32]

Radical rhetoric

In some ways, the rhetoric of the Army of God is similar to that of the Christian Coalition. This is most likely due to both groups' acceptance of Schaeffer's political theology – and the consequential influence it has had on their development. While the Christian Coalition looks to Schaeffer to justify legal political participation, the Army of God echoes Schaeffer in their justification of more dramatic measures.

However, in contrast to the Christian Coalition's focus on society's role in permitting the concept of abortion to continue, and the individual's moral responsibility to reform their neighbor's worldview, the Army of God emphatically focuses on the doctor's role in destroying a human being. With this alteration comes the shift in the appropriate moral response to a wrong – meaning that no longer is it morally responsible to patiently and persistently seek to change society one neighbor at a time. In fact, this approach is portrayed as ludicrous in light of the thousands of babies dying every week. Instead, when the baby is viewed as a human being equal to any child that lives outside the womb, the concept of abortion as murder extends to the realization that doctors who perform abortion must consequently be murderers.

This manner of problem identification manifests itself in two ways in Army of God discourse and literature. In order for the enemy to be identified, it is necessary to first identify the victim. The ubiquity of sin in humanity is a pervasive theme in Christian theology, and one with important implications in problem identification. If everyone is recognized to be a sinner, it is challenging to mobilize movement members against an "enemy" as theology prevents any one person from being deemed any worse a sinner than those moving against them. And most Army of God members are quick to mention the salvation that Christ offers to all humanity[33] – even those who have had or performed abortions in the past. The Army of God thus does not focus on the battle between Army members and Army opponents. Instead, they spend much energy emphasizing the plight of the unborn child – a child which most members believe to be sinless. Thus, the battle is established to rage not only between pro-life and pro-choice, but between innocence (the unborn) and evil (the doctors that would destroy the innocent).

To emphasize this contrast, the Army of God uses a variety of terms to refer to the unborn babies they endeavor to protect. Discourse centers on protection of "the innocent," "the womb-children," and "unseen babies." Never are the babies referred to as fetuses. To physically reinforce the frame of the humanness of the child threatened by abortion, the Army of God makes extensive use of graphic pictures of aborted babies. Lokey, a reclusive truck driver living in a rundown trailer, has invested thousands of dollars in a giant billboard along an Alabama highway – a billboard with a horrifically graphic picture of a dismembered baby, based on the belief that if passersby see the violent nature of abortion in direct contrast to the humanness of a child, they will renounce their support of the practice.[34]

In an interview with the author, Lokey recounted his first experience with anti-abortion activism. He was in prison for murder in California when *Roe* v. *Wade* took place, and having had a very dramatic spiritual conversion while incarcerated, he was horrified by the news of the judicial development. He was inspired to paint a graphic picture of his understanding of the violence of abortion, and spoke glowingly of the picture's effect on others. He says that convicts, the police and guards all looked at the picture and cried, and he says that he has been attacked (since his release from prison) for showing women what would be done to their child in an abortion.[35]

While Lokey is an extreme example of the violent anti-abortionists, his penchant for graphic art is not exceptional among his activist peers. However, while the Army's method of "shock therapy" is effective in reminding them why they do what they do, it only exacerbates the gap between themselves and the more moderate members of the fight (to say nothing of what it does to their relationship with the opposition).

Some supporters of the Army of God are aware of the effect of their radical rhetoric in isolating them from the greater community. Dave Leach is a music teacher, and he endorses the use of force in preventing abortion. Yet, when this author questioned Leach about his own actions for the movement, he said that while he supported the force used by other Army members, he "excused [himself] from the burden because [he] has no experience with explosives or bombs."[36] He went on to suggest sometimes the radical rhetoric of the Army is "like telling a beginner to deal with 16th notes" in that it asks too much of people too soon. Leach emphasized the nature of the Army as directed by God alone, and thus noted the personal nature of each individual's calling to the use of force. He extolled the courage of those who had already heeded the call to use violence, but emphasized that his own call had not yet come.

John Brockhoeft did receive his call, and attributes his shift to the use of violence to a protest he attended in which seven babies aborted in the third trimester were carried around in miniature caskets. He recollects,

> They were all intact (not dismembered) because they'd all been killed by saline poisoning. There they all lay, naked in their caskets. At the times of their deaths, of course, their bodies had long since been completely developed with perfect little arms, hands, fingers, feet, toes, facial features, and full heads of fine baby hair. Those little fingers bore prints no one had ever borne before, nor ever shall again. All of their little eyes were closed in death. All of their bodies were perfectly formed, but their skin was terrible to look upon because of how they had been burned alive by the terrible solution.... My heart was broken not only from the knowledge that these innocent, helpless, precious little babies had been slain for no good reason, but I

was also crushed by imagining the horror and physical agony they had surely experienced during the long hours that these unspeakable crimes were being committed. My heart was full, not only of grief, but rage as well.[37]

Seeing the "perfectly formed" babies in coffins emphasized to Brockhoeft that abortion was not a theoretical issue – it was the murder of real human beings.

> Here you've got these unseen babies, a little blond-headed boy there, a little black-haired girl over there, and you know for a fact, that they're there even though you can't see them. You know, definitely, that you're not dealing with hypotheses, but with real, actual, already existent, living human beings. And you know they are going to be killed within 48 hours unless you do something effective. Here you've got these little babies who have waited for thousands of years in the heart of God. The Lord has held them in His Sacred Heart and known them, and loved them since the beginning of time, and now, only a few months ago, he sent them, incarnate, into this world for the only chance at life they'll ever have. But an appointment has been made for them to be killed in 48 hours.[38]

Once Brockhoeft framed the issue in this way (he pictured each baby as a child with real and unique characteristics, as well as with a real and horrific appointment with death in two days' time), his passion became an urgent responsibility. When he began to view each child as an individual, every day that he did not act to prevent their death became a time when he was morally culpable for their murder. In his words, "Passively declining from doing an evil thing isn't the same as actively doing what is right."[39]

Brockhoeft has endeavored to convey the urgency of the plight of the unborn to others. Michael Griffin, the first Army of God member to kill a doctor who performed abortions, was one individual affected by Brockhoeft's personalization of the issue. Griffin says:

> Since January of 1993, when I first met John B. and I saw for the first time, an abortion in a jar, I have tried endlessly to express how outraged I was at this and the thousands that happen every day.[40]

The second part of the frame is created in the way that the doctors performing abortions are conceptualized. Logic entails that if someone is being murdered, there must inevitably be someone else acting as a murderer. Doctors who perform abortions are murderers, butchers, or criminals, and likened to Nazis in Germany.

Enhancing this frame is terminology devoted to identifying the place in which abortions occur. The term "abortion clinic" is ridiculed by some members of Army of God, "[s]ince, as we all know, a clinic is a medical facility where life and health are administered to people, and never a place set aside specifically to kill people, therefore there is no such thing as an abortion clinic."[41] Instead,

Army of God discourse identifies these places as *abortuaries, satanic alters, butuaries* and *abortion chambers.*

Again, these techniques strengthen the frames that characterize the organization, but they also eliminate potential means of communication between movement members and those who do not already agree with them. The result is that the rhetoric of the organization actually forces them further from the political arena they actively seek to change.

Activists identify themselves as being in a catch-22: if they abandon their "radical" rhetoric in an effort to gain a genuine opportunity for change, then they undermine their ability to convey the urgency of the cause they represent. Many Army members look with loathing on organizations like the Christian Coalition for this very reason. For the Army members, it is inconceivable that one could sit calmly while writing a letter to one's congressman while thousands of children are dying every day. As Army member Chuck Spingola graphically describes it,

> As cream rising to the top of the milk, so the Christian terrorist rises above the huddled masses of churchgoers and the many voices which denounce their violent attempts to defend the innocents from their murderous assailants. Regarding abortion, the testimony is clear: the Christian Terrorist has the Word of God and a testimony of loving, albeit terrifying (to the wicked) actions. The huddled masses of churchgoers have the Word of God alone, interpreted through fear and colored glasses and played upon tinkling symbols and sounding brass.... Adding insult to injury they not only discriminate against the pre-born, but also denounce those who will not do likewise.[42]

However, by "accurately" representing the crisis as genocide on a mass scale and condemning all those who do not share in the urgency of their cause, they are forgoing their opportunity to play a part in the political process. In this sense, what began as an ideology not markedly different from that of the Christian Coalition has manifest itself into a rhetoric that is vastly different indeed. With a rhetoric as deliberately inflammatory as the Army of God's, the organization is perceived by even those who might share the ideology as being dangerously radical. This limits the political access granted to such an organization and accordingly confirms their belief that society (both secular and otherwise religious) rejects their message.

In the following section we will see a similar pattern play out between the Muslim Brethren and al Jama'a al Islamiyya.

Rhetoric in the Brotherhood and al Jama'a al Islamiyya

Current events have propelled the Muslim religion to the forefront of discussion tables across the world. This has had both positive and negative effects. As Human Rights lawyer (and former member of al Gama'a al Islamiyya) Monatasser al Zayat explains:

> Since September 11, 2001, the Western world has more or less placed all
> Islamic movements in one category, that of extremism and terrorism....
> Few scholars care to study the intellectual and social origins of Islamic
> resurgence, and even fewer point out that the majority of Islamic move-
> ments, although barred from politics, have not resorted to violence against
> the state.[43]

In some cases, efforts are made to distinguish between radicalism and moderation, yet the requisites used to distinguish one from the other are so removed
from reality that it causes those seeking to apply them to conclude there is no
such thing as moderate Islam at all[44] – when in reality the dearth is not to be
found in moderate Islam, but in the existence of individuals prepared to identify
the difference.

All this is to say that scholars are sorely in need of a sensitive and realistic
appraisal of the elements that separate non-violent from violent Islam. Such a
study will not only assist in clearing the one-dimensional cobwebs spun by
would-be experts on a complex subject, but will also provide another piece for
the puzzle of explaining religiously motivated violence.

Some of the confusion regarding the distinction between violent and non-
violent Islam can be traced to the fact that most of the violent groups in existence today are off-shoots of the first modern Islamic organization – Al-Ikhwan
al-Muslimin. This section will attempt to clarify the distinctions between the
organizations (where they can be clearly made) and highlight the rhetorical differences between them.

Islam is the solution

The Muslim Brethren owes its existence in part to the mundane circumstances
surrounding its creation. Al-Banna was not from a prominent family, and was
stationed in a teaching position in a small village when he first decided to start
the organization. Ironically, it was the remoteness of his position with lower-
class workers that enabled him to later rise to prominence. Because al-Banna
was not working with rich or influential members of society when he began to
promote the Society, and as its popularity swiftly increased, no one of consequence paid attention. Thus, the Muslim Brethren was given time to grow and
strengthen in a way that it may not otherwise have been able.

And grow and strengthen it did. Within five years of its creation, the Brotherhood boasted 50 chapters. The primary purpose of the organization at this time
was to promote Islamic living, and in its earliest years, al-Banna focused more
on the growth of the organization under this vague umbrella than on developing
a more precise ideology.

In the 1930s, al-Banna began to articulate a more precise ideology for the
organization. He placed a huge emphasis on the importance of action within
Muslim living, arguing that to believe and have faith was worthless without the
clearly demonstrated action to back up a believer's claim. To this end, the

Muslim Brethren developed an extensive social program, which only increased the success of the movement as it was seen to alleviate social problems in a way the government and other organizations failed to do.

Much like Reed's efforts in developing the Christian Coalition, al-Banna's response to conflict or dissent within the group was to stick to vague ideologies that would unite large groups of people. He called for the "return to Islam" and promoted uncontroversial slogans like "the Qur'an is our Constitution."[45] These non-contentious ideas kept the group from becoming fractionalized over specifics of theology and enabled unification toward a broad and appealing goal. Al-Banna identified the specific purpose of the Brotherhood as being to "establish Allah's sovereignty over the world. To guide all of humanity to the precepts of Islam and its teachings."[46] Al-Banna avoided articulating the precise system of government that was necessary to implement Islamic rule, saying that anything besides communism and secularism could be found in Islam and would work in Egypt. This principle ultimately became the slogan of the organization. "Islam is the Solution" had become a refrain sung over and over again by the Brothers in an effort to assuage doubts about the personal power interests of members of their organization.

Although al-Banna attempted to run for Parliament in the 1940s, he still adhered to his belief that unity came before controversy. He focused on issues he believed were clearly defined in the Qur'an. He emphasized the importance of work, the right of individuals to private property and called for the nationalization of Egypt. Al-Banna articulated three basic principles he deemed necessary in an Islamic government: Representation, Unity of Nation and National Will.[47]

Al-Banna's strongest ideological stance during the early period was that Muslims did not need to seek solutions in education, politics, philosophy or any area of life from other places. Islam was the solution, and it offered all that was needed.

In an essay written in 1927, al-Banna criticized the Sufi ideology that called for adherents to remove themselves from society in order to practice discipline and devotion. He contrasted the influence of the Sufis with that of school teachers, saying that the latter were actually superior because teachers influence society through daily interaction with Egyptian youth.[48] The creation of the Muslim Brethren was al-Banna's attempt to demonstrate that Islam called Muslims to far more than religion. In an essay titled "Our Mission" he explained:

> We believe that Islam is an all-embracing concept which regulates every aspect of life, adjudicating on everyone its concerns and prescribing for it a solid and rigorous order. It does not stand helpless before life's problems.... Some people mistakenly understand Islam as restricted to certain types of religious observations or spiritual exercises, and confine themselves and their understanding to these narrow areas and determined by their limited grasp. But we understand Islam very broadly and comprehensively as regulating the affairs of men in this world and the next.[49]

Rhetorical pluralism

In much the same way that the Christian Coalition capitalized on the "normalcy" of their cause, the Brotherhood has maintained al-Banna's interest in endeavoring to be non-controversial. Hudaiby's grandson noted in an interview with this author that the Brotherhood is presently a better representation of al-Banna's vision that it was in the 1950s and 1960s. Al-Banna's sudden death in 1949 left an organization unclear on how to proceed. Some members believed that violence was the solution, and the organization is accused of having planned an assassination attempt on Nassser in 1954, and of an attempted revolution in 1965.[50] It was during this time that Sayid Qutb's writings were first published, and shortly thereafter, al Jama'a al Islamiyya emerged in the universities. According to Hudaiby, the Brotherhood's rhetoric of this time was far more rigid that it had been under al-Banna. But he notes that as the differences between the two organizations crystallized and they officially split into different organizations, the Brotherhood returned to its pluralistic roots.[51]

Hudaiby's observations are underlined by the variance that can be found among members regarding the purpose of the organization. When this author asked Hudaiby about this subject, he explained the organization's purposes as being "the establishment of freedom: freedom of the press; freedom of expression; the freedom of choosing our own government."[52] When the author commented that the goal didn't sound necessarily religious, Hudaiby insisted it was entirely so. He explained that freedom's base was found in religion generally and Islam specifically. The purpose of an Islamic government is to allow people to live in freedom according to God's laws.

Dr. Futouh, another member of the organization, had a different goal. In an interview with the author that lasted almost an hour, he scarcely mentioned the religious nature of Islam at all. Instead he was interested in sharing his understanding of Islam as a civilization. He considers the difference important because Islam as a religion is limited to its impact on Muslims, while an Islamic civilization could include Christians and Jews as well.[53] In fact, according to Dr. Israel Elad Altman, Dr. Futouh "considers the Caliphate to be a purely political, non-religious matter," and "advocates true political pluralism, equal citizenship for all the country's nationals, regardless of religion and rotation of power on the basis of people's choice."[54]

But Deputy General Habib had yet another perspective. He emphasized the promulgation of Islamic principles, to be disseminated through society, to bring change from a grassroots level. He noted that he most appreciated the comprehensive nature of Islam, because it was a system that worked in all areas of life including economics, politics, etc.[55]

In another interview, a lower-level member emphasized the goal of the Brotherhood to instate a government in reaction to the fallen Caliphate. He explained that such a government would rebuild a free Egypt.[56]

These different answers are not striking because they are necessarily contradictory – but neither are they identical. While one might expect to see dissimilarities in theology in a political organization, it was surprising to find such different emphases on something as innocuous as the purpose of the organization. That such differences do exists suggests that the Brotherhood has been successful in maintaining al-Banna's commitment to a vague ideology in favor of a broad political base.

Further evidence of this plurality is seen in the very method the organization promotes. The Brotherhood has long endeavored to change society one member at a time, and government one election at a time. Termed by some authors as "political accommodation,"[57] the Brothers have endeavored to work within the existing political system. In an authoritarian state, involvement in the political process is rife with obstacles for the opposition, and the Brotherhood in the 1980s and 1990s was admirable in its forbearance in reaction to these challenges.

In 1984, the Brethren won 7 of twenty-five seats in the Doctors' Syndicate's governing council, and eight years later they succeeded in winning the majority of seats in the general council. This same year, the Brothers won a majority of seats in the Lawyers syndicate. The Brotherhood has been denied the right to form a political party since its founding. This prohibition has limited the organization's success in national elections. To combat this legally, in 1984 the Brotherhood aligned itself with the New Wafd Party – despite significant ideological differences between the two organizations. This strategy resulted in the Brotherhood gaining eight seats in Parliament.[58]

Yet, there are conflicting viewpoints on the goals of this new strategy of the Brothers, with some indicating that Al-Ikhwan al-Muslimin's decision to become involved in the syndicates was a direct reaction to regime repression[59] and others arguing that the Society's involvement in the Syndicates reflects an effort to appeal to the Egyptian middle class, just as the Society's historic involvement with private social organizations has targeted the lower classes. Whatever the motivation, the result is a Brotherhood that was gaining ground in all classes of Egyptian society.

Three years later, the Muslim Brethren won a total of 36 seats in the 1987 election.[60] The organization's willingness to accommodate even the limitations of the political system illustrates the principle that inspired author Abdel Azim Ramadan to say of the Brotherhood, "they are a part of the political system, not an Islamic alternative to it."[61]

The Brotherhood, much like the Coalition, has focused its efforts on maintaining access to the political system – choosing to align with ideologically dissimilar organizations, and playing by the very rules they decry as un-Islamic. Doing so has at times left the organization open to criticism from more radical elements as having sold out to the political system.

The discussion up to this point could arguably be said to suggest that the Brotherhood has never addressed the issue of violence at all. This not the case. The existence of the Secret Apparatus and al-Banna's apparent awareness of it indicates that al-Banna was not adverse to violence in some circumstances. However, his emphasis on reform at a grass-roots/societal level indicates that neither did he perceive of violence as a moral duty for the implementation of his purposes.

But if al-Banna was purposefully vague about his feelings on violence, Sayid Qutb was anything but. Raised at a time when Egypt was essentially ruled by the British, Qutb was quick to condemn the moral depravity of Western society. He came to believe that Islam alone could fill the moral void that existed.

Although, as was mentioned earlier (page 000), the Brotherhood responded favorably to Qutb's ideology, the methodology he proposed in pursuit of his ends ultimately separated the Brotherhood from future violent organizations. Qutb persuasively argued that Muslims must fight against Jahiliyyah, instead of talking about it. He claimed that actions speak louder than words, and to agree in theory with Islamic doctrine is nothing compared with actively – and, if necessary, violently – working toward its implementation in society.

Although it was ultimately rejected by the Brotherhood, Qutb's philosophy continues to be pervasive in Egyptian politics and society, in part because when the Brotherhood made the official decision to embrace an ideology of non-violence, a significant portion of the membership left the organization to found one of their own.[62]

With the Brotherhood floundering in the 1970s, and Sadat searching for legitimacy on the right, Qutb supporters found fodder for their more radical rhetoric in the universities. When Sadat came to recognize the power of the organizations he'd allowed to flourish (a power that indirectly threatened his own), he moved to thwart their influence. However, this provided the opportunity for Qutb's doctrine to be applied to Sadat's regime and al Jama'a al Islamiyya began opposing the regime in earnest.

At this time, although still technically illegal, the Muslim Brethren was one of only a few Islamic organizations, and it was certainly the only one with such an advanced structure and system of operations. At the universities, there were a number of informal clubs that sponsored Islamic activities (Qur'anic readings, memorization sessions, etc.),[63] but the number of students involved in these activities was far smaller than that of the traditional power base of Nassirists and Communists.

Sadat began releasing many members of the Brotherhood imprisoned by Nasser, and even sought to consult with a number of them in the drafting of the new constitution. Further, the Egyptian press began printing positive reports of the activities of the Islamic activists. These reports were a significant indicator of the regime's new acceptance and support of Islamist organizations as the newspapers were heavily influenced by the Egyptian government. Correctly reading this and other acts as acceptance by the new regime, university Islamists began to exert themselves in skirmishes with the Nasserites and the Communists.

Interestingly, in the early stages of their emergence, the Islamists recognized their own weakness and rather than offer totally new ideas in existing debates, they carefully reworded traditionally accepted Leftish ideas into a Muslim context. For example, the ongoing confrontation with Israel was changed from being a nationalist struggle for Palestinian autonomy in the face of Western imperialism to a case of jihad against infidels seeking to extend their influence in the land of Islam.[64] In so doing, the Islamists were able to gradually glide into the consciousness of the populace and ultimately replace the other groups.

The Islamists further distinguished themselves from their leftist counterparts by extending their role far beyond ideological jargon into the realm of practical solutions to everyday problems. As a result of Nasser's education imperatives, the number of students enrolled in university jumped from 200,000 in 1970 to 500,000 in 1977.[65] All university graduates were guaranteed a job by the Egyptian government, thus leading to mass over-enrollment and significant problems within the university system.

Additionally, classes were vastly overcrowded with students sharing seats and instructor/student ratios exceeding 1:100. This led to significantly uncomfortable lecture environments wherein students were literally sitting on top of one another. Couple this with the fact that many students were women in a society in which male/female interaction was strictly limited, and the problem compounds itself.

Women complained of being harassed both in the classrooms and on the overcrowded buses to and from the university. The university Islamists developed an initiative demanding separate seating areas for women in lecture halls and organized an all-female bus service. For women to take advantage of these sought-after opportunities, the Islamists encouraged (and later insisted) that women veil themselves in the traditional Islamic style. Given that they were anxious to avoid the harassment so prevalent in the crowded conditions, many women willingly accepted the dress code and, intentionally or otherwise, demonstrated support for the Islamist organizations.[66]

Sources are contradictory about precisely when these different Islamic clubs officially coalesced into the organization now known as Al-Jama'a al Islamiyya, which, when translated, literally means "the Islamic Group." Tal'at Fu'ad Qasim, a founding member of the organization, cites its origin as the mid-1970s in Minya. He claims that the organization began when nine individuals met to study a number of famous works of the modern Islamic movement. He says that the organization was officially formed sometime after this group of individuals successfully pressured universities to segregate men and women, and before they took over the student union.[67]

Dr. Abdel Mun'em Abul Futouh – now a leader in al-Ikhwan al-Muslimin, but also one of the founding members of al Jama'a – confirms this timeframe, but he emphasizes that the organization began to confront the strength of the nationalist sentiment that was dominating the universities. Futouh recalls a growing realization among some students of the time that nationalism had, in many ways, lost sight of the elements that truly defined Egyptian culture – the most prominent element being Islam. Futouh and others endeavored to bring Islam back to the forefront of Egyptian thinking by demonstrating its ability to fill the moral vacuum which the socialist/nationalist agenda never could.[68] In an interview with the author, Dr. Futouh explained that he supported the founding of the organization because of his concern that nationalism in Egypt had come to supplant the Islamic roots of the country.[69] According to Futouh, in Egypt there has always been a strong culture of religious piety, and that religion is actually the "nature of Egyptians," and it is something that makes them distinct from other people. It was, for Futouh, Nassir's disregard of this dominant element of Egyptian character that made the founding of al Jama'a al Islamiyya necessary.

Futouh recounts his experience in the early 1970s of entering the university to find that the nationalists (he called them Communists) dominated the student groups and campus newspapers, and shaped the social dialogue. He remembers that anyone expressing Islamist sentiments was derided for being anti-modern, and he concluded that something must be done to counteract this influence. The Brotherhood was not the answer, as many members were in prison during this time. The solution, in the mind of Futouh and his fellow founders, was al Jama'a al Islamiyya.

With the implicit blessing of the Sadat regime, the Islamic Group grew in strength, reaching its pinnacle in 1976. During this year, the organization controlled the student unions of universities across Egypt. This success offered them access to the publishing committee of the unions, which they used to re-produce important Islamic tracts and writings.

Having achieved success at the universities, the group began to turn their attention to the larger Egyptian society. Whether in an effort to maintain good relations with the regime or out of genuine belief, the group focused on reform at a societal level. Al-Jama'a al Islamiyya began making efforts toward making entire universities and towns "Islamic." Members of the organization began attacking those not adhering to the social norms of Islam – that is, Islam as defined by members of the group. Violations of these norms included the viewing of popular films, dancing and listening to contemporary music.[70] Abul Ela Mady clarifies that al Jama'a al Islamiyya turned to violence after a number of the founding members left the organization to join the Brotherhood.[71]

In 1989 al Jama'a al Islamiyya published *Mithaq al-Amal al-Islami*, or *The Charter of Islamic Action*, describing the goals and strategies of the organization. Interestingly, and much like the similarities of purpose seen between the Christian Coalition and the Army of God, the goal of al Jama'a does not differ markedly from that of Al-Ikhwan al-Muslimin. Where the Brothers call for the establishment of "Allah's sovereignty over the world," and endeavor to "guide all of humanity to the precepts of Islam and its teachings,"[72] al Jama'a al Islamiyya desired to

> follow the commands of God and the Prophet Mohammed in all that they do and ... to establish Islam as a totality in each soul, and over each handbreadth of land, in each house, in each organization, in each society.[73]

The difference between the organizations becomes more evident in the statement of their chosen methods. The *Mithaq* notes that the implementation their goal is dependent on the organization's ability to "make people worship their Lord" and establish a Caliphate.[74] Later, in a section of the charter devoted specifically to enunciating the *tareeq*, or method, the authors introduce an idea that would prove dominant in their discourse for years to come: undertaking the good, and forbidding the evil.[75] The second statement in this section of the charter indicates that the emphasis of the organization is on the latter, rather than the former. This section defines jihad as disciplined struggle to "change the ways of those who abandoned the good in favor of the forbidden."[76]

According to Sheikh Rifa'ey Ahmad Taha, a leading member of Al Jama'at in the 1990s, the goal of the organization is to establish "an Islamic vice regency in accordance with prophetic guidance and to seek the pleasure of Allah, the Lord of the Worlds."[77] Again, this statement does not indicate an ideology markedly different from that of the Brotherhood. But the Sheikh goes on to identify the organization's program as "to fulfill the law of Allah and to adhere to all that has been required of us, with respect to the religion of Allah, commanding decency and forbidding indecency, and to strive in the path of Allah."[78] While the first half of the statement is not discordant with the platform of the Brotherhood, the second clause, which is the first indicator of method, is significantly inharmonious. In an interview conducted by the author of this book, Brotherhood Deputy General Guide Dr. Mohamed Habib presented a very different picture of the method pursued by the group. The author asked whether, if elected to power, the Brotherhood would enforce the veiling of women. Dr. Habib indicated that, while veiling was a practice called for by the Qur'an, the practice was an outward indicator of an internal commitment. He said that forcing women to veil defeats the purpose of veiling. In other words, the Brothers view vice as something that must be rejected by the individual – not physically prevented by the authorities.

While the *Islamic Action Charter* only vaguely identifies the organization's enemy as "the oppressors,"[79] the organization discourages alternative religious frameworks as dangerous, making specific reference to people who branched off in the founding days of Islam and were killed by the Prophet Mohammed.[80]

Another interesting distinction between the rhetoric of the Brotherhood and al Jama'a al Islamiyya is found in Sheikh Taha's statement regarding the ruling authorities: "The reality is that the Egyptian regime did not just participate in the destruction which took place in Egypt, the Egyptian regime is destruction itself."[81] This sentiment is much like that of the Army of God when they focus on the "murderers" who perform abortion over the act of abortion itself. By shifting the emphasis from the effects of destruction onto the perceived embodiment of it, al Jama'a has ratcheted up the intensity of their rhetoric and limited the manner in which the regime can consistently be dealt with by the organization. If the regime is "destruction itself" then the regime loses all authority – much like the Army of God suggest the American government has as a result of the legalization of abortion.

Once this is perceived to be the case, it becomes easier to distinguish between "good" and "evil," as Sheikh Taha does in the following statement:

The time has come for a complete demarcation. There is no longer any room for flexibility controlling the distinctions and drawing the boundaries. Either you are amongst the secularists and under their sovereignty, or you are with the Religion and Islamic Law. Either you are entrenched with the transgressing despot or with the suppressed Muslim people.[82]

Interviews conducted with leaders of al Jama'a al Islamiyya in the 1990s have in common the leaders' insistence that the organization was not adversely affected by regime repression. Hisham Mubarak interviewed Tal'at Fu'ad Qasim in the mid-1990s and commented on the group's waning influence as a result of regime crackdowns. Qasim defensively responded:

The Jama'a exists in eighteen provinces, including tens of centers and hundreds of villages. Up to now, the state has not won one battle in any of the thirteen centers, just in the province of Asyut.... For every member killed, twenty join. Contrary to what some think, the power of Jama'a is on the rise.[83]

The interview transcript indicates that Mubarak (the author, not the president) stated he disagreed with Qasim, and specifically identified evidence of dwindling numbers. Qasim boldly responded that Mubarak was entirely wrong. His assertion was supported by the 1997 interview with Sheikh Taha, if not by actual numbers. Taha indicated that, in 1997, "many are continuing to join the Jama'a." He describes the flourishing cells of al Jama'a all over Egypt, including in trade and charitable organizations. He argues that the numbers seem smaller because "the situation does not permit for them to openly declare their affiliation."[84]

Qasim's statement brings up an interesting point in the discussion, on which the Brothers and al Jama'a evidently agree. The Brotherhood rejects the use of violence in favor of spreading the message of Islam with truth. As General Guide Tilmisani stated, "There exists a holy interdiction against aggression and offensive attacks. Instead jihad prescribes justice towards enemies and the guidance of Muslims to show mercy and respect."[85] However, though they condemn violence as misunderstood Islam,[86] they see its cause as the government's repression of all Islamists. Because the government limits the organizational capacity of the Brethren, they are not in a position to restrain violent off-shoots of their organization.[87] The argument of the Brotherhood here is not unlike that being made in this chapter as a whole: the further organizations are excluded from the political process, the greater the likelihood that they will use more radical methods to emphasize their cause. This will be better illustrated with a further historical account of the organization.

As they had during their university years, members of al-Jama'a pursued change at the social level, wanting to serve as the impetus for a mass movement through public sermons and actions. In a manner that would make them famous in the mid-1990s, they took it upon themselves to "forbid vice" by physically attacking members of society that they judged to be acting immorally. However, the methods the Islamic Group employed were frequently criticized as not going far enough to bring about the implementation of an Islamic society. Some members of al Jama'a argued that the targeting of perpetrators of vice did little to solve the ultimate problem of an unjust government. As a result, al-Jihad was born.

There is no real consensus among scholars as to the relationship between these two groups. Diaa Rashwan, a leading expert on violence in Islamic movements, identifies the organizations as fully separate groups, tracing the origins of al-Jihad back to 1967 or 1968, with its full recognition as an autonomous organization coming toward the end of 1980.[88]

Rashwan notes that al-Jihad began as clandestine meetings between teenagers in the 1960s. Abul Ela Mady argues that the two groups began as separate institutions but merged into a single consultative council in late 1980. He says that both were involved in the assassination of Sadat. When members of the merged organization were imprisoned in response to the assassination, they separated back into the two entities.[89]

However, other authors, including Gilles Kepel,[90] indicate that the organizations are far more closely linked – that al-Jihad emerged out of al Jama'a. Whatever the confusion, it is certain that the two organizations share significant ideological similarities. Both accept Qutb's argument regarding the jahilyya society, and both have denounced the Egyptian state as *kufr* (non-Islamic – literally: infidel). Further, the organizations agree that "the use of violence is necessary to change the situation in Egypt.... Revolution is necessary to uproot the evil system and replace it with an Islamic system."[91]

In either case, around 1980, after the Islamic Group was well established, Mohammed Abdel Faraj emerged to unite the disparate jihad organizations into a single entity.[92] Part of this unification effort resulted in the publication of *Al Faridah al Ghaibah* – or *The Neglected Duty*, a book written by Abdel Salam Faraj, one of the five individuals executed for the assassination of Anwar Sadat.

On October 6, 1981, Khaled al-Islambuli shot and killed President Sadat, yelling "I am Khalid al-Islambuli, I have killed Pharaoh, and I do not fear death!"[93] Author Gilles Kepel carefully details the ideology that inspired Islambuli's action, and he identifies Islambuli as a leader of the Islamic organization Al-Jihad.[94]

Most scholars of Islamic violence agree with Kepel's identification of Islambuli as a member of al-Jihad, an organization that allegedly developed in reaction to al-Jama'a. However, there are other reports (to be discussed in more detail below, page 000) that question the legitimacy of this understanding and, indeed, others still that question the existence of the organization al-Jihad at all.

Whether the result of the actions of al-Jama'a or al-Jihad, or some combination thereof, the assassination of Sadat led to significant changes in the ruling party, but few changes within the state system – which had been the goal of the assassins. Up to this point, Sayid Qutb had been the primary driving force in the definition of jihad among Islamic activists. But Faraj, in *The Neglected Duty*, criticized the implementation of Qutb's conclusions. He argued that jihad must not be fought with an eye toward avoiding antagonizing the state – as he charged most organizations had done to this point. Rather, jihad must be against the state, with concerns for the Islamic education of society playing a distant second.

Greater attention to Faraj's argument regarding the duty of the Muslim to overthrow the state will be paid later in this book. For the purposes of this part, it is sufficient to note that Faraj's views were in accordance with others who had left the Brotherhood, disillusioned by the incremental change the organization pursued. In 1980, Faraj met up with Karam Zuhdi, at the time the leader of a southern branch of al Jama'a al Islamiyya. At the time of their meeting, the two men decided to merge al-Jihad and al Jama'a into a single organization, united under a consultative council. They invited Omar Abd al-Rahman[95] to serve as their mufti. He agreed and began issuing fatwas condoning the actions and proposed actions of the organization.

The al-Jihad members of the now unitary organization largely operated out of Cairo and other parts of lower Egypt, while the original al-Jama'a members dominated the south. Between 1980 and 1982, several joint operations occurred, including an armed robbery of a jewelry store to finance further operations, multiple attacks on police stations and other security forces, and the killing of 82 police officers. But the most famous of these incidences had far greater consequences for the organization and the Egyptian state.[96]

Khaled al Islambuli was a Faraj sympathizer and a lieutenant in the artillery corps of the Egyptian Army. His brother, Muhammad al-Islambuli, was a low-level leader of the Islamic Group at Asyut University. In September 1981, Muhammad was arrested for his association with the Islamic group. Khalid was furious when he learned of his brother's arrest and approached Faraj about a plan to assassinate Sadat. Records show that the members of the organization had hoped that the assassination would spark a popular revolution that would, in turn, overthrow the state structure. Instead, Vice-President Mubarak took over, and the state remained relatively unchanged. Over 350 individuals were charged in conjunction with these acts, as well as Sadat's assassination, and much of the leadership of the conjoined groups were imprisoned.

According to some sources, after the military tribunals came to an end, the organization split back into two parts with al-Jihad under the leadership of Abbud al Zamr, and al Jama'a al Islamiyya under Karam Zuhdi. Accounts of al-Jihad after this point become sketchy, but al Jama'a al Islamiyya grew in strength.

Rather than confront them directly, Mubarak chose to isolate al Jama'a from state influence. The organization was allowed to conduct activities in specific areas in upper Egypt and greater Cairo – provided the activities did not threaten the ruling power of the regime.[97] The group used their influence in the region and established bands to forbid vice, including interaction of the sexes, concerts, etc.

For instance, members of the group would visit wedding parties with belly-dances and offer the bride and groom a choice to remove the dancers or face the consequences. They frequently burned video stores and beauty salons, declaring

them sacrilegious.[98] The group held large conferences in the areas they controlled and employed paramilitary members to protect them from the regime. In
all other parts of Egypt, groups were required to have a security permit for any
large conferences. The Jama'a's flouting of this law demonstrated their ability to
evade the grip of the regime in certain situations.

This is not to say that al Jama'a served only as a source of moral intimidation
in the towns they influenced. In fact, much like Al-Ikhwan al-Muslimin, al-
Jama'a was responsible for establishing many new social services in the regions.
They handed out food to the hungry, provided school supplies for poor families,
and established conflict-regulation committees to resolve community conflict
from an Islamic perspective.[99] Much as they had in the universities in the 1970s,
al Jama'a sought to protect the honor of women by monitoring inter-gender relations. In other words, al Jama'a provided services in the towns they dominated
that the government was ill-equipped to provide. This perhaps goes some way
toward explaining why the Egyptian government was so slow to step in as al
Jama'a began growing in strength.

A war between the "states"

The uneasy toleration that linked the state and al-Jama'a ended in 1990 when the
official spokesman of al Jama'a al Islamiiyya, Ala Muhyi al-Din, was assassinated by the state. The group responded by assassinating Rifat al-Mahjoub, the
former speaker of parliament. The government, in turn, began arresting thousands of suspected Islamists all over Egypt.

In 1992, Sheik Gaber Mohammed Ali, a self-proclaimed leader of al Jama'a,
began announcing in interviews with foreign journalists that al Jama' al Islamiyya had turned the area of Imbaba into a state within a state. Described by one
author as having "the charisma of Ayatollah Khomeini, the street smarts of a
mafia don, and the empathy of Robin Hood,"[100] Gaber controversially informed
the world that

> Islamic law is applied in many areas of Imbaba. We first use our tongue. If
> people don't listen, we threaten them, and if they still don't adhere, we use
> force. It annoys the government that we are a state within a state. But thank
> God we are not only a state within a state, we have become a state in
> itself.... God willing, Holy Law will be applied in all Egypt."[101]

Gaber's boasts were picked up by the Western media, and Mubarak began to
fear that Egypt was in danger of losing her place as a "democratic, moderate ally
of the West." To demonstrate his commitment against the Islamic cause, President Mubarak launched a war on Imbaba. The state led a massive campaign of
arrests. In 1992, 16,000 soldiers were sent to release the grip of the al Jama'a on
Imbaba. In 1993, another 8000 soldiers sought to uncover all members of al
Jama'a living in Masarah, Dairut, Manshiyat Nasir, Sanab, and Dairut al-
Sharif.[102] Al Jama'a then responded with unprecedented levels of violence.[103]

This series of events is an excellent example of the argument being made in this chapter. When al Jama'a had limited its influence in Imbaba to a role that subtly compensated for the state by provided services – both social and financial – that the state could not, the Mubarak regime was content to ignore their growing strength. But when word of Sheikh Gaber's radical claims (about Holy Law gaining influence in all of Egypt, and his boasts about the strength of al Jama'a) reached an international volume, Mubarak acted swiftly and ruthlessly to close the window of opportunity that had previously been open.

In the next five years, attacks on both sides continued sporadically. Al-Jama'a began directing attacks against Egyptian tourists, which al Jama'a leader Tal'at Fu'ad Qasim justified as follows:

> First, many tourists activities are forbidden, so this source of income for the state is forbidden. Striking at such an important source of income will be a major blow against the state. It does not cost us to strike against this sector. Second, tourism in its present form is an abomination: it is a means by which prostitution and AIDS are spread by Jewish women tourists, and it is a source of all manner of depravities, not to mention being a means of collecting information on the Islamic movement. For these reasons we believe that tourism is an abomination that must be destroyed. And it is one of our strategies for destroying the government.[104]

In 1993, moderate Islamists attempted to reconcile the demands of al-Jama'a with the Egyptian interior ministry,[105] and a delegation of moderates was established to meet with Interior Minister Abdel Halim Musa. One member of the delegation stated that Aboud Zumur was supportive of mediation efforts and was potentially willing to renounce violence. Hafez reports that Zumur met with an Egyptian general and asked for the "release of Islamist leaders and prisoners, an end to mass arrests and torture, and the return of private mosques to Jama'a along with a promise that the state would not interfere with their preaching activities."[106]

Qasim, however, denies that al-Jama'a was ever prepared to compromise, saying that

> [t]here will be no dialogue until one side is victorious over the other, or the Islamic Regime is established.... After coming to power, perhaps we will enter into a dialogue with the leaders about how they can leave the country.[107]

Further, Interior Minister Musa was dismissed by President Mubarak shortly after the alleged meeting took place, indicating Mubarak's own unwillingness to compromise with the organization that had brought such unrest to his regime. From 1993 to 1997, al-Jama'a initiated ten more attacks in locations across Egypt.

Then, in 1997, al-Jama'a secured national recognition when it claimed responsibility for a massacre in Luxor that killed 58 tourist and four Egyptian nationals. On November 17 of that year, six gunmen disguised as police officers emerged from the cliffs surrounding the popular tourist attraction – the Temple of Hatshepsut – and began firing indiscriminately on tourists. Some reports suggest that the attack lasted over 45 minutes, with the attackers "engaging in a gruesome game of hide-and-seek among the ancient columns with terrified men, women and children."[108]

In 1999, Swiss federal police confirmed al-Jama'a's responsibility for the attack, noting that it was ordered by al-Jama'a military commander Mustafa Hamza. Hamza had, by that time, been sentenced to death in Egypt three times for assassination attempts against the Egyptian information minister in 1994 and President Mubarak in 1996, as well as for armed attacks in Minya.[109]

Potential for conclusions[110]

Al Jama'a al Islamiyya developed as a result of direct support from President Sadat. During this time, their activities were confrontational, but not directly violent. But within only a few short years of the founding of the organization, Sadat saw his influence spiraling out of control. At a similar time, he embarked on one of the most controversial policy undertakings of Egyptian history by seeking peace with Israel. This event was a clear indication to organization members that their access to political influence was rapidly waning – and this understanding was reinforced by Sadat's "Autumn of Fury." During this time, the organization began engaging in violence – in one instance killing dozens of police officers. This time period culminated in Sadat's assassination.

When Mubarak came to power, like Sadat he initially reached out to the Islamists, allowing them some degree of autonomy – although this was contingent on their activities taking place far outside Cairo. But, like his predecessor, when Mubarak began fearing the strength of the organization, he began a campaign to eliminate them entirely. They responded with unprecedented levels of violence.

Al Jama'a al Islamiyya did not embrace the pluralism that the Muslim Brethren say they endorse. To have access to their protection even in the early days of their existence, women had to wear the veil – and in so doing support the specific ideals of the group. Islam Lotfy, a member of the Brotherhood, told this author that the organization rejected violence for both moral and pragmatic reasons. He argued that if the Brotherhood desired to change the heart of society, violence was not a practical means of achieving that change.[111] Implicit in this statement is the acceptance that must inevitably accompany a commitment to gradual change. Dr. Habib echoed these sentiments in his comments about the Brotherhood's position on the veil. While he stated that the veiling of women was "fixed"(required) according to the Qur'an, his emphasis remained on the individual's choice. As he said, "We want the heart to choose."[112] This choice could be influenced by exposure to faithful living, academic lectures, articles and dialogues, but ultimately the organization has lost its purpose if it pursues morality using a gun.

In a society as diverse as Egypt, it is not surprising that Dr. Habib's compassion and Dr. Futouh's "Islamic Civilization" carry more resonance in society than did al Jama'a al Islamiyya's forcible efforts to bring about change. The consequence of this is that the Brotherhood, while still unquestionably subject to repression and exclusion, has never lost their footing entirely in the political process. Unlike democratic systems, exclusion from government power in an authoritarian state is more the norm than the exception. Accordingly, attention must be paid to exclusion from other spheres as well – most notably civil society. The Brotherhood's continued success in the syndicates is firm evidence that they still have significant levels of access to the Egyptian process. This is in contrast to al Jama'a al Islamiyya which was eventually exiled to upper Egypt, and then later cut out of the process entirely.

This chapter has attempted to illustrate that the severity of religious rhetoric and action influences the speed with which political windows of opportunity close. As a result, the more radical groups face greater limitations to their political access, in contrast to the more moderate groups which maintain some degree of influence despite their religious method. The consequence of this is that radical groups are pressed further to the edges of society, while moderate groups maintain a position far closer to the secular center.

In the next chapter we will explore the effects of this pressure on the development of structure within an organization. It will be demonstrated that location at the fringe of society requires more secretive methods of organization. However, at the same time, these organizations must develop alternative means of sustaining the ties between members to ensure continued support for their cause.

6 The power of structure

It has been demonstrated elsewhere in the book (see, for example, page 000) that religious movements have reacted to the advance of secularization by engaging in the political process to an extent not seen in recent history. Chapters 4 and 5 argued that organizations within movements use different degrees of rhetoric to draw supporters to their cause, and that the type of rhetoric influences the location of the movement in relation to opportunities for political access. The organizations that use less-radical language and imagery in their campaigns are granted greater access to the political process. Organizations that continue to use language that reflects the severity of the crisis they perceive are expelled from the political arena. This chapter will argue that the location of a movement influences the type of organizational structure a group is able to develop and that where limitations on organizational structure threaten to decrease the strength of ties between members, organizations compensate with stronger ideological frames.

The significance of this argument is evident only if structure is recognized as an informative variable in the prediction of organizational action. For this reason, this chapter will begin with a discussion of two divergent disciplines that arrive at two seemingly different conclusions about the relationship between structure and action. A review of behavior theory in the field of social behavior in the first section will reveal that hierarchal structures have traditionally been identified as increasing the likelihood of violence, because the strength of ties between members (and, by extension, the weakness of ties between members and the surrounding community) decrease the moral dissonance an individual might otherwise feel when engaging in violent behavior. A subsequent examination of the treatment of structure in social-movement theory will show that hierarchal structures in social movements have traditionally resulted in greater movement success and, consequentially, increased access to the political arena. The resulting paradox presented by these two arguments (how can hierarchy simultaneously increase an organization's access and thereby decrease their likelihood to use violence *and* decrease their ties with other members of society thereby increasing their likelihood to use violence?) will be explored in light of the four case studies. The final section of the chapter will argue that the increased secularization of politics simultaneously causes those within the arena to look with suspicion on more radical organizations, and those within radical organizations to look with contempt on those still in the arena. State suspicion (and prosecution) of radicalism has limited the ability of organizations to establish hierarchal structures. However, rather than limiting the violence that organizations undertake, the inability to form hierarchal structures has instead influenced the establishment of alternative measures to strengthen ties between members and their cause. Precisely what these alternative measures are will be explored in Chapter 7.

Social behavioral understandings of organizational violence

Since the end of World War II, hierarchy has been accused of making good people do very bad things. When Hannah Arendt first coined the phrase "the banality of evil," psychologists, philosophers and political scientists were only just beginning to explore the effects of structure on the actions of individuals. Arendt's work on Eichmann was disturbing because it argued that evil is not a characteristic that can be identified among the aberrants of society; rather, it is an outcome of the tendency that drives ordinary people to follow orders and conform to mass opinion. As another author described it, "Situations can be created in which it is possible to enlist ordinary participants in the commission of evil and in the process, the participant is transformed into a creature capable of autonomously and knowledgably committing evil actions."[1]

Philip Zimbardo explored this idea in his now notorious Stanford Prison Experiment.[2] Operating on the hypothesis that some individuals are predisposed to cruel behavior, Zimbardo and his team set up a mock-prison environment in the basement of a Stanford building in 1971. The team selected 24 participants from a pool of 75 volunteers. Each participant was asked whether he would like to play a guard or a prisoner. Without exception, all requested to play prisoners. Zimbardo's team randomly divided the group into prisoners and guards. The guards were given instructions not to harm the prisoners, but to establish in them a sense of powerlessness. Prisoners were not referred to by name, but by number.

The results of the study were very disturbing, and mirrored what Arendt had argued. The prison experiment had to be shut down by Zimbardo after only six of the projected 14 days due to the inhumane conditions that had developed in that short time. Within 24 hours of the start of the experiment, the guards began to exhibit sadistic and cruel behavior toward the prisoners – individuals who were indistinguishable from themselves only 24 hours before.[3] Zimbardo concluded from this experiment that structure – and the roles it establishes for individuals to fill – is a powerful catalyst in the move toward action.

In essence, individuals are linked to their social environments by identification with a particular role in that society. Typically, an individual internalizes the rules or norms of his/her society and then comes to act as an advocate for those rules or norms in the future. In this way, the structural norms of society enforce the actions that the individual will commit on behalf of that society: "If society is asking that individuals obey orders resulting in evil outcomes, still these enforcing forces move the person towards obedience."[4]

What Zimbardo, Arendt and others have argued is that evil, cruelty and violence are not entities or acts chosen for their own sake. Instead, "each step is so small as to be essentially continuous to the next one. After each step, the individual is positioned to take the next one. The individual's morality follows, rather than leads."[5] Zimbardo, Arendt and their contemporaries concluded that behavior is shaped by the environment of the individual, and thus structure is a critical element in understanding behavior.

Lifton carries this assumption further, contending that structure can actually transform the essentially good individual into an essentially evil one. He says this of his own study of Nazi doctors: "Nazi doctors were banal, but what they did was not. Repeatedly in this study, I describe banal men performing demonic acts; and in carrying out their actions, they themselves were no longer banal."[6] Darley concurs: "The encounter begins a process that morally alters the person who participates in the process."[7]

The point that Darley and Lifton make is slightly different than Milgram's. Milgram believes that individuals are all capable of good or evil, and sometimes both. Their interaction within a structure that promotes evil action may cause them to do evil, but they will not be fundamentally changed by that structure – they would still have the capacity for good in a different set of structural circumstances.[8]

Milgram's study tested two variables for inducing individuals to commit violence against other individuals. The first was the physical proximity of the victim, and the second was the physical proximity of the authority commanding violent behavior. Hierarchal organizations are well suited to control both of these variables.

For example, Milgram demonstrated that as less contact occurs between an individual and his victim, a greater the willingness to use violence against the victim develops. Milgram says, "The concrete, visible, and personal presence of the victim acted in an important way to counteract the experimenter's power and to generate disobedience."[9]

Hierarchy provides a system of rules and norms that insulate members from their culpability in committing violence. The structure has the potential to isolate the would-be perpetrators from the would-be victims, so as to minimize the potential guilt a perpetrator might feel. When the perpetrator has little or no interaction with his victim, he or she is less likely to perceive the individual as a person deserving of empathy and, as a result, the perpetrator is not forced to identify with the victim or feel guilt for the pain he or she has caused.

Hierarchy rests on vertical bonds between an individual and his or her superiors – as there is usually far less horizontal interaction between the individual and others. The rigid structure can ensure that the individual's primary interaction occurs within the group, thus reinforcing violent behavior without outside forces tempering the effect.

Just as hierarchy decreases the interaction between an individual and his or her victim, it can also increase the interaction between an individual and the authority demanding violent action. In Milgram's study, the individuals were less likely to disobey the order to cause the victim pain when the experiment director was in the room. The reason for this is two-fold.

The first relates to Arendt's conclusion that banality is a function of an ordinary person's tendency to follow orders and conform to mass opinion. When the experiment director was in the room directing the individual to increase the level of electric shock, he was shaping the individual's perception of mass opinion. In the same way, hierarchal systems reinforce at every level the commands coming from the authority. With this vertical system of communication, "mass opinion" becomes that which is dictated from the top, and lower-level members will be more likely to conform. In this way, hierarchal organizations are those identified as having the greatest potential for violence, because hierarchal organizations have the most efficient structure of coercion.[10] The second reason centers on the distribution of culpability. The presence of a chain of command eliminates individual responsibility and, instead, it places the impetus for moral judgment on the system, rather than the individual.

In order for organizations to assure obedience among their members, they must limit the encounters members have with forces that could challenge the pre-eminent ideological framework. Further, they must insure that they have an ability to explain contradictory interactions in a way that is not dissonant to the frame, but an enforcement of it.[11]

The studies mentioned above would suggest that hierarchal ties serve to reduce the horizon of encounters and to detract from the importance of any resulting inconsistencies. From this, it is possible to conclude that efforts to end religiously motivated political violence should center on preventing the establishment of hierarchal structures within opposition movements. For, if organizations are unable to control the interactions of their members with the rest of society, they will also be unable reduce the dissonance members will experience engaging in violence. According to this line of argument, we should expect to see a clear difference in structure between violent and non-violent organizations. More specifically, we should see the organizations using violence exhibiting distinctly hierarchical structures that reinforce the framework of violence they support.

But hierarchy is not the only structural argument being made about organizational violence. Within the field of social movements, arguments come to a conclusion completely at odds with the one explored above.

Political-process theory would suggest that the structure of the arena constrains the opportunities available to social movements, and in so doing influences their timing and methods. But as this discussion established earlier, and as Schattschneider so aptly put it, "the flaw in the pluralist heaven is that the heavenly chorus sings with an upper class accent."[12] Theories oriented around the elements of the political process cannot explain the actions of those that do not have a place in that process.

Early studies of social movements centered on the assumption that only the deviant members of society were prone to protest, and thus sought to identify the characteristics that separated social-movement activists from the rest of productive society. But, as these studies progressed, scholars concluded that previous assumptions about the type of individual likely to pursue contentious politics were at best incomplete. Scholars – notably including Oberschall,[13] Tilly,[14] and Zald and McCarthy[15] – endeavored to move the study of social movements out of the realm of the pathological and exceptional and into a predictable framework that emphasized the importance of structure and organization.

This epistemological shift did well to address the issue that most participants of social movements were far from the marginalized members of society that previous research presumed them to be. Recognizing that movements most commonly were undertaken by members of a pre-existing organization explained why movement participants were usually well integrated into society. Thus, the previous question of how disparate and marginalized individuals were able to successfully maintain social protests over prolonged periods was answered by the recognition that the individuals were neither disparate nor marginalized, and were using existing organizational ties to sustain movement momentum.[16]

Further research shows that pre-existing organizational ties affect more than just the sustainability of the movement; indeed, such ties can have a significant impact on the types of actions employed by movement participants. In fact, certain organizational structure can decrease impulsive inclinations toward violence. Ties between individuals in strong families, churches etc. can facilitate members' willingness to conform in society overall. In fact, when individuals are isolated from society and the structure of strong network ties, they are predicted to be more likely to engage in violent behavior.[17]

Tilly has demonstrated that the type of organizational base influences the type of actions undertaken by movement participants. For instance, association-based organizations are more likely to undertake actions that are "planned, scheduled, bounded and disciplined,"[18] in contrast to the smaller and less-organized actions frequently undertaken by communal organizations. Thus, one can also posit that the origin of organization influences the range of actions undertaken.

But even with these conclusions, one is still left unable to explain *why* organizations with similar origins and comparable intentions still sometimes undertake dramatically different methods of action. To address this, it is expedient to draw on more recent social-movement research that correlates not the origin of organization, but the structure of organization, with the likelihood of success of the movement.

What we find is that formal organizational structures can offer certain benefits to their members that makes violence less likely. Formal structures delineate clear lines of collective identity and a coherent worldview.[19] The absence of a formal structure, then, offers at best poorly defined parameters of thought, action and success. The incentives for members of these groups are amorphous.[20] The inverse of this argument is quite important: movement success is dependent on the organizational capabilities of a movement – and that hierarchies have been proven to offer the greatest efficacy in organization. By this reasoning, we can expect that organizations with hierarchal structures are more likely to gain access to the political process, and as their access to the process increases, their willingness to use violence will decrease. This becomes doubly significant in light of the realization that it is the perceived increasing limitation of access to the political process that drives organizations to undertake more radical action

This reveals the second of the two competing elements at work in the structural influence of social protest: the first element is drawn from the previous pool of research, which argues that hierarchal organizations are more likely to induce violence by their members; the second is that hierarchal organizations are more efficient, and tend to be more successful in achieving the aims of the organization. The aim of a social movement is to change the environment in which it operates in such a way that its issues are respected and acted upon. In other words, social movements seek access to the political process, and the efficiency that a hierarchy produces assists those movements in gaining such access. The consequence of this understanding is that the efforts undertaken to restrict radical movements from establishing hierarchal structures (as a means of preventing violence) are undermined by the constraints such limitations put on the organization's opportunity to access the political process.

This is a very important point – particularly in light of the recent form of development of religious organizations across the globe. Likely responding to increases in technology and law-enforcement, organizations are becoming less likely to build a hierarchal structure that can be easily monitored and infiltrated. Instead, from the famous example of al-Qaeda to the cases of this study, organizations are not building hierarchies at all. Instead, we see violent action somehow flourishing in a structure of organization that superficially appears to be the polar opposite of a hierarchal structure: cell composition.

Recognition of the dual nature of hierarchy in opposition organizations brings us closer to the understanding of the selection of methods, because it focuses the discussion on the alternative structures that are being developed and leads to a recognition that, when coupled with the right rhetorical frame, cells can be equally effective (and markedly more secretive) in inducing violence among members. This turns the discussion to an attempt to understand how the physically opposite cell and hierarchal structures can affect comparative influence over the violence used by their members.

The efficacy of the cell model in the use of violence

Louis Beam, a self-described seditionist, has most articulately explained the problems with hierarchy in opposition movements. He argues that hierarchal organizations are dangerous for insurgents because

> an infiltrator can destroy anything which is beneath his level of infiltration and often those above him as well. If the traitor[21] has infiltrated at the top, then the entire organization from the top down is compromised and may be traduced at will.[22]

Advances in technology have made the infiltration of hierarchal organizations relatively easy, thus rendering pyramid organizational structures essentially useless.[23] We have seen a concomitant rise in cell-structured organizations, in which single members operate without the direction of a central management structure.

But can such a type of organization actually serve the purpose for which it has developed? If hierarchal organizations are the most efficient, these utterly decentralized and seemingly chaotic webs of philosophical connections seem to be about as far on the other side of the spectrum as one can get.

Beam argues that leaderless resistance does not reflect an inability to issue orders and make use of a chain of command; rather, it reflects the dearth of a need to do so:

> Since the entire purpose of leaderless resistance is to defeat state tyranny, all members of phantom cells or individuals will tend to react to objective events in the same way through the usual tactics of resistance. Organs of information distribution such as newspapers, leaflets, computers, etc. which are widely available to all, keep each person informed of events, allowing for a planned response that will take many variations. No one need issue an order to anyone. Those idealists truly committed to the cause will act when they feel the time is right, or will take their cue from others who precede them.[24]

Organizations with this leaderless structure are often mistaken for being disorganized or underdeveloped by outsiders and members alike.[25] But scholars are slowly coming to recognize that this lack of a structure actually allows for a greater flexibility in adversarial circumstances. The cell structure "supports rapid organizational growth in the face of strong opposition, inspires personal commitment, and flexibly adapts to rapidly changing conditions."[26]

Beam also extols the ability of the cell structure to inspire personal commitment, pointing out that it quickly weeds out those not fully committed to the cause. He notes that some cells will be no larger than a single person, a daunting structure for someone just dabbling in opposition. However, for those devoted to the cause, it is an ideal scenario, because the cell's ability to maintain secrecy is best for the endurance of their purpose.

So, while the recognition of the increased efficiency of hierarchal structures may be appropriate for organizations operating safely inside the political arena, for those endeavoring to change that arena (and suffering from government opposition to their cause), cell organization may actually prove more expedient.

One of the stalwarts of the structural behavioralist experiments was the encompassing nature of the structures they were mimicking. Gurr's far reaching hypothesis on the effects of relative deprivation on a person's tendency to rebel becomes relevant if one considers the ability of a hierarchal organization to reduce an individual's deprivation by providing for his or her physical needs, thereby indebting the individual to the cause the organization promotes.[27]

But what if relative deprivation is not limited to physical needs? While the cell structure of leaderless resistance will do little to assuage hungry bellies, it has great potential to alleviate a different kind of pain – moral hopelessness. Stern distinguishes between the fulfillment of physical and moral needs by identifying what she calls "inspirational leadership." The relationship between leaders and followers is sometimes unclear, with the goal of the leader being the transformation of the follower into a relatively independent moral agent: "They use moral suasion rather than cash to influence their followers, appealing to higher-order deficiency needs in the Maslow hierarchy, including the desire to be part of a community and to gain recognition for one's achievements."[28]

Most members of the Army of God lament a government that has betrayed them and failed in its function to protect the rights of the innocent. They express outrage at the false legitimacy they see converged on a government which has long abdicated its purpose. They speak of feeling helpless when they think of the children being murdered with the sanction of the government.[29] The cell structure of the Army places action directly into the hands of those feeling the moral outrage. They can endeavor to diminish the powerlessness they feel through violent action – and they do not need to wait for permission from the leaders of the organization. Thus, their moral needs are more than adequately met by the structure of an organization which puts "salvation" in their hands.

And so, although structurally the organization is quite disparate, the emphasis on individual decision and action gives each member the opportunity to confront the helplessness they feel about the murder of innocents. The implication is that the more dangerous (violent) the action, the greater the blessing on the individual committing it. The organizational ties are not founded on consistent physical interaction, but on a shared understanding of the value of actions committed. The byproduct of this structure is as Beam predicted it would be – that those who remain members are fully committed to the use of violence.

One of the other most significant elements of a hierarchy in producing violence by its members is the strong ties between the members and the authority calling for the action. When these ties are strong, the ties between members and their victims are necessarily weak, and the traditional violence inhibitors are nullified.

Social psychologists have long argued that individuals seek consistency in their belief systems. When an event or interaction takes place that calls into question a person's beliefs, that person will act to reduce the dissonance between the event and beliefs. This can be done by changing their beliefs or by reframing the event to fit into what they already "know."[30] The shelter of a hierarchal organization can reduce the dissonance to which its members are exposed and limit the likelihood of a change in beliefs.

On the face of it, it would seem impossible that the cell structure of organization could produce the same results – especially given that the purpose of the structure is to blend in with the surrounding society. If the very purpose of a cell structure is to blend into the surrounding society, it would seem that opportunities for dissonance, and thus a restructuring of belief, would be common.

But as we saw in the chapters on rhetoric, the more isolated an organization is from the political process, the more radical the rhetoric they use. Conversely, organizations with greater access to the political process demonstrated more pluralist rhetoric. As we will see in the discussion of structure in the cases in this book, there is evidence of a trade-off between strength of hierarchy and specificity of rhetoric. In the final chapter of Part II, it will be argued that organizations that have been thrust to the fringe of the political process tend to structure their organizations in the more secretive cell formation, and that the strength of the rhetorical frame they construct compensates for the opportunities for dissonance reduction offered by more traditional hierarchal structures.

But first, it is useful to examine the structure of each of the cases being studied in this book in light of the competing explanations of hierarchy and political opportunity.

The structure of the Christian Coalition

While the ideology of the Christian Coalition is what most frequently makes the news, in many ways it was the organizational structure that revolutionized politics. In one action-plan letter sent to an emerging county chapter, the state leaders reminded their members of the following:

> We must focus on our short term goal, and that is establishing county chapters of the PA Christian Coalition. After getting the organization going, you will have time to get involved in the issues. But for now, stay clear of the issues and focus on ORGANIZATION.[31]

It is not surprising that the Coalition focused so heavily on organization. To distinguish the organization from its predecessors, and to take advantage of the support Robertson had gained in his presidential campaign, Reed was determined to create a grassroots organization.

Members were mobilized to hand out voter guides and go door-to-door to educate their neighbors on the issues (estimates suggest that over 33 million voter guides were distributed in the 1994 Congressional elections). This resulted not only in a very substantial budget for the organization to further influence the political scene, but the availability of a "rapid response network" allowed the Coalition to exert powerful influence very quickly.

Current Coalition Legislative Director Jim Backlin recounts the power of this fluid structure in the case of a 2002 bankruptcy bill.[32] The Coalition had no objections to what Backlin described as "common sense legislation" until Senator Chuck Schumer of New York inserted into the bill what Backlin refers to as a "pro-abortion clause."[33] The legislation was delayed until after the 2002 election and then placed abruptly on the Senate agenda with only two hours' notice.

The national Coalition office immediately hit the phones, calling key state and local representatives, urging them to call their House leaders immediately.

The chairmen, in turn, called the members underneath them in the hierarchy and urged them to pick up the phones as well. The bill ended up being defeated by 71 votes, and Backlin accords the Coalition all the credit. He noted that the same bill came up again in 2004 without the abortion clause and passed readily. Backlin boasts that, although the banking lobby supporting the bill was powerful,[34] it was no match for the grassroots mobilization of the Christian Coalition.[35]

The grassroots element of the organization meant that local efforts had to be made to start local and state chapters. But once that initial interest was expressed, the national office provided organizational assistance to local chapters. Some key county-level decisions were made by the state chapter – including the appointment of the county director and chairman.[36] In an outline of the organizational structure of county chapters, there is an underlined reminder that

> starting a chapter will not necessarily be done through a democratic process. Instead, chapters will start by the state office assigning the position of county director and temporary chairman to one person who will put together an executive committee. The eventual goal is to organize the precinct level in every key precinct in each county. In order to help the County Chapter achieve the goals set forth by the state office, the state office will provide help through what we are calling a "County Staffer". The job of the county staffer is to make the job of the volunteers easier and more manageable.[37]

The state offices suggest meeting formats, methods for member contact, and they even provide pre-written letters appealing for local support, complete with blanks to be filled in with the specific county information. The meeting formats include ten-minute breakdowns of the monthly two-hour meetings, including a list of state-generated agenda items.

While Robertson and Backlin both stress that local and state chapters do have autonomy from the national organization, it is clear that the autonomy is determined within a very carefully structured and largely hierarchal organization. For a time, the hierarchy and meticulous organization paid off – in the 1990s the Coalition was a powerful force in the Republican Party.

The structure of the Muslim Brethren is in many ways remarkably similar to that of the Christian Coalition, and for that reason we will break with organizational precedent set by the first five chapters of this book and turn to a discussion of the Muslim Brethren next.

The structure of the Muslim Brethren

Initially, the structure of the Brotherhood organization centered primarily on the compelling persona of al-Banna. However, in 1931, a conflict arose between al-Banna and other members of the organization. Accounts of the dispute differ, but the problems seem to have centered around al-Banna's choice for his deputy – with some members criticizing the low social standing of the individual selected. The matter was further complicated by charges that al-Banna had inappropriately used funds of the organization. The matter was resolved when the dissenting members of the Muslim Brethren resigned, but al-Banna was inspired by the conflict to more carefully articulate the structure of the organization. Changes were made over the next 15 years and, by 1948, the structure that exists today was largely in place.

The Brotherhood is led and represented by a single General Guide, elected by three-quarters of the Consultative Assembly. To be eligible to serve as General Guide, an individual must have been a member of the Consultative Assembly for at least five years, be "at least 30 lunar years of age," and demonstrate the values of "morality and practicality."[38]

The General Guide, upon his election, takes an oath to be a "faithful guardian over the principles of Al-Ikhwan al-Muslimin, the interests of the Muslim Brethren according to the book and the Sunna and with the advice and opinions of those around him."[39] The Guide is expected give a full-time commitment to his post, and he is not to have any economic interests in any company, even those affiliated with or supported by the Brotherhood. The appointment is for life, but the governing articles of the organization do allow for the possibility of the Guide's removal should he fail in his expected duties.

The General Guide sits at the head of the Guidance Bureau, composed of 12 members of the Brotherhood: nine from Cairo, the remaining three from other Egyptian governorates.[40] Members of the Guidance Bureau are also required to be at least 30 years old and are expected to demonstrate the same qualities of morality and practicality as their leaders. Members themselves are elected to the Guidance Bureau by the Consultative Assembly. Once elected, these members serve a renewable two-year term. Given the legal restrictions on the Brotherhood, the Guidance Bureau rarely meets as an entire group, preferring instead to meet in groups of two or three so as to avoid detection.[41]

The Consultative Assembly is composed of 100 members of the Brotherhood elected from each province and is responsible for establishing and maintaining the strategy of the organization. For example, it was the Consultative Assembly that made the decision in 1980 that the Brotherhood should pursue efforts to become an official political party. However, it was the job of the Guidance Bureau to implement and oversee these efforts.[42]

The Consultative Assembly and the Guidance Bureau oversee the rest of the Brotherhood, which is further divided into the Technical and Administrative apparatuses. The Technical Apparatus is divided into several subsections dealing with specific elements of the organization – Policy, Finance, Media and Law – and the Administrative apparatus is itself divided into three subcategories of District, Branch and Family.

There are administrative offices all over Egypt, usually corresponding with the division of provinces in the state. Each administrative office has a chairman, a deputy, a secretary, a treasurer and a representative of the Guidance Bureau. The GB representative is considered advisory, and he does not vote in matters pertaining to the district.[43]

The structure of the Ikhwan is based on concentric circles of membership.[44] General membership is the widest circle of membership. As explained by the website, "In this category of membership, the focus is directed to faith, loyalty and training. This stage is a test of confidence which shapes and defines the next stage."[45] Once satisfactory attainment of the characteristics required of a general member are attained, a member can move on to Active membership, which "stands for the member who has got the characteristics of piety, obedience and jihad." Finally, a member gains the opportunity for jihad membership:

> It stands for the person entitled to practice education and training, to take the pledge of allegiance, to participate in organization decisions and to know the MB secrets. Moreover, he has the right to lead. This necessitates a high degree of training, which makes eligibility limited to a few people.[46]

To move from one circle from the next, members engage in religious training. The Ikhwan's website promotes the "study circles system" as one which best promotes the knowledge of "da'wa."[47]

What is interesting about the structure of the Muslim Brethren is that, although it is highly organized and very hierarchical, there is a regulated autonomy at each level. The hierarchy enables fast responses to developing issues quite similar to the Christian Coalition. In fact, one member interviewed estimated that news or commands issued from the Guidance Bureau could be disseminated among all the hundreds of thousands of members throughout Egypt in less than six hours, thanks to the streamlined structure of the group.[48]

As mentioned earlier, the Consultative Assembly and the Guidance Bureau work in tandem to make strategic and ideological decisions, but day-to-day decisions are left almost entirely in the hands of each locale. A confidential Egyptian government report notes that

> [g]roups can organize activities as long as they stay within the limits of the movement's policy and that there is no use or call for violence. There is no need of prior authorization from the hierarchy before launching an initiative. For example, after the killing of Hamas leader Sheikh Yassin in Palestine, students at Al-Azhar launched the first demonstration at 6:00 a.m., one hour after the killing, with no consultation from the hierarchy.[49]

The result of this structure is that members are intensely and continuously involved with their surrounding community. One member of the Brotherhood pointed out that, in some ways, it is the constant repression they have suffered from the regime that has led to such a strong grassroots movement. He explains that because the Brotherhood is banned from practicing official activities, they cannot rely on media advertisements to get their message across or recruit new members. Instead, they are required to rely exclusively on personal interaction with society on a face-to-face basis. This, coupled with their relatively vague ideological rhetoric, allows them to appeal to a vast base of individuals. As a result, there are extremely strong lines of communication and levels of support between the Brotherhood and their surrounding communities.[50]

Ibrahim Hudaiby[51] explains that the organization is a necessary mix of control and flexibility. New membership is constrained by the regime's watchful eye toward expansion. As a result, Hudaiby says that potential members are recruited by current members, rather than current members being approached by those hoping to join, in order to thwart the regime's intentions of undercutting the organization.[52] This function serves to maintain the hybrid elements of structure and flexibility in that current members must be involved with their communities, if for no other reason than to spot opportunities for expansion. But new members enter the organization with existing ties to their recruiter, enabling the preservation of hierarchal order. Like the Christian Coalition, this organization has proven remarkably successful, with the Brotherhood boasting extensive membership in all classes of society.

The cases of the Christian Coalition and the Muslim Brethren offer support to Oberschall's theory that hierarchal structures increase organizational efficiency and success. Does this necessarily mean that the social psychologists have it entirely wrong, and that hierarchies had been falsely accused of being more likely to produce violence? The following discussion regarding the Army of God and al Jama'a al Islamiyya will argue that the elements of a hierarchy that allowed for the promotion of violence are not relegated exclusively to hierarchies. Rather, these elements can be mimicked in other types of seemingly opposite structures.

The structure of the Army of God

The Army of God could not be more different from the Brotherhood and the Coalition. In interviews, several members echoed the sentiment articulated in the *Army of God Manual*: that they are a real Army with God as their general. They look to fellow Army members for support and inspiration, but not orders. Henry Fellisone, a minister and a supporter of the Army of God, demonstrates his understanding of leaderless resistance, saying, "So we have the Army of God, which in the future will organize and coalesce like those of Europe who had centuries of underground work, and there will be skilled assassins and skilled saboteurs after the abortion industry."[53]

Leaders of the Army do not command their supporters to commit certain actions. They are not involved with the day-to-day upkeep of the organization at all. Rather, they encourage the spirit of resistance and offer a variety of methods for its implementation. In the preface to the *Army of God Manual*, the author explains:

> My main goal is to encourage others to take certain actions at certain times in solidarity with the resistance effort. In other words, when the [unintelligible type] begin to smoke, add some wood to the fire. We desperately need single lone-rangers out there, who will commit to destroy one aborttuary before they die.[54]

Stephen Jordi is one such lone-ranger. He saw an interview with some of the Army supporters on television, was impressed by their biblical argument, and felt compelled to act himself. He declines to speak of any interaction he had with them before he planned the bombing of an abortion clinic.[55]

In the Army, emphasis is not on specific action, but on doing "God's will." God's will is relatively well-defined and firmly entrenched in scripture, but the moral impetus for action is on the individual. As Shelly Shannon explains:

> Prayer is the key. Pray and obey. Once you know for sure it is the right thing to do, and that you too must do what is right, just keep following God and let him be the Master builder. Your work will probably not be like anyone else's.[56]

Part of the "hands-off" leadership style of the Army entails publishing personal accounts of individual action, which are technically nothing more dangerous than an innocuous biography. However, most are written in such a way as to not only tell the story of the author, but to provide knowledge of how a reader could commit the same action him/herself. Shannon's account of her first attempt to blow-up a clinic is almost tedious in its attention to the nuanced detail of making fire bombs out of milk cartons ("the kind with pop-off tops").[57]

The *Army of God Manual*, which is essentially a 100-page picture tutorial of methods for sabotaging abortion clinics, starts off with a legal disclaimer reading:

> The information contained in this book is intended solely for the interest and/or amusement of, and what it may be worth to, the reader for information purposes only. It is not intended to encourage the activities mentioned and described here. Kids, don't try this at home.[58]

The pages that follow are filled with helpful "hypothetical" information about things that have the potential to shut down abortion clinics. Consider, for example, "Project Noah":

> Babies have been known to send mail to abortionists through the mail slots in their front door. They will use the abortionist's water hose, or import one of their own (using gloves or Godfather tape), placing it through the slot, turn it on, and let gravity do the rest. A variation to Project Noah is Project Drought. In many communities, the water meters with their associated shutoffs are located in a hole in the ground near the premises they serve. A small bag of Sackrete concrete mix can be dumped in the hole, covering the meter. A few short pieces of steel reinforcing rods or galvanized pipes can be shoved in also. Then a bucket of water (and some calcium chloride, if you like) can be poured in.... Obviously this little tactic has the potential to greatly irritate the city utility people, so don't get caught.[59]

The tactics change as the reader moves on through the manual, as do the legal disclaimers. Once the reader finishes the manual, he or she has the opportunity to read through the appendices, the first of which is preceded by the following note:

> The Appendix that follows is intended for the serious and committed covert activist. If you decide to read and use the information in the following appendix, be careful, be thorough, and remember, as far as men are concerned, you are on your own. But what we do, we do for the babies, and God Knows, and God helps. God Bless.[60]

In the section that follows, readers are informed how to use a rifle to destroy the car of an abortionist so he is unable to commute to work, or how to use toxic waste to shut down clinics, or seriously endanger the staff within them.

The final section is identified as being for those with "Terminal Courage," and is considered a "once in a lifetime tactic." The wording in this disclaimer is particularly disconcerting evidence of a powerful frame at work in a very non-hierarchal organizational structure:

> Not everyone will be blessed with this opportunity. With family ties, it would be most difficult.... You may not be afraid to die. You are afraid of living a lifetime in bonds. Understandable. Yet, you have faith. You look forward to meeting our lord face to face. The time has come.... It would only take a few activists practicing terminal courage to drive the entire killing industry underground. Maybe the Spirit of God has been hounding you to take certain actions on behalf of his children and you have not obeyed. Here is your last chance.[61]

In this section, readers are informed how to create effective firebombs to dismantle clinics permanently.

The manual ends with admonitions for solidarity – in thought, if not in physical presence. The author argues that the government deliberately emphasizes the arrests of Army members and then underemphasizes the number of clinics destroyed in an effort to make members feel they are alone in their outrage, as well as alone in their actions. The manual explains that over 250 abortion clinics have been totally destroyed since *Roe* v. *Wade*, and that only one out of every 100 activists is caught. The author implores the reader to realize that the organization is not as vulnerable as the government would have them believe. He reminds his readers repeatedly that "you are never alone."

Whether or not this is true is not clear, but also not entirely germane to the present discussion. The Army of God is remarkable for its ability to circumvent the benefits conveyed by a hierarchal organization in their own structure, which is anything but. They have used the unique features of religion to inspire and sustain solidarity, despite the fact that members rarely interact with one another. In a hierarchal organization, numbers, authority and prestige matter. In the structure that the Army has developed, these elements are irrelevant except in the members' judgment of themselves in relation to the accounts posted by others. Ultimately, God is their judge *and* general – and it is His orders, His authority and His interaction with members that matters.

The structure of al Jama'a al Islamiyya

The case of al Jama'a al Islamiyya is in many ways (at least structurally) a synthesis of the other cases that have been examined. Al Jama'a al Islamiyya developed as an organization intended to prepare cadres trained in weaponry to enforce the implementation of Sharia law.[62] According to Dia Rashwan, one of the primary differences between al Jama'a al Islamiyya and al-Jihad was that al Jama'a never endeavored to be a secret organization. Their activities were a mixture of public works (education, infrastructure, etc.) and the call for a turn away from jahiliyya.[63] In many ways, the organizational structure is very similar to that of the Brotherhood.

There are eight members of the Majlis al Shura (Consultative Council), and seven others at a second level of leadership. There are local branches as well, and decision-making is a combined action of the national and local councils.[64] Also like the Brotherhood, and for similar reasons, al Jama'a did have to be relatively secretive in whom (and how) they recruited. The level of secrecy increased as the organization became more brazen in challenging the regime, and was paralleled by increasing standards for membership.

In the 1970s, when the organization was supported by Sadat, "required readings" were no more controversial than the Qur'an and the hadiths. As the actions of the origination became more violent, potential recruits were required to read Sayid Qutb and Ibn Tamiya.[65] Further, as violence became more commonplace, participation was expected by all the members, and lines of authority were clear.[66]

However, quite unlike the Brotherhood, al Jama'a al Islamiyya formed an official armed wing, and each local region established its own armed wing with an autonomous commander.[67] So, al Jama'a al Islamiyya presents a case with a unique structure in that it is, in many ways, identical to that of the non-violent cases discussed earlier, but it also mirrors some of the significant elements of the cell model. According to Hafez, al Jama'a in the 1980s had clear leadership roles, but saw many decisions delegated to the local levels.[68]

But, by the 1990s, the hierarchy had largely fallen to the necessity for secrecy, and a 1993 Egyptian government report identified the organization as "a decentralized conglomeration of militant groups."[69] Indeed, after much of the organization was imprisoned in the 1990s, the chain of command became entirely tangled. This was emphasized by the contradictory reactions to the 1997 ceasefire issued by some of the organization's leaders. Omar Rahman denied its legitimacy and urged those not in prison to continue the fight.

Structural violence?

What we can conclude from the case studies is that the Christian Coalition and the Muslim Brethren built hierarchal organizations, and in so doing achieved a level of efficiency that enabled them to achieve some degree of political access. This access reinforced their belief that change could come from legal opposition. The adherence to legal opposition kept the window of opportunity open (the level of openness varied – particularly in the Egyptian case). However, the Army of God and al Jama'a al Islamiyya looked at the window afforded to their predecessors and thought it not open wide enough. They called for more dramatic change, and in so doing found themselves under suspicion. Accordingly, they began to operate more secretly, but were forced to give up a modicum of efficiency, thereby restricting their ability to achieve effective change.

Most social-movement theorists focus on the effect structure has on the efficacy of the group, without considering what effect the efficacy of the group has on structure. The difference is subtle, but important nonetheless. If it is recognized that exclusion from the political process prohibits the establishment of an organizational hierarchy, and that organizational hierarchy increases an organization's ability to gain access to the political process, then the excluded organization will experience an increased intensity in their level of exclusion and seek to strengthen their influence in a different way.

The question that remains, then, is: despite being unable to establish a hierarchal structure, how do violent organizations sustain member loyalty to the cause? Recognizing that violence for its own sake is rare, how does a disorganized organization maintain sufficient levels of control of its members to convince them to undertake illegal and ultimately costly acts of political subversion?

In the next chapter, it will be argued that, while structure has traditionally been accredited with the most comprehensive explanation for the development of violence, the frame of religious belief acts as an intangible alternative to structure because the "hierarchy" is not headed by a person, but by God. Consequently, the member who questions the cause is also questioning God. And to question God produces far greater dissonance than an act of supernaturally justified violence.

7   The impact of ideological frames

Many of the violent religious organizations making news headlines in the present time are turning previous explanations for the causes of violence on their respective heads. Behavioral theories, which explained group violence in terms of a leader's ability to sustain reduced levels of dissonance for organization members through strict hierarchal structure, are unable to explain the very disparate organizational structure that is seen in the majority of violent religious organizations today. In fact, the individuals in violent religious organizations are active members of their communities and are not constrained by traditional hierarchal structures at all. In the previous chapters, it was argued that these more-disparate structures have developed in response to the organization's exclusion from the political process. The task presently at hand is to assimilate previous understandings of violence with present manifestations thereof.

It will be argued in this chapter that religious organizations are unique because the presence of belief in the supernatural opens up a wide range of choices not accounted for in the study of secular movements. Further, the presence of religion ensures that even when a hierarchy is present, the leader is constantly constrained by how well the individual leads according to his or her followers' perception of God. But where there is no hierarchy, God remains, and for this reason there is still a very strong force linking members to a particular cause. In fact, it will be demonstrated that when belief is framed so as to make violent action not only a right, but a responsibility, movement participants will endure severe resistance without turning from their cause.

This argument is based on two simultaneous understandings. First, there are relevant differences between secular and religious social movements. Second, once the differences between secular and religious organizations are taken into account as important, it is possible to identify uniquely religious elements which serve parallel purposes as structural functions within secular social movements. It will be argued that the elements of structure that have traditionally been understood to increase propensities of violence (namely strong ties between members and their superiors, fostered by a hierarchal structure) are supplanted by members' belief that God has demanded their action. Specifically, while violent organizations are forced by their exclusion from the political process to form cell-structured organizations rather than hierarchies, the same reduction of dissonance is achieved as a result of a frame that characterizes violence as a sacred duty. The discussion will turn to the scholastic understanding of framing as a motivator for action and then contrasts the pluralistic frame of the Christian Coalition and al-Ikhwan al Muslimin with the rigid frames of the Army of God and al Jama'a al Islmiyya. Following this, it will be illustrated that the violent organizations have not only developed far more specific frames than their non-violent counterparts, but how these frames shift the understanding of justification from the justification of violence to the justification of non-violence. In other words, the *violent* organizations argue that violence is not a right of its members, but a responsibility of all God-fearing individuals.

Religious exceptionalism?

In the first part of this book, it was noted that religiously motivated political violence has typically been treated either from the perspective that religion is not an informative variable (in other words, that religious movements are no different from secular ones) or that religion is so exceptional that its very presence is an indicator of potential violence. The problem with the first explanation is that researchers who consider religion to be no more than a superficial variable are unable to recognize its explanatory power. The question these scholars ask is not, *What is it about religion that leads to political violence?* but instead, *What are the conditions of individuals that lead them toward violent religion?* Seen in this way, religion is perceived as a mask for other variables. Yet the trouble with the opposite end of the spectrum is that studies linking religion and violence generally fail to account for the enormous number of religious individuals, organizations and institutions that never resort to violence at all. If monotheism is so destructive, then why are *all* monotheists not inspired by religion to commit acts of political violence?

This book has aimed to link these two seemingly contradictory understandings, by recognizing there are unique elements of religion that can influence religious adherents to engage in violence, and by arguing that these elements can best be understood using tools refined in the study of secular movements.

Part I examined some of the arguments that were made in relation to the rise of the anti-abortion movement in the United States and the case of the Islamists in Egypt. It was demonstrated that a political source is found to be responsible for this deprivation, and action is coordinated to undermine the legitimacy of this source.[1] Here, the likelihood to act violently is calculated by measuring the gap between the entitlement one feels toward certain resources and an assessment of the likelihood of the actual attainment of such resources. As this gap increases, the individual's belief in a non-violent way to bridge it decreases – increasing the likelihood of engaging in violent behavior.[2]

A number of explanations identify the political, social and economic conditions that lead to these feelings of deprivation. Modernization is frequently labeled as a culprit. The rapid growth rates and structural changes in the economy that accompany modernization also serve to intensify group competition for similar and scarce resources, thereby increasing levels of deprivation.[3] Rapid urbanization is credited with dismantling established rural networks, leading to feelings of isolation, loneliness and alienation.[4] This can result in efforts to establish new networks, increasing an individual's susceptibility toward recruitment into extremism.

Further, existing state structures are not always prepared for the rapid influx of migrants during times of increased urbanization. Potential for mobilization decreases, while at the same time migrants are in much closer proximity to elites, thus raising their awareness of their own deprivation.[5] The introduction to this study discussed the results of Norris and Englehart's research,[6] and these results are compatible to this argument. As individuals become increasingly aware of their relative deprivation, they are more likely to seek out the conditions of security that accompany belief in a supernatural force.

The underlying theme of all of these arguments is that religion is not born of a rational belief, but out of a subconscious effort to deal with adversarial economic or social conditions. In a sense, it is inaccurate to call such research a study of religion, as the entire purpose of such studies is to explain not religion, but the conditions of reality it masks.

Other scholars object to a focus on religion from a more methodological perspective. All too frequently, gross generalizations are made about particular religions and the adherents thereof. Edward Said explains that amateur scholars of Islam typically fall into one of two camps:

1   those that promote the religion as a dangerous adversary to modernization and democratization, and
2   those that can see only its virtues as a promoter for peace, humanism and development.[7]

Said bemoans the "semantic field of Islam" as "fundamentally narrow and constricted," often leading to academic inquiry that is equally plagued. The realization that any effort to define Islam – or any specific religion – inevitably constricts one's understanding of other manifestations of the same religion, and it leaves many scholars loathe to account for its existence at all.

A related criticism is that religion is simply culture, alternatively named. Schwedler points out:

> All red haired Caucasian females born to protestant blue-collar families in Detroit in 1966 probably do not identify collectively, and we cannot know that they would even if they lived in close proximity and shared social experiences.... It is just as impossible to know the significance of Islamic identity for every individual Muslim and assumptions are frequently spurious.[8]

As one would be scholastically bankrupt to predict the political actions of the red-haired girl from Detroit based only on the fact that she is a red-haired girl from Detroit, so also (the argument goes) is the scholar attempting to predict the political actions of the Muslim based solely on his or her practice of Islam. And certainly, if one is unable to predict the political actions of Muslims based on their Islamic beliefs, neither can one predict the political actions of Christians based on their belief in Christ.

Unquestionably, there is validity in these concerns. But often, instead of serving as cautionary reminders to tread carefully when conducting research about religion, these concerns instead result in the failure to appreciate the necessity of religion in understanding many aspects of political violence.

But the truth is, religion does have some impact on action. We know that individuals will rarely become involved in contentious action when they believe that such actions are condemned by their religion.[9] Conversely, where religious approval is offered in support of contentious tactics, believers are far more likely to engage in protest. This confirms that religion impacts on the range of actions available to actors, and thus necessitate studies that seek to understand this impact. When religion is viewed only as a mask for other secular variables, some bold assumptions are then made about religion as an outcome of certain unfortunate political or social circumstances based on preconceived ideas about the epistemology of religion. By doing so, scholars perpetuate the assumption that religion is non-rational and reinforce the very mechanisms this discussion aims to circumvent by avoiding its study.

In an age of secularization, it is critical to assess the significance of belief, if only because it is that which is most likely to be overlooked, as it is not a variable traditionally understood to be rational or predictive. Political science has, unsurprisingly, and perhaps even appropriately, evolved to reflect the secularization of society. As a discipline, political science is designed to study activity of the public realm, the predicted retreat of religion from the public realm into the private behooved religion's removal from the discipline.

Research is structured in such a way as to avoid normative approaches, and it reflects a fundamental understanding of political actors and political institutions as "understandable, explicable, and knowable by way of human reason and methods."[10] The problem with this type of discourse is that it inevitably limits one's ability to understand the actions of actors driven by something other than secular human reasoning. That is, when epistemology is limited to the understanding of human reason, it is unable to offer insight into the actions of those believing themselves to be guided by divine truth. Ironically, by refusing to study the significance of religion, scholars fundamentally narrow and constrict the semantic field of religion as much as they do with superficial studies.

Thus, by moving the discussion into the narrower field of social movements, one can recognize that the primary and significant difference between secular and religious social movements is found in the source of justification for the acts undertaken. Only religious actors can claim that their acts (violent or otherwise) are justified, condoned and often compelled by a being capable of judgment superior to any earthly courts. While Communists may speak for the proletariat, and environmentalists may speak for the ecosystems, neither of these entities is capable of offering justification. Environmentalist can act violently to further their cause, and they may consider *themselves* justified in deviant behavior. However, the trees they protect are not capable of similar justification, as they do not possess the capacity for judgment at all. In contrast, religious activists frequently justify their actions not on *behalf* of the God they serve, but rather at His *bequest.*

When individuals believe themselves to be acting at the bequest of a divine being, their entire structure of rational choice shifts. Traditionally, rational choice is measured based on the gains (or potential gains) made by an individual within his or her lifetime. Yet, religion just as frequently pertains to what happens *after* one's lifetime. Thus, to understand the actions of religiously moti-vated individuals, it is imperative to extend one's analysis to account for the potential gains achieved after (or in) death. While members of secular opposition movements may be willing to die for their causes, they infrequently pursue death.

Furthermore, to act at the bequest of a divine being, one must presumably have some manner of communication with that being. While there are certainly examples of this communication being conducted through a religious leader, this does not necessarily have to be the case. In fact, as will be shown in the cases of this study, the elements of hierarchy that promote violence can be equally present in a disparate structure if the individual members are directed by a per-ceived notion of God's will. This will be more clearly articulated in the follow-ing pages.

In the previous chapter it was noted that, although hierarchy is traditionally accredited with being best suited to reduce the dissonance generated by the use of violence, hierarchal organizations are also the most efficient at achieving their political objectives. The resulting paradox – that organizations prevented from forming hierarchal structures are condemned to less-efficient organizational structures and thus less likely to ever gain access to the political process, and consequentially are more likely to use violence to bring attention to their cause – was explained by the realization that contemporary cell structures are demon-strating the ability to provide similar functions in promoting violence as past hierarchies did. Where hierarchies reinforced the commitment of individual members through constant interaction with leadership, cells demand full com-mitment from members because blame cannot be shifted up the hierarchal chain of command. A secular government won't appreciate that God demanded action, and individual members are aware (indeed, are exultant) of their "culpability" when they join. Second, while hierarchies can assuage the physical needs of their followers with money and food (and thereby secure support via physical depen-dency) religious cells provide a moral power to their members, filling the empti-ness religious individuals feel when confronted with an immoral society. Finally, hierarchy is recognized to be critical for reducing the dissonance that is present when violence is committed by one human being against another. By limiting the interaction of individuals to such only within the organization itself – and primarily via a strict chain of command with organization leaders – movements can diminish any moral qualms a member might otherwise feel. However, in the previous chapter it was not explained in detail how this critical component was accomplished in cells.

In the remainder of this chapter, it will be argued that religious organizations are able to reduce dissonance not by limiting the interaction of their members with the surrounding community (in fact, the cell structure makes interaction more common, not less), but by framing the act of violence in the context of a moral duty rather than a legal right.

Hierarchy is believed to reduce the number of interactions a member has with anyone likely to challenge the belief he or she holds. However, what we will see in the case of the Army of God is that interaction is not valuable for its own sake. Few individuals who stop at the grocery store at the end of a long day's work can remember the name of the cashier that sold them their dinner. Individuals are capable of carrying out interactions without engaging themselves in a relationship with the other party. However, if the same individual had been told prior to the grocery trip that the cashier in check-out lane 10 had a crush on him/her, suddenly the individual would be far more likely to be able to recall not only the cashier's name, but personality traits and physical characteristics.

Essentially, individuals interact with specific frames in mind. These frames can be shifted and altered, but they directly impact the significance of each interaction.[11] All individuals are governed by frames, but most individuals – often without even realizing it – allow these frames to shift as they encounter new experiences.

The Army of God has established so comprehensive a frame that it has the power to envelop and dissipate the dissonance that is produced as a result of everyday interactions. Thus, rather than being forced by interaction to alter their frame, the frame causes the restructuring of the perception of the interaction.

This tension between interaction and frames is seen most clearly in the ongoing dialogue between Army members and supporters of the non-violent anti-abortion movement. One might expect to see some solidarity between the two perspectives, for the goal is the same (to end legal abortion) even though the means are dramatically different. Instead, Army of God members are quite vocal about their disparagement of non-violent anti-abortionists.

For example, Reverend Bray repeatedly lambastes other Christians who do not accept the use of violence in the pursuit of the cause:

> Those pro-life organizations which have scurried to re-purge themselves and get their press releases out in condemnation of James Kopp, thwart the very movement they think to be protecting. By condemning defensive action, they belie themselves and nullify all their pro-life proclamations, reducing themselves to noisy gongs. Their "dignity of man" protestations ring hollow, and their earnest pleas for the lives of the innocents are as cogent as the hollerings of a glossolalist on a hot tin roof. Rather than advance the effort to contend for justice for the womb children in our land and in the world, these "anti-violence" dupes, with their irrational rhetoric, continue to turn the movement backward.... I call all pastors who have condemned James Kopp

false. They have failed to handle God's word soundly and they have failed to guide our fellow citizens into good citizenship, leading them instead into the same sinful condemnation of a righteous fellow citizen. Moreover, they, by such condemnation contribute to the prolongation of this bloody scourge.[12]

There are two particularly interesting things about Bray's comments. The first is his condemnation of pastors committed to non-violent protest as "false." This sentiment is remarkably similar to one seen later in this discussion that distinguishes the violent and non-violent Islamic movements. The right to judge whether or not someone is a real Muslim is a distinct dividing line between the two methods, and it is fascinating to see a similar practice here. Bray could have simply questioned the judgment of these pastors, but instead, he questions their right to be pastors at all.

In many ways, it is the non-violent pro-life movement that has the greatest potential to cause dissonance for Army members. After all, most share the belief that abortion destroys innocent life, and that this life comes from God. But rather than dwell on these similarities and wrestle with the difference in methods, the Army determines that their opponents are not real Christians. In so doing, they eliminate the dissonant elements of the discourse and are free to comfortably maintain their structure of belief.

The second interesting element in Bray's statement is his assertion that these "false Christians" are actually the ones causing the "prolongation of this bloody scourge." While more time will be spent in the next chapter discussing the frame that the Army of God has constructed, it is sufficient here to say that the members are consistent in shifting the need for justification to those who are not violent.

Despite hundreds of pages of exegesis, and hours of recorded interviews and statements in which Army members panegyrize violence as a moral virtue, here Bray almost concedes that the violence is not a good thing. However, this concession is embedded in the assertion that it is the fault of the false Christians that true believers find themselves in a position where violence is necessary. And thus, the discord between the violent and the non-violent Christians is dealt with on two levels.

First, there is the question of whether the non-violent Christians are really Christians at all; and second, there is the assertion that the failure of non-violent Christians to obey God has led to the situation in which the violent Christians must take radical action. In both cases, the issue is not frequency of interaction, but the ability of the frame to account for the dissonance sewn as a result of the interaction.

Bray also has something to say about political leaders who condemn violent action. After James Kopp shot and killed Barnett Slepian, then attorney-general John Ashcroft issued a statement saying, "Kopp committed a heinous crime that deserves severe punishment. We need to send a strong message that whatever our differences, violence is not the solution."[13] Bray then responded by arguing:

[t]his is a lie. This is rhetoric designed to placate Ashcroft's abortophilic political opponents. Mr. Ashcroft does not believe this. Killing a serial killer to stop the murder of innocents is not heinous – it is glorious.... Mr. Ashcroft knows this, but cannot, as an effective politician say what he believes.[14]

Mr. Ashcroft is well known for his Christian fundamentalism, and some Army members consider him a friend to their cause.[15] But when Ashcroft condemned the killing of Dr. Slepian, the Army had to (consciously or unconsciously) figure out how to reduce the dissonance this created. In this case, rather than question the hero status of Mr. Ashcroft, or the consequences of a hero condemning the behavior of the organization, it was asserted that Mr. Ashcroft supported their actions secretly, but he was simply prohibited by his role from expressing it. This reframing of Ashcroft's position by the Army aligned nicely with the anti-government perspective of most of the members, and it reinforced the idea that violence was something only the truly courageous could actively support.

Thus, it is evident that the right frame enables the traditional factors which make structure so important to exist, even when structure does not. In other words, when the frame is strong enough, it has the force to provide moral ties that are as strong as what its hierarchal ties may otherwise be. As a result, the effects of the observable structure of the organization are superseded by the strength and type of frame.

It appears from the case of the Army of God that the "disorganized" cell structure has the potential to meet or even succeed the level of violence that can be produced by a hierarchal organization when the moral needs of supporters are being met, as long as the organization is still capable of reducing dissonance that occurs as a result of increased interaction.

The looming question, of course, is how can dissonance be reduced despite the increased levels of interaction a cell structure produces? The pages that follow will argue that, framed appropriately, the ideology of an organization has this capacity. There are two conditions of this occurrence. First, organizations must establish an ideology that reinforces the expectations and experiences of those it would seek to transform. Second, it will be argued that when religious movements develop a frame that shifts the use of violence from being a right of a politically oppressed organization, to being the responsibility of a true believer, the believer begins to see future actions through this lens, making him or her less likely to accept alternatives to violence, even should they be offered.

A framing of opportunity

It was mentioned in the previous chapter that the cell-structured organization can be as effective, if not more so, in inducing violent behavior from its members because it ensures that those involved are fully committed to the cause. In the same way, secrecy and limitations to membership – be they structural, pragmatic or ideological – perform the important function of ensuring that those who are active understand the ideas that make their action necessary.

Thus, it will be demonstrated in this chapter that the ordered structure of non-violent cases is possible and necessary due to the relatively vague ideology of each group. In contrast, this study's violent groups are united by a carefully articulated and well-promulgated ideology, and membership is largely contingent on the demonstrated acceptance thereof.

Ideology is not created in a vacuum – rather, it is shaped by the social origins of those who would abide by it.[16] One can conclude from this that the most compelling and transformational ideology will be one that reinforces the beliefs and experiences of those it would compel and transform. The subsequent pages will also serve to prove this reality.

When ideology is framed to capitalize on existing beliefs, it takes on the ability to transform future beliefs and experiences of the ideologue. In other words, when situated in the appropriate framework of structure and experience, ideology gains the aptitude to color and ultimately transform future interactions in such a way as to reinforce the ideology. Violent action then becomes a self-perpetuating cycle.

Foucault defined discourse as

> ways of constituting knowledge, together with the social practices, forms of subjectivity and power relations which inhere in such knowledge and relations between them. Discourses are more than ways of thinking and producing meaning. They constitute the "nature" of the body, unconscious and conscious mind and emotional life of the subjects they seek to govern.[17]

In this sense, discourse is a means of transmitting ideas into knowledge and then practice. More significantly, as Foucault indicated with his plural use of "ways," belief can be constituted into practice by different methods. And thus, a different result from the same belief is not at all impossible.

Studying the framework of a social movement allows researchers to focus on the development of ideas and meaning within the movement. Prior to the advent of this discipline, there was an underlying assumption that social movements carried ideas and meanings that grew automatically out of the structure of the movement or existing ideologies.[18] But, by studying the process by which these ideas and meanings develop, scholars are able to understand actors within a movement as agents involved in the creation of meaning.[19]

Framing is described as the process of selecting an aspect of one's perception of reality and emphasizing it through a text, speech or tactic (etc.) in such a way that a particular problem definition, causal interpretation, moral evaluation and treatment recommendation is identified. The researcher's purpose is to identify these aspects of a frame and then reach an understanding of their development, maintenance and success or failure. Thus, by studying the frames that make up a discourse, scholars are better situated to understand the way that belief influences action.[20]

Chapter 5 of this book showed how the Christian Coalition and the Muslim Brethren chose to engage in more moderate rhetoric, and in so doing were able to secure some degree of access to the political process.

The frames that the Coalition employed were designed to decrease the perceived radicalism of the group and appeal to a wide base of potential constituents. While still clearly identifying the liberal elite as the enemy, and thus implicitly indicating a need for combat, the call to arms was worded in such a way as to minimize the cost to potential participants. For example, in his presidential announcement speech, Robertson said the following:

> Human cruelty, human selfishness, alcoholism, drug addiction and sexual promiscuity will always bring in poverty and the disintegration of society. The answer does not lie in institutionalizing aberrant behavior ... the answer lies in a new rise of faith and freedom that will give every American a vision of hope ... a vision that will take us past these troubled days and show us the promise that lies ahead for each of us.... Of course some would say, doesn't that upset the atheists in our midst. Studies done for us by George Gallup show that 94 percent of all Americans believe in God.... I do not believe that the 94 percent of us who believe in God have any duty whatsoever to dismantle our entire public affirmation of faith in God just to please a tiny minority who don't believe in anything.[21]

Robertson framed his argument in such a way as to emphasize the normalcy of his fight, and by extension, that of his supporters. This is the quintessential Coalition argument – the shared understanding they presented to the country they were trying to reach always hovered over the justification that they had the right to be in the arena at all.

But how does this explain the totally different method the Army of God opted to pursue? Many psychological studies of violence dabble in dissonance theory – the idea that most people work to avoid dissonance in their thinking. If a person has two understandings that conflict with each other, this produces dissonance, and an associated effort to reduce it by resolving the contradiction.[22] Most individuals' conception of self is based on three goals of preserving a consistent, competent and moral self. The measurement for these qualities can be drawn from social norms, perceptions of a spiritual order or a combination of these two.

The Coalition's frame successfully reduces the perceived differences between a spiritual and a secular worldview. That is, it draws on shared understandings of Christian values, but does not require individuals to put themselves at odds with social mores in order to see those views implemented. Indeed, the frame emphasizes the compatibility of the Christian worldview with the societal "norm." In this sense, dissonance never becomes an issue, or at least not as a result of their political participation.

However, the Army of God emphasizes the inconsistency between their spiritual worldview and the political practices around them. The human tendency to reduce dissonance would require they somehow diminish this contradiction, and they see violence as the most appropriate means of doing so. But (and this is where it gets really interesting) a reduction of the inconsistency of their spiritual thought and the political world around them requires acts that would challenge the third goal in the conception of self. In other words, the reduction of inconsistency has forced them to undertake actions that are not typically considered moral.

Typically, one would expect at this point to see a frame that justifies this "immoral" behavior. Elliot Aronson argues that "[i]f we hurt someone it causes us to justify our actions by derogating our victim. This impels us to feel more hostility towards him, opening the door for further aggression."[23] This can be accomplished by creating frames which simultaneously dehumanize the victims, euphemistically avoid acknowledgement of a crime, and justify the actions that were taken.[24]

Although they were not employing violence, the Christian Coalition did, in some sense, follow this model. They were constantly focused on justifying their contention of the political norm – and then when the secular humanists (or, as Robertson prefers to call them, the liberal elite) fought back, they had further justification for their fight. But fascinatingly, this is not the model that the Army of God has chosen to follow at all. Instead, the Army has used their frame to paint an entirely different picture, where justification is not sought for violence, but for non-violence. By doing this, they have shifted the juxtaposition between the method by which they reduce inconsistency and the method by which they extol morality. Violence is not justified *despite* its inconsistency with the moral self, but instead actually becomes a consistent and morally inspired response to dissonance.[25]

Members of the Army of God who have engaged in some form of violent action describe a period in their life in which they came to be compelled as to the necessity of extreme action. Paul Hill speaks of his fear – up to the day that he killed George Tiller – as a fear that was endured based on his knowledge that his actions would save thousands of babies from death.[26] Shelley Shannon "couldn't imagine killing a fly, much less attempting to kill a person...." Over time, though, she came to consider the plight of the babies in greater detail and with deeper empathy, saying, "Surely I would be willing to do more than block a door or stand around with a sign if they were about to kill me."[27]

Likewise, Michael Bray cites his encounter with a woman who had had four abortions before *Roe* v. *Wade* occurred. Meeting this woman put a face to the issue of abortion for Bray which no other theoretical argument had before. In reaction to this meeting, Bray wrote to a federal judge saying, "It became impossible for me to continue to permit the tragedy to continue without direct intervention."[28]

Brockhoeft came to believe he had failed God, by failing to do all he could to prevent abortion:

My heart was overwhelmed with grief and love for the babies, fury and rage toward the criminals ... and ... deep shame and embarrassment before God. I was ashamed of being an American ... ashamed of being part of a luke-warm church. I was also ashamed of myself for having done nothing ... namely the exertion of actual force to prevent the slaughter of my people.[29]

While Army of God members are careful to point out that only God can command His soldier to use force in their writings, these same soldiers are extolled over and over for their bravery, holiness and commitment to the cause, as evidenced by their violent actions. Reverend Donald Spitz, the current web-master of the organization, said in an interview that

I support defensive action. If a born person were being murdered right here, it would be our duty to defend him. It would be wrong to allow him to be murdered before our eyes. It is also our duty to defend the unborn. An unborn person is not less a person than you or me.[30]

That duty is clearly very real to members of the Army who have not yet engaged in violence. Jonathan O'Toole, who became involved in the movement when he was still a teenager, has spoken proudly on television and elsewhere about his involvement in the Army of God. He also assists in the maintenance of Neal Horsely's "Christian Gallery" website,[31] home of the notorious *Nuremberg Files*.[32] In one interview, O'Toole makes a statement that emphasizes how well this frame has worked. He says that whenever he thinks about the giants of the violent anti-abortion movement, specifically mentioning Paul Hill, he (O'Toole) is "put to shame" because he himself has not yet done something so dramatic for the cause.[33]

The benefits of violent action in American politics are few and far between. Members of the Army of God who have not engaged in violence, but have been unwilling to condemn the violent acts of their fellow soldiers, have been subject to intense government scrutiny, and in some cases (according to those involved) harassment. Those who have used violence find themselves in prison, or in the case of Paul Hill, dead.

But, interestingly, while few Army of God members feel any love toward the government they perceive to have failed them, few are bitter about their situa-tion. In fact, many boast about their persecution, or in the case of John Brock-hoeft, refuse to speak of their violent acts, lest they be accused of bragging. Speaking with and reading the works of the individuals in the Army of God is in many ways like entering a rabbit hole into Wonderland – suddenly up is down, wrong is right and dark is light. While it is a disconcerting experience, it is also evidence of a powerful frame at work.

A violent duty

Using a frame to its full potential can reap great rewards for the successful social movement. Frames can be used to interpret or define problems and offer a course of action.[34] The job of the movement, then, is to take the sentiment that exists and convince the public that the cause of the social movement embodies that sentiment. In the case of the Army of God, one can see the exploitation of traditional religious values. They do this by developing metaphors and alternative definitions that support their unique interpretation of this frame.

In a chilling essay warning of the consequences to any doctor that would ever perform an abortion for one of his family members, Michael Bray uses biblical heroes to portray his threat as just:

> Therefore I declare as follows: I would not allow the murder of my children or grandchildren to go unpunished. As the government would not bring just vengeance against the murderers of my children, I would assume this duty, the right of a kinsman, and personally execute them.... Should any of my children, by human frailty and confusion ever commit such an atrocity, I would personally opt not to assume any obligation to execute them, but judge them to suffer a type of "temporary insanity". I would limit my obligation as an "avenger of blood" to the execution of the hired murderer of my grandchild.[35]

He then admonishes other fathers to do the same: "May fathers rise to the task of loving and protecting their children, and thus our nation from the calamity and destruction it is facing. May they keep their promise to love and protect their children."[36]

Bray calls on the characteristics of biblical patriarchs from both Old and New Testaments to frame his actions. In so doing, he implies that, given the opportunity, these legendary men would do the same. Thus, individuals who choose any other means of pursuing their ends are acting unheroically and unbiblically.

Brockhoeft also couches his actions in an interesting mix of supernatural justification and American jargon – "Preborn persons are endowed by God with the inalienable right to life."[37] Brockhoeft articulates the moment he decided to employ violence as the moment he learned to love the baby as if it were he, himself. He explains that to garner the courage to bomb the abortion facilities, he had to picture the face of the babies that would die in that facility the following day. To impress that image onto himself, he recalled the Bible command to "Love thy neighbor as thyself." Reasoning that if he were to witness his neighbor's baby being brutally tortured and killed, he would not hesitate to intervene – even at risk of harm to himself or the perpetrator – he concluded he had the same moral imperative to save the babies about to be aborted.

To further drive home the urgency of their plight, Brockhoeft did the following:

> I had superimposed myself onto that one, certain, real baby. He was real. He really existed. He was alive, still alive, somewhere in the Cincinnati area. In my heart, I became him. I was about to be killed, horribly, so, without question, I had every right to fight for my life, didn't I? While I was

superimposing the desperation of the baby's circumstance onto myself, I remembered that I must not also assume his helplessness. If it was still the baby who was about to be killed he wouldn't be able to fight for his life. I could fight for my own life and I would fight for his. Moreover, if I was indeed, helpless like him, that's what I'd want others to do unto me. I wouldn't want others to merely protest my death, but to fight for my life. And passive resistance wouldn't be good enough for me. That's not fighting. No, I would want someone to fight for my life. So I had to do it for him.[38]

Paul Hill uses different words, but he shares the same manner of justification as Brockhoeft. He argues that there is a moral law found in both the Old and New Testaments of the Bible that calls for individuals to defend the innocent. Hill says:

When murder, thus, has been legalized, and thousands are being slain every day, there is an overwhelming moral obligation to maintain and promote the means necessary for saving those threatened.... The Moral Law (as summarily comprehended by the Ten Commandments) requires the means necessary for defending innocent people. The unborn are innocent people. Therefore, the Moral Law requires the means necessary for defending the unborn.[39]

But Hill's argument is even more encompassing than this. He later states,

Those who have failed to uphold this duty should be reproved and warned of the consequences of persisting in this neglect. Both defending people with the means necessary, and upholding the obligation to do so are such obvious duties of the Moral Law that God will not excuse those who neglect these responsibilities on the basis of false pleas of ignorance.[40]

He goes on to quote Proverbs 24:11–12:

Deliver those who are being taken away to death, and those who are staggering to slaughter, O Hold them back. If you say, we did not know this, does He not consider it who weighs the hearts? And does He not know it who keeps your soul? And will He not render to man according to his work?

It is common for Christians and non-Christians alike to support pacifism by referring to the sixth commandment that "Thou shalt not kill." But Paul Hill meticulously endeavors to demonstrate that not all killing is evil. He argues that in Hebrew, there is a word for *kill* that is entirely different from the word used to communicate *murder*. It is the latter which is used in the sixth commandment, implying that "wrongful killing" is forbidden by God.

Capital punishment, on the other hand, is not only condoned, but required.[41] But after demonstrating the Biblical defense for capital punishment, Hill is careful to explain that his actions were not an effort to employ public justice. He says, "I did not kill John Britton to punish him for his past murders, but to prevent him from continuing to murder. My actions, thus, serve as an example of necessary individual defense – not public justice."[42]

John Brockhoeft, imprisoned for destroying abortion facilities, argues that violence intended to end abortion can be categorized as any of the three biblically justified types of homicide. In support of the capital-punishment justification, he argues that individuals in the "complete absence of any legitimate, legal authority ... have the right, the duty, to appoint themselves as upholders of genuine justice. And their self-appointment can be perfectly legitimate and wonderfully authoritative."[43] Brockhoeft contends that the United States government erred so grievously in the legalization of abortion that it relinquished its legitimate authority, creating a vacuum that others (read: members of the Army of God) are morally compelled to fill.

Just War

The *Army of God Manual* contains a declaration in its epilogue which states the following: "We the remnant of God-fearing men and women of the United States of America do officially declare war on the entire child-killing industry."

While the origins and consequences of the chosen title "Army of God" are controversial, it is certainly apt that the most frequently understood defense for the use of violence comes from the theory of Just War.

Just War theory was developed by the ancient Greeks and then adopted and expounded on later by a number of influential Christians, including Augustine, Aquinas and Grotius. The early Christian Church was largely pacifist, taking literally Jesus' example to approach conflict in a conciliatory and peaceful way. Early Christians disputed the right to bear arms, and military converts were encouraged to seek forgiveness for their sins of violence and to disengage themselves from future military commitments. But when Christianity became a religion of the state under Constantine, this pacifist doctrine became untenable.

As religion and the state became intertwined, the precepts of pacifism threatened to interfere with a state's ability to defend its borders and its citizens. Over time, the mainstream Christian Church came to accept the moral justification of war in certain situations. Aquinas developed the most comprehensive theory of Just War, and others have modified and debated it ever since. Yet for purposes here, it is sufficient to consider the broad criteria that is generally agreed upon by its proponents.

- War must be waged by the proper authority.
- War must be waged with the right intention (to right a wrong or redress a grievance – it is not sufficient to seek monetary gain).
- There must be a chance of success.
- The type of war waged must be proportionate to the offense.

While the Army of God uses the term *just war* quite liberally, it is not always apparent from their words that they understand it in the same way Aquinas did. Nonetheless, it is possible, and indeed helpful, to consider the way they have framed their actions to emphasize the similarities where they exist. Accordingly the discussion will now turn to an investigation of each of the above criteria.

Identifying the proper authority

Brockhoeft explains that the only element differentiating between abortion and murder is government sponsorship of the former and condemnation of the latter.[44]

But, given the foundations of the American government, including *the inalienability of the right to life*, the passing of a law that would violate this inalienable right results in the nullification of the law, and the government which passed such a law becomes illegitimate. Abortion then becomes a crime of war, and the government which passed a law that is in such dramatic violation of the principles upon which the government was founded, becomes an illegal government with no legal or moral authority.

Absent of these forms of legitimacy, the government no longer has authority to distinguish between abortion and murder. Brockhoeft argues that it was a situation precisely as this one that inspired Thomas Jefferson to say, "whenever any form of government becomes destructive of these ends, it is the right of the people to alter or abolish it."[45]

Hill concurs:

> Most people recognize that there are circumstances under which it is justified to intentionally use lethal defensive force, but some mistakenly limit this type of defense to the armed services and the police.... But under the rare circumstances when the police are not discharging this obligation for the people, but are rather using snipers to protect known and habitual murderers, the use of this means is not restricted to the government.... If the police cannot, or will not use the means necessary to defend the people's children on their behalf, this duty necessarily reverts to the people.[46]

This is complementary to Bray's earlier use of the biblical patriarchs to condone his threat to any would-be abortionist. In another section of the same essay, Bray argues that the government has certain duties, duties which are evidentially and miserably neglected when abortion is made legal. Thus, God-fearing individuals have a moral duty to step in and fill the absence created by the resulting moral void. In so arguing, Bray, Hill and Brockhoeft are able to refute those who contend the state is the only institution with the right to use force.[47] Thus, by denying the legitimacy of the state, they are then able to identify themselves as the proper authority, with not only a right, but a responsibility to protect their "citizenry."

War must be waged with the right intention

According to the *Army of God Handbook*,

> Mercy, rather than justice is the driving force behind our actions. Or to say it another way, we are merciful in our pursuit of justice, in our pursuit of peace.... The average abortionist has become so used to the daily carnage he or she commits it is on the order of flushing a commode. By permanently removing their ability to commit the crimes, one has given them a tremendous gift. Only by being forced to back away from the life they now live can they ever begin to see themselves as they truly are. Thank God for the braveness of those who have repented of their crimes. For the rest, I think thumblessness a small price to pay ... "better to enter life maimed."[48]

Brockhoeft makes a similar point in his diaries, making clear that he harbors no grudge against those he would harm – rather he simply loves those he would save far more.

There must be a chance of success

Despite their high rate of incarceration, Army of God members are remarkably upbeat about their chances for success within their movement. Hill viewed his action as valuable for its own sake (that is, for its success in preventing Dr. John Britton from aborting any more babies), but perhaps even more valuable for its potential to bring light to what he sincerely believed would be a contagious movement to outlaw abortion. Hill calls other abortion foes to act against abortion and says that "[i]f enough people were to openly promote this duty, legal abortion would soon come to an end. It is, therefore, imperative that you prayerfully consider taking this step."[49]

Activists believe that much of society is currently blind to the crime of abortion. By dramatically speaking and acting against it, they believe they force individuals to face the crime being committed. They claim that even the doctors performing abortion benefit from the violence committed against them. Not only is the death of one such doctor likely to deter another from continuing in his or her chosen profession, but even in cases of violence that stop short of murder, the activists believe their actions force the doctors performing abortions to re-evaluate their role.

In many ways, using violence serves two ends for the Army of God. In the first place, there is the physical consequence of their behavior. Whether the weapon is C4 aimed at dismantling a clinic, or a bullet aimed at dismemberment, or even a shotgun aimed at the heart, the end result is an incapacitated clinic or clinic practitioner. But more than this, by using violence (or justifiable force), Army of God members believe they are forcing their fellow Americans to view the fight against abortion as a war in which they must choose a side. And, the assumption goes, most Christians that are currently "moderately pro-life" will then join the battle on the side of the Army of God:

Every act of abortion is an act of aggressive, unjust warfare that defiles our land and incurs the wrath of God against us. When Christian Americans accept this, they'll be able to shed more of their moderation, perhaps all, and will be poised to assume the position where we can actually win the war.[50]

But equally, if not more significantly, the Army of God identifies the plausibility of their success in one other way – assurance given by God Himself. Army of God literature refers constantly to the "when" of their success, never the "if." To be sure, though, the understanding of how this success will manifest differs from one member to another.

For instance, Bob Lokey views success in terms of abstract spiritual warfare. He claims that he has finished fighting, and he spends his days waiting for the end that will play out as a result of his actions. He explains that he knows precisely how this end will unfold, and that it will be a great success for the pro-life movement. However, he is vague in his description, saying only that "[v]ery soon I will be able to stand on the midst of rubble and look around and say, see, this is what I have done."[51] But he is quick to point out that this end will not be brought about by his hand alone. He likens himself to a baby in comparison to the other [spiritual] forces at work in the war.

In contrast, Brockhoeft identifies success as temporal, saying:

You can be absolutely assured that this will happen – that the zealous among God's people will fill public seats of authority. History gives endless proof of it, and the Bible declares it will happen in the end.... The pendulum has never stopped swinging, only pausing briefly, at the beginning and end of each cycle. But one day it will stop. It will come to rest on the right side – on God's side – the side where truth and justice lie.... You leftists, you who kill babies, you who participate in this evil in any way, repent now.... But if you wait until this changing of the guard appears imminent, and only then make a show of "repentance" to save your own skin, it will be too late. Too late.[52]

Neal Horsley is even more specific, describing the success in the form of a new political party – the Creator Rights Party. He contends that this Party will, with God's power and providence, put "an end to legalized abortion in the United States of America."

The action must be commensurate with the offense

One of the more interesting side issues in the debate surrounding the use of force to stop abortion is the interaction and commentary between the anti-abortion advocates themselves. Members of the Army of God look upon the pro-life leaders that condemn acts of violence with derision. Equating their own acts with those who endangered their lives to end the Holocaust in World War II, the Army of God members have condemned the anti-force Christians as "good

Germans." Army of God members point to the inconsistency of those who say that abortion is murder condemned by God, but who are then unwilling to be God's hand in defending unborn babies from such murderers.

Yet the anti-force pro-life leaders often carefully distinguish between nuances in force – arguing that the Army of God, in killing doctors who perform abortions, have used far greater force than necessary. Hill explains that seeking to use the least degree of force to save a child is neither pragmatic nor appropriate. He implicitly concedes that there are less forceful means of preventing a doctor from performing abortion, but claims that to seek these means is to place a higher value on the life of the guilty doctor than on the life of the innocent child.

> When someone decides to kill people for a living, he thereby subordinates his right to be protected to the rights of his intended victims to be defended. When an innocent person's life is threatened, the primary goal should be to prevent the intended harm. Saving the life of a murderer should not be given priority over saving the lives of his intended victims.[53]

Hill also points out that the very lethal nature of his action serves as a deterrent to other doctors who offer the same services, thereby increasing the effectiveness of his action in relation to the original offense.

In response to the argument that lethal force can result in "collateral damages," Hill urges his critics to do the math by comparing the number of unborn people killed and the number of innocent bystanders killed by people defending the unborn. Recognizing the millions of unborn killed in contrast to the few unintended casualties, Hill considers his actions well-balanced on the scale of commensuration. In interviews before his execution, Hill argued that if lethal force were not used, doctors who perform abortion may well go back to performing abortions after receiving the injury. Bray is on record lamenting that the man Shelly Shannon shot went back to work the next day, despite her efforts to impair his arms.

There is even evidence of the construction of a frame of moral duty within this subset of the framework of Just War. Hill addresses the qualms over excessive force as "men's inventions." He says:

> The Bible does not annul force that is reasonable, under very pressing circumstances, nor condemn anything but the absolute minimum force that can be conceived by someone sitting in a distant armchair. Rather, the Bible justifies, and as in Abraham's case blesses, the use of lethal force in circumstances where lesser force could have been employed.

As he goes on, one can see the frame shift:

> To reject anything but the minimum degree of force that could conceivably be used places an unreasonable burden on the defender that may endanger both his own life and the lives of those he is defending. If one fails to use

the means necessary to defend the innocent, for fear of harming the attacker more than necessary, this may amount to culpable negligence.... If you condemn anything other than the least degree of force that could possibly be used .. you condemn God for justifying lethal defense in Exodus 22:2, and for blessing Abraham after "the slaughter of kings" in Hebrews 7:1.[54]

Hill's words here are significant. Notice that he is not only suggesting that violence is necessary, but he is condemning those that would question its use as people who "condemn God." In social-behavior theories of violence, the hierarchy serves as a powerful restraint on members' opportunities to question their actions because leaders are constantly present to reinforce the frame that justifies violence. But this same restraint on questioning is present in the Army of God because they follow an omnipresent God as their general. Further, the omniscience of God means that the individual has no opportunity to question the frame, as to question is to condemn the general with ever-present access to their thoughts.

Seen in this way, the cell model has equal, if not greater, consequences for violence than the hierarchal model. When members of an organization have access to each other, a constant subtle refinement of the ideological frame is at work. Members agree in principle on the broad elements of that frame, but will inevitably have slight differences in the best way to see the frame implemented. The hierarchy addresses this by establishing a clear chain of command – but still cannot eliminate all forms of inner-group dissonance. In the Army of God, members rarely interact with one another except to read accounts of "heroic" deeds, and exultations for strength and courage. The individual that has accepted the frame that identifies violence as a duty, and doubt a grievous sin, only interacts with God about the particulars. For this reason, he or she does not face the same opportunities for inter-group dissonance as an alternatively structured counterpart.

As for dissonance produced by interaction with the external community (interaction fostered by the cell model), Schwartz's conception of the religious Self versus the non-religious Other takes on added significance.[55] This distinction between religious and non-religious is fostered in all forms of monotheism – violent or not – and delineates clear lines of influence. In letters to this author, Stephen Jordi speaks very derogatively of former Attorney-General Janet Reno, in turn questioning her sexual orientation and her classification as a human being. Reno was seen by Jordi as the antithesis of everything he stood for. Contrast this to Michael Bray's characterization of Attorney-General John Ashcroft as a man just doing his job – despite that Ashcroft had just called for the capture and merciless prosecution of an Army member – while calling his act a "heinous crime." Ashcroft, unlike Reno, is a "believer" and thus has a credibility among other believers that Reno cannot attain. This characterization of the religious Self in contrast to the non-religious Other is so ingrained as to siphon meaning out of even repeated interactions between the two.

It has been argued that the Army of God is able to incite violence from its members because it has constructed a frame that simultaneously makes violence a responsibility of the true believer, and condemns those who question the use of violence as a sinner who questions God. In the following pages we will see a similar occurrence in the operation of the Muslim Brethren and al Jama'a al Islamiyya.

Frame construction in the Muslim Brethren versus al Jama'a al Islamiyya

To understand the difference in frame between the Brotherhood and al Jama'a al Islamiyya, it is necessary to begin by looking at the works of Sayid Qutb. While Qutb was a member of the Brotherhood, Hassan Hudaiby – the General Guide of the Brotherhood at the time of Qutb's writings – ultimately rejected the frame Qutb constructed. However, many others did not, and relics of Qutb's philosophy are clearly evident in the thinkers who shaped the frame of al Jama'a al Islamiyya.

Milestones on the path to violence

Qutb believed that the purpose of politics was to establish harmony in the world by restructuring society to reflect the parameters of absolute truth:

> Politics should be about maintaining the community, and the maintenance of the community requires unanimity among men in conformity with the will of God. Political activity must, therefore, be directed towards ascertaining the will of God, putting it into practice and ensuring that dissenting practice does not rupture the harmony thereby established.[56]

As was discussed earlier, Qutb identified all aspects of life as under the authority of God – and thus required to be in alignment with God's governance. Recall that Qutb believed that humanity needs government (in the form of Sharia law) to fulfill their purpose. A government created in accordance with Islamic principles allows God to be in control, and to promote the proper order of things.[57]

In this, Qutb and the Brotherhood were in full agreement. Both agree that when Islam is recognized as a fully integrated religious doctrine and comprehensive political system, there is no need for laws made by humanity. Indeed, government should never be more than the humble servant of Allah – fully recognizing that leaders are no more privileged than those they govern.

General Guide Muhammed Ma'mun Hudaiby explained that

> Muslim scholars and jurisprudents over the ages and all Islamic countries unanimously agreed that the rulers are not more than human beings who can be obedient or disobedient to Allah, right or wrong, and that none of them is infallible. Therefore, while the government in Islam is required to abide by the principles of the Islamic Sharia, it is still a civil government that is subject to accountability.[58]

So both Qutb and the Brotherhood have identified the protagonists of this frame as those who submit fully to God and His laws in all aspects of their lives. Qutb goes on to identify the antagonist as jahiliyyah – those movements in society that would threaten to destroy the harmony established by true believers. He says that jahiliyyah "is based on rebellion against God's sovereignty on earth. It transfers to man one of the greatest attributes of God, namely sovereignty, and makes some men lords over others."[59]

Hudaiby also acknowledges the existence of those who do not follow the practices of Islam, but rather than identifying these individuals as infidels deliberately hindering the progress of Islam, he defines them as individuals with the potential for change. He says:

> The Muslim Brotherhood does not pass judgments on those around them, e.g. denouncing other Muslims as infidels, kuffar. On the contrary it judges individuals on the basis of their actions and words. A sinful Muslim is not a Kafir, since he may change at a later time; hearts are the domain of Allah, the Merciful, Who provides them with Piety and to Whom all are accountable. We, the Muslim Brotherhood, always consider ourselves "Du'ah" not "Qudah" (preachers but not judges). Therefore we have no intention of forcing any person against his faith or ideology, bearing in mind the Qur'anic guidance "Let there be no coercion in religion."[60]

This stands in stark contrast to Qutb's efforts to ratchet up the intensity of the existence of this Jahiliyyah. In what he says next, Qutb seems to be acknowledging the tendency of even "true" believers to think of Islam as theology, not reality:

> This Jahiliyyah is not an abstract theory. In fact, under certain circumstances, it has no theory at all.... When Jahiliyyah takes the form not of a "theory" but of an active movement, in this fashion, then any attempt to abolish this Jahiliyyah and to bring people back to God, which presents Islam as merely a theory will be undesirable, rather useless. Jahiliyyah controls the practical world, and for its support there is a living and active organization. In this situation, mere theoretical efforts to fight it cannot even be equal, much less superior to it.[61]

And, in so saying, he is shifting the frame from one that values thought and purity of heart to one that follows thought with action. This same principle is evident in the Charter of Islamic Action, published by al Jama'a al Islamiyya discussed in Chapter 5. In the charter, the authors emphasized the importance of action over complacency – a clear echo of Qutb's denunciation of Islamic theory here. Less directly, it may be this passage of Qutb's work that informed the third section of the charter, which articulates al Jama'a's understanding of Islam. In this section, the authors indicate that "the majority of Muslims have a distorted understanding of their religion."[62] This contrasts with the words of al-Banna early on in the Brotherhood's history. Writing to clarify the beliefs of the organization, al-Banna stressed that the beliefs of the organization were such that "the entire Islamic Ummah will agree with [him], that this criterion is the book of Allah; from whose streams we refresh ourselves, from whose oceans we draw our sustenance, and to whose wisdom we return."[63]

But even more significantly, Qutb discounts the argument that this struggle for God's purpose should be fought in the hearts of individual believers:

> The Muslim society cannot come into existence without this [action]. It cannot come into existence simply as a creed in the hearts of individual Muslims, however numerous they may be, unless they become an active, harmonious and cooperative group, distinct by itself, whose different element, like the limbs of the human body, work together for its formation, its strengthening, its expansion, and for its defense against all those elements which attack its system, and which prepares for the strengthening and widening of their Islamic character and directs them to abolish the influence of their opponent – the jahili life.[64]

This jahili can – or, really, *must* – be dealt with from two angles. On the one side, it is "through preaching that [false] beliefs and ideas are confronted," but it is only through "the movement that material objects are tackled." He reiterates:

> Thus the two – preaching and the movement – united confront the "human situation" with all the necessary methods. For the achievement of the freedom of man on earth it is necessary that these two methods should work side by side. This is a very important point and cannot be over emphasized.[65]

Indeed it is one that is prominent in al Jama'a's charter, and evident in their methods.

Qutb also confronts Muslims that would cite the Qur'anic verse that "[t]here is no compulsion in religion" as a call against violence. Qutb explains that anyone who follows laws created or established by humanity is guilty of worshipping humanity over God. Qutb argues that Muhammad accused even Christians and Jews of being idolaters, because "[w]hatever their priests and rabbis call permissible, they accept as permissible; whatever they declare as forbidden they consider forbidden, and thus they worship them."[66]

Thus, for Qutb, as long as someone or something other than God is being worshipped, the worshippers are subservient to humanity instead of God. And, as long as someone is subservient to their fellow, then he or she is not free to experience the freedom in Islam. So, while Qutb does not condone the use of violence to force someone to believe, he actually promotes it in an effort to create an environment conducive to the development of belief. He says:

> It is not the intention of Islam to force its beliefs on people, but Islam is not merely belief. As we have pointed out, Islam is a declaration of the freedom

of man from servitude to other men. Thus it strives from the beginning to abolish all those systems and governments which are based on the rule of man over man and the servitude of one human being to another. When Islam releases people from this political pressure and presents to them its spiritual message, appealing to their reason, it gives them complete freedom to accept or not accept its beliefs.[67]

And then:

Anyone who understands this particular character of this religion will also understand the place of jihad bis saif [striving through fighting] which is to clear the way for striving through preaching in the application of the Islamic movement.[68]

Also, note the contrast between what Qutb says above and what Hudaiby says here:

In the past years, the Muslim Brotherhood have repeatedly stated that they are involved in political life and have committed themselves to legal means and non-violent methods. Their only weapons are the honest and truthful words and the selfless dedication to social work. In so doing, they are confident that the Ummah's [community of believers'] conscience and the people's awareness are the rightful judges of all intellectual and political trends which honestly compete with one another, within the limits of the constitution and the law. Thus, the Muslim Brotherhood reiterate their rejection of any form of violence and coercion, as well as all forms of coups which undermine the unity of the Ummah because such plots allow their organizations to supersede the political and social realities; but it would never give the masses the opportunity to practice their free will.[69]

Where Qutb argues that only by violence can the world be prepared to actually hear the words being preached, and thus have the freedom to embrace the truth of those words, Hudaiby (and, by extension, the Brethren) argues that the very acts of violence impair the freedom to choose. In other words, Qutb believes that violence serves as the vehicle for allowing the presentation of truth, and Hudaiby argues that violence is the greatest hindrance toward the dissemination of truth.

Here Qutb is laying the groundwork for the assertion of a duty to forcibly reject jahiliyya. But much as the Army of God shifted the emphasis from justifying the use of violence to forcing non-violent supporters of their cause to justify their non-violence, Qutb suggests that the impetus is on those who promote preaching to justify their unwillingness to fulfill their greater duty to create a world in which the words they preach can actually be heard. In other words, he is implying that those who would use violence to achieve their ends are not, as many would suggest, doing so despite their beliefs, but instead are the only ones truly living them.

Having established the reason for the use of violence, Qutb next outlines its scope:

> Since the objective of the message of Islam is a decisive declaration of man's freedom, not merely on the philosophical plane, but also in actual conditions of life, it must employ jihad. It is immaterial whether the homeland of Islam, in the true Islamic sense, is in a condition of peace or whether it is threatened by its neighbors. When Islam strives for peace, its objective is not that superficial peace which requires that only that part of the earth where the followers of Islam are residing remain secure.[70]

With this passage, the frame Qutb was constructing is largely complete. He speaks in other portions of his work about the fallacy in justifying jihad as a defensive war, thus making it subject to the Western moral and legal restraints of such a war. For if Qutb can convince Muslims that Islam's survival and purpose is dependent on the freedom of potential recruits to hear its message, then he can convince those same Muslims that non-violent action is not just another alternative, but is actually a perversion of what Allah intended.

The Neglected Duty

Qutb was executed by the Egyptian government in 1965, and for the next several years there was little activity. But, as was discussed earlier in this book, when Nasser died, Sadat came to power and sought influence among the religious population. He sponsored the establishment of religious organizations within the universities in an effort to secure a political base. But Sadat was also saddled with Nasser's untenable economic model, and was compelled to seek foreign aid, which he did in a remarkably dramatic fashion by pursuing sudden peace with Israel. This set Sadat at odds with the Islamist movement he had helped to create, and suddenly Qutb's characterizations of jahiliyya took on renewed importance. It was into this mix that Abdel Salam Faraj entered with his work, *The Neglected Duty*.

Faraj accepted Qutb's definition of jahiliyya, but argued that Qutb did not take the consequences of his argument far enough. Where Qutb had suggested state antagonism should be avoided where possible, Faraj believed the overthrow of the state was an excellent place to start.

Much like Qutb, Faraj framed jihad as a very real – and fully obligatory – struggle in which believers were duty-bound to contend. He opens his work with the argument that

> Jihad for God's cause, in spite of its extreme importance and its great significance for the future of this religion, has been neglected by the ulama of this age. They have feigned ignorance of it, but they know that it is the only way to the return and the establishment of the glory of Islam anew.[71]

This dual theme – that violent jihad is an obligation for all true Muslims and that the many that would call themselves true Muslims and yet would reject this obligation are actually thwarting God's purpose and committing apostasy – is continued throughout the rest of his work.

He insists that the Qur'an is clear in its establishment of the duty of violent jihad – and that those who argue otherwise do so deliberately rejecting God's purpose for the world:

> There is a duty which is rejected by some Muslims and neglected by others although the proof for the obligatory character of the establishment of the state is clear, and made obvious by the Book of God – (blessed and supreme is He), for God (Glory to Him) says: and that you must rule between them according to what God sent down.... Whosoever does not rule by what God sent down, those, they are unbelievers.... God's prescripts are an obligation for Muslims. Hence the establishment of an Islamic state is an obligation for the Muslims, for something without which something which is obligatory cannot be carried out becomes itself obligatory. If a state cannot be established without war, this war is an obligation as well.[72]

Again reflecting the works of Qutb, Faraj elaborates saying that

> [i]t is obligatory for the Muslims to raise their swords under the very eyes of the leaders who hide the Truth and spread falsehoods. If the Muslims do not do this, the Truth will not reach the hearts of men.

Much later in the manuscript, Faraj quotes Muhammad and puts the issue in its clearest form: "Someone who does not fight for his religion, or someone whose soul does not talk to him encouraging him to fight for his religion, dies as a pagan."[73]

Just as Qutb did (and just as the Army of God continues to do), Faraj has removed the need for the justification of force. No longer is force justified by the unjust actions of those it targets. Instead, with this frame, it is those who would not use force that must justify themselves. In fact, the abstention from force becomes the position of the weak, the cowardly – and most importantly – the one who has rejected God.

This is made particularly clear in Faraj's discussion of the argument that paints jihad as an internal or any other sort of peaceful struggle. To those who characterize jihad as principally an internal struggle, Faraj dismisses them as ignorant and cowardly. He concedes that jihad has an internal element – but insists that it must take place not prior to violent external fighting, but in conjunction with it.

To those who argue that jihad is only a verbal struggle, one in which preaching is the most powerful weapon, Faraj says this:

> Fighting is prescribed for you. This refutes the view of whoever says that jihad is indeed a duty and then goes on by saying: "When I have fulfilled the

duty of engaging in missionary activities for Islam (da'awa) then I have fulfilled the duty of jihad because engagement in missionary activities for Islam is jihad too." However, the real character of this duty is spelled out clearly in the text of the Qur'an: It is fighting, which means confrontation and blood.[74]

Faraj also mirrors Qutb in his position on the source of all law: just as Qutb reasoned that law was from God, and any law created by humanity was thus a law denying God, Faraj does also.

He argues that the Qur'an (and the Hadiths) contain "everything which is good, and forbid everything which is bad" and as such, render any other laws useless. Accordingly, citizens who would create laws that are not specified in the Qur'an deliberately shun the perfect system that God created. In doing so he becomes "an infidel and he must be fought until he returns to the Rule of God and His apostle, and until he rules by no other law than God's law."[75]

But, even more encompassing, and also like Qutb, this emphasis on God's law even supersedes a political system in which a Muslim presides over something other than Sharia. Any Muslim who does not commit fully to the implementation of God's clearly outlined plan is targeted for fighting. Faraj draws on the work of Ibn Taymiyah to enforce this point:

> Any group of people that rebels against any single prescript of the clear and reliably transmitted prescripts of Islam has to be fought ... even if the members of the group pronounce the Islamic Confession of their faith (by pronouncing the double formula "There is no God but God, and Muhammad is his Apostle") but at the same time refuse to carry out the five daily prayer ceremonies, then it is obligatory to fight them. If they refuse to pay the zakat (religious tax), it is obligatory to fight them. Similarly, if they refuse to keep the fast of the month of Ramadan.... If they refuse to forbid abominations, or anything else that is forbidden by the laws of Islam.... In all cases that are equivalent to these things, God says "Fight them until there is no dissention and the religion is entirely God's."[76]

Supporters of Faraj articulated their frustration with the Brotherhood's aimless efforts toward the Islamization of society. The efforts to transform the state by first transforming society struck many members of the organization as a slow and potentially futile effort at reform. These individuals were impressed by the urgency with which Faraj called for armed jihad against the state.[77] Individuals sympathetic to his message organized into informal groups in Cairo.

Throughout the 1980s and 1990s, the violent Islamists kept up a running commentary on the ineffective and cowardly methods employed by the non-violent Al-Ikhwan al-Muslimin. When asked about the common thread of Qutb's ideology, Tal'at Fu'ad Qasim explained the dramatic difference between the Brotherhood and the Islamic groups:

There are two points here. One is our relation to the ideas of Qutb; the other is the extent to which Qutb's ideas are those of the Brothers. Qutb has influenced all those interested in jihad throughout the Islamic world. At the time there were many interpretations and we were in need of direction. This Sayid Qutb's teachings provided. The Muslims Brothers have abandoned the ideas of Qutb.[78]

One can readily see evidence of the frame at work even here. Qasim is condemning the Brotherhood for its abandonment of the principles that Qutb articulates. Were violence merely justified, there could be no abandonment – merely a rejection of its use. Rather, it is because violence is a sacred duty that its rejection serves as a dramatic severance between the two organizations.

The Brotherhood, as discussed extensively earlier, still maintains the importance of the implementation of Sharia, but it endeavors to achieve this goal by changing the government from within. Leaders of the violent side of the movement condemn this behavior as fulfilling the sinful objectives of the regime far better than the regime alone ever could: "The presence of Islamists inside the regime's legislative assembly bestows upon the regime legitimacy it never dreamed of. The mere direction of Islamists toward the ballot box guarantees the fulfillment of the state's goal."[79]

In comments like these, one can hear the admonitions of Qutb and Faraj regarding the encompassing nature of God's laws, as well as the culpability of any who would participate in a government devised by humanity. The frame that is established by shifting the responsibility for justification onto those who would not use violence casts a suspicious shadow over organizations that have similar objectives. The result is that violence is no longer just a means to an end: it is now a necessary end in and of itself.

Concluding remarks

In both the Army of God and al Jama'a al Islamiyya, violence has been transformed from an extreme act requiring justification by external events to a moral responsibility whose abdication must be justified. In the case of the Army of God, failure to use violence (indeed, even questioning the use of violence) is a rejection of God which results in the death of innocent children. For al Jama'a al Islamiyya, failure to use violence is a rejection of the sanctifying properties of Sharia, which prohibits others from living rightly before God.

When secular movements dominated the political opposition, hierarchy was a respectable predictor of violence because of its capability for reducing dissonance. But when secularism became the dominant political paradigm, religious organizations found themselves in opposition. The unique elements of religion (actions are committed at the bequest of, rather than on behalf of, a superior being) meant that the restrictions to the development of hierarchy were circumvented because each individual was acting as the highest leader (God) had called them to. In other words, while structure has traditionally been accredited with the most comprehensive explanation for the development of violence, the ideological frame of religious belief can act as an intangible alternative to the violence-inducing elements of structure. This is most clearly seen when the ideological frame of the organization casts violence as a responsibility, rather than a right, and makes the questioning or rejection of violence the questioning and rejection of God.

The final part of this book will explore the way this argument can inform the development of future religiously motivated political violence. The religious-settlers movement in Israel has many similarities to the American and Egyptian movements already explored, and yet it has not split into distinct violent and non-violent organizations. The following Part will explain why this is the case and then will speak briefly about the consequences on the future of the movement.

Part III

Exploring new terrain

The future of religious opposition in Israel

8   Breaking new ground

The religious-settlers movement in Israel

The previous two parts of this book have argued that the development of religious social movements is a predictable response to the increasing secularization of society around the world. It has been demonstrated that violence is a product of three interacting variables: inflammatory rhetoric, covert-cell-like structure and ideological frames that promote violence as a religious duty. We have seen that these variables offer insight into the interaction between the state and its opposition, and within opposition movements themselves. The cases examined presented clear distinctions between the actions and the justification of violent and non-violent organizations. This final part will explore a religious social movement in which the distinctions have not yet been so clear.

The following pages will show that the religious-settlers movement in Israel exhibits characteristics of each of the four case studies examined in previous parts, but has not segmented into distinctive violent versus non-violent organizations. It will be argued that this is because Israel has not yet irreversibly secularized and has consequently left significant room for the religious-settlers movement to operate in the political arena. However, this part will also show that the current arrangement cannot last, and that when it fails, the religious-settlers movement in Israel is primed to react much as the Christian and Muslim movements did in the United States and Egypt.

This part will proceed with a history of the development of the religious-settlers movement in Israel and its symbiotic relationship with the Israeli government. It will be clear that, although the relationship between the movement and the government has never been smooth, only once was it violently adversarial. It will be shown that the Israeli government and the religious settlers have served compatible functions within the state that have forestalled more direct confrontations. In the next chapter, the discussion will turn to the three critical variables identified in the previous parts of this book. Religious-settlement organizations will be examined from rhetorical, structural and framework perspectives.

Historical context

The present-day state of Israel has only been in existence for 60 years, and the circumstances of its creation might, at first, appear to render its development a unique case. Ehud Sprinzak calls Israel "one of the most unnatural states in modern history," because of its role as a post-colonial settlement of skilled immigrants and as a refuge following one of the most horrific attempts at genocide in history.[1] And yet, interestingly enough, while the political development of Israel is distinct in many ways, the development of violent political opposition and contentious Jewish movements shows many similarities to the American Christian and Egyptian Muslim models.

The history of the Jews is simultaneously one of consistent persecution and resilience. From the time that the Second Temple in Jerusalem was destroyed in AD 70, Jews lived as an ethnic minority all over the globe, frequently forming a mercantile class as traders, jewelers and craftsmen.[2] In the Middle Ages, Jews were eventually expelled from Italy, France and Spain, and many emigrated to parts of Eastern Europe, including Russia and Poland. Yet Eastern Europe served as no more a safe haven than Western Europe had, and Jews were restricted in where they could live and the professions they could engage in.

It was this abiding persecution that eventually led such thinkers as Leo Pinsker and Theodor Herzl to advocate the formation of a distinct Jewish state. Pinsker concluded that anti-Semitism was an incurable psychological condition exacerbated by the transient nature of the Jewish minority. The only response to such a condition was to create an independent Jewish nation.[3] Doing so would afford Jews the opportunity to engage with the rest of the world as autonomous equals at political, social and economic levels. Herzl arrived at a similar conclusion by different means. He argued that anti-Semitism was not born of theological incompatibility, but social dislocation:

> It is no longer – and it has not been for a long time – a theological matter. It has nothing whatsoever to do with religion and conscience. What is more, everyone knows it. The Jewish question is neither nationalistic nor religious. It is a social question.[4]

In *The Jewish State*, Herzl argued that the "misery of the Jews" was so significant as to make the formation of a state critical to the survival of the race and, ultimately, the world. He says, "The Jewish State is essential to the world; it will therefore be created."[5] In this way, whereas in the United States and Egypt nationalism grew as a consequence of the creation of the state, in the case of Israel, the state grew as a consequence of Jewish nationalism.

When the idea of a Jewish state first attained international consciousness, the location of the state was not fixed. Herzl, a political pragmatist, entertained locations as diverse as Kenya, Cyprus and Argentina in his quest for Jewish sovereignty. In *The Jewish State*, Herzl articulates the contrasting benefits of Palestine and Argentina, noting that while Argentina was "one of the most fertile countries in the world" and Palestine was "our ever-memorable historic home." The Jews "shall take what is given us, and what is selected by Jewish public opinion."[6]

Herzl was perhaps overly optimistic about the existence of a uniform Jewish public opinion, but his oversight probably has much to do with the very encompassing nature of the program he proposed. As inclusive as his strategy and vision were, he may not have realized the controversy he brushed over so lightly. It is not surprising, then, that although Herzl himself was committed to a secular Jewish state, he was not averse to working in tandem with religious Zionists as well. His comments regarding the theocratic elements of his envisioned state highlight an issue that continues to divide Israel today:

> Shall we have a theocracy? No, indeed. Faith unites us, knowledge gives us freedom. We shall therefore prevent any theocratic tendencies from coming to the fore on the part of our priesthood. We shall keep our priests within the confines of their temples in the same way we shall keep our professional army within the confines of their barracks. Army and priesthood shall receive honors high as their valuable functions deserve. But they must not interfere in the administration of the State, which confers distinction upon them, else they will conjure up difficulties without and within.[7]

It is interesting that, within a single paragraph, Herzl apparently unknowingly identified the three initially complementary and ultimately competing characteristics that would plague Israel over the course of its existence: religion, violence and the state.

Encountering religion

Much like Christianity and Islam, Judaism traces its roots back to the beginning of humanity with Adam and Eve in the Garden of Eden. The Jewish race began with Abraham, a man called by God into a holy covenant. God promised Abraham as many descendents as there are stars in the sky. He also promised Abraham a Holy Land in which his descendents will live.

History follows the descendents of Abraham from Isaac to Jacob and then Joseph into Egypt, where the Hebrews are enslaved for several generations. God calls Moses, a Hebrew who had been adopted by an Egyptian, to lead His people out of Egypt and into the promised Holy Land. During the Exodus, Moses encountered God on Mount Sinai, and it was there that God established the laws of the covenant that would separate the Israelites as a nation under the one true God.

After 40 years of exile in the desert, God uses a man named Joshua to lead the Israelites to conquer the Holy Land, then known as Canaan. The Israelites lived under a government ruled by God, but enforced by judges. The judges were ordained with leadership by God. After several generations of judges, the Israelites approached Samuel – the current leader – and protested their system of government. The Israelites complained that the system of judges gave them a disadvantage when interacting with other kingdoms. Samuel was grieved over the Israelites' complaint, as he saw it as a rejection of God as their ruler. But Samuel (and God) agreed to give the Israelites a king. Saul was the first king of Israel, though Samuel still held the position of judge. When David ascended to the throne after Saul, he unified the religious and political leadership into a single position. Before his death, David appointed his son Solomon as king, and the nation of Israel achieved great wealth during Solomon's 40-year reign.

The period following Solomon's reign is characterized by the themes of exile and redemption that will be evident for the rest of Israel's history. The kingdom was split into two parts (Judah in the south and Jerusalem in the north), and according to God's displeasure at His people's rebellion, both portions of the kingdom were ultimately conquered and sent into exile. The Jews were eventually allowed back into Judea where they established a relatively autonomous government, albeit under Roman control. Over time the Roman influence became more invasive, and in AD 66 Judeans initiated a revolt against the Roman leaders. Rome quashed the revolt, but Jews remained in Judea until AD 135 when they underwent another revolt and were exiled once again. The Jews in exile had to determine how to continue to practice Judaism without a temple or a state. Rabbinical Judaism developed in response to this, and was the primary interpretation of Judaism well into the twentieth century.

From the time of the exile to the end of the nineteenth century, Jews existed as a minority in communities in the Middle East and all over Europe. Until the late eighteenth and early nineteenth centuries, the nature of the feudal system ensured that most ethnic groups remained isolated in their clans and Jews were no exception. In fact, the persecution that Jews suffered over the centuries reinforced this separateness and assisted in maintaining the purity of the culture. But when the structure of society began to change and the city became the center of social life, Jews were presented with the opportunity to adopt social roles that could overshadow their cultural and religious backgrounds.[8] The concept of being Jewish became voluntary instead of fixed.[9]

There were significant benefits that came from moving beyond the cloister of Jewish culture, as well as important cultural compromises. To enjoy the economic and social benefits of integration, Jews had to be willing to designate the observance of some religious laws to a secondary level of importance, if they maintained observance at all.

Zionism was conceived as a result of the merging of liberal Western and Jewish thought.[10] The themes of nationalism, liberty and independence began to sweep through Western Europe with the advance of industrialization and its bedfellow, urbanization. Zionism reflected these values in combination with the cultural elements of Judaism. The idea of self-determination was appealing to the Zionists in light of their persecuted history, but was dependent on a land in which to practice it. The secular Zionists viewed the return to the Holy Lands from a political perspective and highlighted social themes of biblical history. As Karpin and Friedman note, "The prophets of Israel were sanctified not because they preached obedience to God but because some of them protested social exploitation; their religious morality was transformed into a message of 'social justice'."[11]

But to the Jews seeking to remain unaffected by the changing nature of society, the idea of a Jewish state was an anathema.[12] The symbiotic themes of exile and redemption dominate much of Jewish history,[13] and God alone is the protagonist as the story continues to be written. Rabbi Shalom Dov Baer was one such critic of the emerging Zionist movement. In 1904 he wrote:

> The Zionist idea contains all manner of poison which destroys and tears apart the soul. The Zionists will never succeed in gathering themselves together [in the Holy Land] by their own power. All their forces and many stratagems and strivings will be to no avail against the will of God. The counsel of the Lord remains steadfast, for He alone will take us and gather us from the four corners of the earth.[14]

Anti-Zionist Jews argued that a Jew must remain a passive participant in God's plans for redemption and to pursue a return to the Holy Lands was to force God's hand in the redemptive process.[15] Further, because the pursuit of Zionism was based on the themes of self-determination, the nature of the state that would be developed would be adversarial to God's sovereignty in the lives of His people.

Although they were in the minority, there were observant Jews that supported Herzl's idea, if not his ideology. Rabbis Yehudah Alkalai and Zvi Hirsh Kalishner laid the groundwork for a religious Zionist perspective 30 years before Herzl came on the scene by arguing that God is not immune to the desires of His people. They suggested that He could be moved to act even in ways He had not intended, should His people inspire Him to do so: "These stirrings below would move heaven; they would represent the 'beginning of the redemption' which God would complete."[16]

When Rabbi Abraham Isaac Kook entered the Zionist dialogue, he did so from an entirely unique perspective that synthesized the two camps. Kook argued that redemption was not a single act of God for which humanity must wait, but that it was a process through which humanity was currently passing. The very process of claiming the Holy Land for Jews was an act of redemption – even when secularists were at the head of the movement. Rabbi Kook argued actions could be holy, even if those who performed them did not know it. The action had the potential to redeem the individual. Thus the creation of Israel was the first step in the process of redeeming the Jews.[17]

Rabbi Kook emphasized the totality of Judaism – much like Hassan al-Banna did of Islam when he formed the Muslim Brothers. Rabbi Kook desired to integrate religion into every aspect of life, which was a direct repudiation of the traditional Orthodox method of seclusion.[18] According to this interpretation, Zionism, be it worldly or religious, and the State of Israel, be it a theocracy or a secular state, both embodied sacred developments of messianic redemption.[19]

At the outset, Rabbi Kook's mystical understanding of the redemptive process merged the religious and secular Zionists into a cooperative force. Religious Zionists could rest in the mystery of God's plan while secularists unknowingly pursued religious ends. Suddenly the discussion of a whether a Jewish state would be ruled by halacha (religious law) or by a secular government was not a determinate of participation in the Zionist movement. Once a secular government was understood to be capable of achieving religious ends, religious Zionists could whole-heartedly get behind the state-creation process. The consequence of this manner of thinking was that Israel was created without a consensus regarding the purpose of the state. Both religious and secular Zionists could embrace the participation of the other without confronting the opposing nature of their beliefs.

The religious Zionists who accepted Rabbi Kook's theology were content to use the secular Zionists in pursuit of redemption; and the secular Zionists were anxious to widen the circle of support for their cause, particularly among the observant Jews of Europe.

Speaking years later about the merger between the secular and religious Zionists, Yigal Allon succinctly summarized the relationship: "It was the classic coalition between horse and rider, however, each side thought he was the equestrian."[20]

The presence of violence

This tenuous relationship between the secularists and the religious was preserved because the shared understanding of how to act made extensive discussion of belief unnecessary. Sprinzak argues that the conditions surrounding the creation of the state of Israel resulted in a shared understanding between Israelis about the underlying ethos of a state. He specifically suggests that the shadow of the Holocaust loomed so dark over the creation of the state that most Israelis clung to the light of democratic values with a ubiquitous ferocity.[21] While this may explain some elements of Israel's democratic stability, it is also likely that the heterogeneous recognition of ever-present threats to Israel's existence also played a role. The history of persecution, the recent Holocaust and the unfavorable reaction of Arabs to the presence of an Israeli state ensured that a fierce commitment to security would be a shared value of the Israeli state.

Before the state of Israel was officially created, there were frequent altercations between settling Jews and the Arab inhabitants of the land. Where groups on the far right of the political spectrum advised tit-for-tat reactions to Arab violence against Jews, the secular Zionists, then under the leadership of David Ben-Gurion, advocated a patient response. Ben-Gurion indicated that Arab violence in the face of a tempered Jewish reaction would highlight the character of the battle being waged and result in Europeans supporting the evidently more "civilized" race.[22] Ultimately Ben-Gurion's strategy paid off when Britain conceded the necessity of a Jewish defense organization that would ultimately become the Israeli Defense Forces.[23]

The debate on both sides centered on the strategic benefits rather than the moral qualifications of the actions undertaken. In other words, discussions did not center on whether violence was a morally acceptable response to Arab protest, but rather whether violence would serve the objectives of the emerging Israeli state. In fact, Ben-Gurion was quite comfortable with the possibility of the use of force – even from an offensive, rather than a defensive, position. He explained:

> We must expel the Arabs and take their places. And if we have to use force – not to dispossess the Arabs of the Negev and Transjordan, but to guarantee our own right to settle in those places – then we have force at our disposal.[24]

The agreement about how to protect the state made the disagreement about why to protect it less important. In fact, until peace negotiations became a realistic possibility in the late 1970s, the secularists and religious adherents existed in a symbiotic co-dependent relationship that few questioned. The state was able to capitalize on the ongoing threat from its Arab neighbors as a tool of mobilization and support. The immediate purpose of the state did not have to be philosophically resolved so long as it fulfilled its more-immediate purpose as a protection against physical threats.[25]

From the moment of Israel's conception on May 14, 1948, violence has been a central part of its history. Five Arab armies invaded the country a day after its foundation, committed to destroying it entirely. Israel successfully repelled the Arab forces, gaining even more territory in the process. Immediately after the war, the Israeli government was faced with the challenge of incorporating the variety of non-government militant groups into the Israeli military structure. These groups, including the Stern Gang, and Irgun, had developed in response to Arab hostility to Jewish settlers in Palestine. Several tense years followed the dissolution of these groups in which Ben-Gurion repeatedly demonstrated his iron resolve for a government monopoly of the legitimate use of Israeli force.

Part of Ben-Gurion's success was based on his willingness to liberally and conclusively defend against any threats to Israel's existence, however minor they might be. Raids by Palestinian refugees from the Egyptian and Jordanian border were common, particularly in the early years of the state, and Ben-Gurion did not hesitate to respond to such occurrences with extensive force. But the Israeli government also sought to shore up its resources by increasing the Jewish population within their boundaries. Ben-Gurion typically trumpeted these calls for Jewish immigration as security-enhancing measures, saying that increasing the Jewish population stood to "save Jews from destruction."[26] Ben-Gurion recognized that military conquest could only take the Jewish state so far. He noted, "We have conquered territories, but without settlements, they have no decisive value. Settlement ... is the real conquest."[27]

This strategy merged neatly with that of the religious Zionists who pursued land for its biblical value. As long as the state of Israel was prepared to defend the ever-increasing settlements on land promised to the Jews by God, the Israeli government could be said to be working for religious ends. While the religious Zionists frequently lamented the government's unwillingness to offensively take more biblically ordained territory, the compatibility between the two entities was sufficient to ensure continued co-existence.

But then, in May of 1967, Rabbi Kook's son stood before graduates of the yeshiva his father had founded and expressed his extreme grief over the current borders of the land of Israel. He bemoaned the inability of Jews to live in Hebron in particular, and indicated that the situation was approaching a level of intolerability.[28] Accounts of the speech he gave indicate that his lament was delivered in a strikingly different tone from the rest of his sermon, and the national events that followed only three weeks later lent credence to later suggestions that Kook the younger had been overcome by "a genuine spirit of prophecy."[29] For, in June of 1967, Israel reacted to Egyptian troops amassing at its borders and delivered a crushing defeat to the Arab armies of the 1967 war. In so doing, the Israelis took over the Gaza Strip, the Sinai Peninsula (previously governed by Egypt) and the West Bank (under the leadership of Jordan).

Shortly after the Israeli victory, Rabbi Yehuda Kook stood before the Wailing Wall that was finally on Jewish territory and declared, "We hereby inform the people of Israel and the entire world that under heavenly command we have just returned home in the elevations of holiness and our holy city."[30] The dramatic military victory and consequential enlargement of Eretz Yisrael brought the marriage of religion and the state to the forefront of national consciousness. But rather than force a reckoning between the two perspectives, the victory served to reaffirm their compatibility resulting in an intense increase in both religious fervor and national sentiment: "Nationalism and statehood, permeated by the values of modernism and secularity were suddenly placed in new proximity and sympathy with the values of religion and tradition."[31]

A compatible state

The actions undertaken by both the religious and secularists following 1967 further reinforced the relationship between them. Levi Eshkol, the leader of the Socialist Labor-led government, authorized the building of new settlements in the occupied territories three months after the war ended.[32] Yehuda Kook responded by elevating army service to a near sacramental status: "The current state of Israel embodies that envisioned by the prophets. Therefore, reinforcing the Israeli Army is a vital religious and spiritual matter. At least equivalent to glorifying the Torah by increasing the number of Yeshivas."[33]

The territorial acquisitions of the 1967 war lent credence to Rabbi Avraham Kook's theology that the secular state could achieve religious objectives. Rabbi Kook elaborated on this theology saying:

> With the perfection of our military system … the perfection of the essence of our rebirth is evident. We are no longer considered only to be The People of the Book. Instead we are recognized as The People of God. The Holy people for whom the Book and the Sword descended together from heaven.[34]

The idea that the state and the military establishment represented something sacred took flight in the minds of many following the war.

This perspective was aided by the interactions between the state and the religious settlements that began to be established in the occupied territories. While the government only occasionally officially authorized settlements in advance, the state frequently subsidized settlement-living once Israeli citizens had laid claim to the territory. For example, on June 8, 1967, Ben-Gurion announced that

> We now control Jerusalem, and that is one of the greatest events – one of the first things that must be done is build neighborhoods ... to immediately settle the Jewish quarter. If there are empty Arab houses, we'll put Jews in them as well. The same is true for Hebron.... I am sure that with the current mood, people will go.[35]

Once he was made aware of Ben-Gurion's remark, Rabbi Moshe Levinger (a follower of Rabbi Kook) arranged a "temporary" stay for himself and a small group of followers at a hotel in the Arab city of Hebron. When Levinger's reservation expired, he and his followers announced their presence as the "first group of settlers that has come to renew the Jewish settlement in Hebron."[36] While the government withheld official verbal support of the settlement, the settlers were provided with government-issued weapons and resources.[37]

The government's equivocating response to the settlement issue did not undermine the religious Zionists' faith in the compatibility of their purposes. The vacillating government position could be explained by their as-yet-secular vision of God's intended purpose. But critical to the acceptance of this perspective was the understanding shared by religious Zionists that secular Zionists would eventually recognize the holy nature of their acts.[38] The deterministic faith of the religious Zionists imbued the secularists with a purpose that would ultimately be recognized by all Israelis. The completion of redemption depended on the eventual recognition of the true purpose of the process. The 1967 war and the implicit government acceptance of the settlements were viewed as signposts along a predetermined path.

But if the settlements and the government's blind eye to them were signposts on the road to redemption, the Yom Kippur War was a jarring pothole. Believing themselves to be secure in the new borders established in 1967, and confident in their military superiority, the Israeli government was not prepared for the offensive launched against them by Syria and Egypt in 1973. A week into the October war, Israel were in real danger of running out of ammunition. Only when the United States airlifted in reinforcements was Israel able to turn the tide and secure a narrow victory. The war cost nearly 3000 Israeli lives and destroyed Golda Meir's coalition government.

It was in the aftermath of the Yom Kippur War that Gush Emunim (the Bloc of the Faithful) was established. As the founder of the movement acknowledged, "There was a lack of clarity in Israel after the 1973 war. The dominant spirit was one of depression. The Labor Party didn't know what to do about the Arab territories. We stepped into the breach."[39] The Kookist doctrine that served as the foundation of Gush Emunim provided Israel with a moral explanation for the near catastrophe in the Yom Kippur War. Kook considered the war to be a consequence of the moral decline of Israel. The loss of territories suffered in the war were interpreted as a test imposed by God on His people.[40] The reaction to the test would determine the future course of the nation. Gush Emunim held the answer key.

Gush Emunim was notable for its ability to seamlessly merge a political and religious reaction in the aftermath of the war. Politically, the future leaders of the organization called for the resignation of Golda Meir and Moshe Dayan. But, at the same time, the political solution was explained in light of the religious one: Meir and Dayan represented the worst of secular Zionism, believing that land attainment was a security issue, not a Holy one. Because Meir agreed to a disengagement plan that gave up some of the Sinai territory gained in the 1967 war, there was no guarantee that she would not give up more if the opportunity presented itself. Gush Emunim sought to express God's displeasure with this tactic, and in doing so created a frame that resonated across a shell-shocked public.

Further, Gush Emunim embarked on a campaign that would make future attempts to give away land far more difficult. Gush Emunim encouraged dozens of families to take a stand for the redemptive process by settling – often in little more than tents – all over the occupied territories. While settlements were very small, the consequences were significant. The settlements forced the Israeli government into the proverbial space between a rock and a hard place. On the one hand, the government was bound by international agreement to abide by the stipulations of the Geneva Convention prohibiting civilian settlements in occupied territories. On the other hand, the Israeli government was loath to stand by and watch its civilians be attacked by Arabs angered over Israel incursions into those territories. The official reaction was often a seemingly incoherent response that addressed both issues simultaneously. As in Hebron, while negotiating for the settlers' removal, the government might also provide arms to the settlers for their protection. Or, while insisting the settlers leave, the government would also provide a military contingent to ensure their welfare as they remained.

The result of this progression of events is that Gush Emunim served as a spearhead for future settlements and the expansion of current ones. The fervent believers making up the core of the movement endured the difficult conditions ubiquitous to initial settlement, while the equivocal government response and gradual acquiescence ensured that less-committed believers could soon follow. Over time, the settlements benefitted from government subsidization and support. Consequentially, even some secular Jews came to find low-cost housing an appeal that was hard to resist. The impact of Gush Emunim continued to reverberate and the opposing motivations for policy continued to result in compatible outcomes. As Don-Yehiya explains:

> Expressions of public support for Gush Emunim and the success of its activity encouraged the feeling among its activists that they represented the real will of the people.... Furthermore, in violating government decisions, they were in fact helping the government reconsider their policies and arrive at decisions in accordance with the spirit of the nation.[41]

The impact of Gush Emunim was so significant over the next three years that, for the first time since the creation of the state of Israel, the more right-winged Likud Party won the 1977 parliamentary elections. The defeat of the Labor Party, which had been the governing majority for 29 years, confirmed for Gush Emunim the accuracy of Kook's theology. The replacement of the secular and socialist Labor Party with the more hawkish Likud could be interpreted as Israeli society's acknowledgement of God's territorial designs for the state.

Following his election, Menechem Begin reinforced this understanding of events by standing before a group of settlers and calling for "many more Elon Morehs." Begin was referring to the process of settlement that took place between 1973 and 1975. The initial settlers were repeatedly escorted from the territory they were trying to claim, until the Labor government, led by Yitzhak Rabin, finally conceded them the territory they sought. The Elon Moreh settlement embodied the fluctuating government response to settlement activities, and Begin's promise for many more assured Gush Emunim of a long-awaited full-government endorsement of future settlements.

The election of Begin and what Gush Emunim believed it represented in terms of national consciousness made Begin's participation at Camp David a shock to the religious settlers. Begin had emphasized his religious outlook, and the settlers had believed he shared their views on the sacredness of the land. When it was revealed that Begin had not only made peace with Egypt, but had given up the Sinai Peninsula in order to achieve it, shockwaves resounded in the settler communities. For the first time since the creation of the state, the religious and the secularists were forced to confront the consequence of their differences. To the secularists, the potential security costs of giving up land were balanced by the benefits of trading territory for lasting peace. For the religious, no peace was worth the cost of redemption. The ideological divide that had previously run parallel between the two groups suddenly veered in opposing directions.

Kook's ideology had the power to account for secularists unknowingly acting out the purpose of God. But when faced with secularists deliberately acting in opposition to this power, Gush Emunim was hard-pressed to keep the faith: "The retreat from Sinai and the evacuation of Jewish settlements were considered acts of sin, retreats from the course of redemption."[42] For the first time, Gush Emunim and their supporters were forced to recognize that the inevitable drive to redemption could be led astray by the secular government.

The consequences of this realization were mitigated at least in part by the careful dance Begin conducted with the settlers. Although he agreed to return Sinai to Egypt, he simultaneously supported more settlements in the West Bank. He continued to allow the settlers unprecedented access to his government, and continued including members of the movement in key government positions.

Nonetheless, the reactions by Gush Emunim activists and supporters were mixed. While some called for a measured return to educational efforts, and continued operation within the existing government system, others created the Jewish Underground and developed plans to blow up the Dome of the Rock. Some members of the Underground attempted to kill three Arab leaders in the

West Bank by planting bombs in their vehicles. One of the mayors lost both of his legs, another lost his foot and the third attempt was thwarted before the intended victim got in his car. In a separate incident, several Israelis tossed a grenade into the courtyard of the Islamic College in Hebron, and covered the area with machine-gun fire. Three Palestinians were killed. In 1984 a plot to blow up five Arab-owned buses was uncovered and three-dozen members of the Underground were arrested.

While the attacks conducted by the Underground were atrocious, it is worth noting that they were not acts of political violence. Rather, they were racially motivated acts of vengeance against the Arab population. While this distinction does not in any way justify the crimes that were committed, it does assist in the analysis of the continuing relationship between the settlers and the state. Of the acts committed by the Underground, only the plot to blow up the Dome of the Rock could be considered a political act – and it was ultimately rejected by Underground members themselves. How can we explain the relatively muted reaction of the settlers movement in light of the threat the Israeli government posed to the redemptive process? The answer can be found, in part, in the state's reaction to the discovery of the terrorist organization.

Arnoff notes that the Underground emerged when "the movement had gained access to the highest levels of government which was actively implementing its settlement policy. The government had all but co-opted the movement as its ideological vanguard."[43] Rumors later surfaced that the government could have stopped the attacks, had they been so inclined. Yossi Sarid, a member of the Knesset at the time said, "I'm not saying these people had full knowledge about the underground, I'm saying a number of people had clues which might have been very helpful to the Shin Bet and could have prevented the attack on the Islamic College."[44]

Whether or not the government could have prevented the attacks is unclear, but the consequence of the *belief* that they could have was significant. The government reaction to the incident demonstrates that, by 1984, there was still no resolution to the ambiguity between the religious and secularist policy advocates. The Arab mayors were unsurprisingly unpopular among much of the Israeli community, and a forceful government reaction against the murders would force a confrontation between Menechem Begin and Gush Emunim, an outcome neither side desired. Following Camp David, Begin had shored up some of his political capital on the right by encouraging further settlements in the West Bank, even while forcibly evacuating settlers from Sinai. Further, Gush Emunim was not unified within itself in regard to the use of violence against Arabs. While some of the settlers condoned the spirit of vigilantism that developed in the settlements, many initially condemned the pre-mediated murder attempts as excessive. But Gush Emunim supporters in Likud lobbied for the perpetrators to be pardoned for their crimes. In fact, President Chaim Herzog did pardon half of those involved in the planning once they expressed remorse for their actions – adding to the indistinct relationship between the government and the religious right.

After the discovery of the Jewish Underground, the relationship between the religious Right and the Israeli government returned to its mutually dependent state: "On the one hand, the government gave in to the movement generously and encouraged it, while the other admonished it. In turn, Gush Emunim acknowledged the government, but violated its instructions and provoked and criticized it."[45] But the society in which this relationship flourished had changed with the Camp David Accords. Many Israelis came to realize that the way to peace was the relinquishment of territory – not the preservation of it. The organization Peace Now was born in 1978 and it developed a significant following throughout the 1980s.

The impact of this change in social consciousness was manifested in the 1992 Israeli elections. For the first time since 1977, the Labor Party was able to form a coalition government that did not include any of the representatives of the religious-settlers' interests.[46] More disastrously, the PLO was indicating willingness to recognize the state of Israel, and the Labor government, under the leadership of Yitzhak Rabin, appeared to be seriously considering it. Supporters of Eretz Yisrael were shocked and horrified by the formation of the Labor-led coalition. That Labor's victory had been so conclusive planted a seed of doubt about the Israeli public's ability to participate in the redemption of the land.[47]

The path to the Oslo Accords was far more traumatic to the religious Right than the way to the Camp David Accords had been for several reasons. First, the Camp David Accords were conducted by Menechem Begin, not only a member of the more conservative Likud Party, but also an unabashed supporter of the religious-settlers movement. Even though settlers were furious with Begin's betrayal, his subsequent nebulous reaction to the Jewish Underground, his advocacy for West Bank settlements, and his right-winged, security-based political ideology made his actions during the Accords slightly more palatable. Yitzhak Rabin was another story entirely.

Rabin was an avowed secularist. He ridiculed the religious Right, and made no effort to pretend to support their ideology.[48] Rabin referred to members of the settlers movement as "Israel's Ayatollahs" and "Jewish Hamas."[49] Whereas Begin had been dependent on religious support for his government and its policies, Rabin's coalition was formed largely in opposition to the movement. Rabin's coalition government was formed with Meretz – a Party that embodied the very secularism that the religious movement deplored. Rabin did nothing to undermine the message this sent to the religious movement – even going so far as to appoint Shulamit Aloni, an extreme feminist icon, as the minister of education and culture.[50]

Further, the Rabin government made the Arab parliamentary bloc a part of the governing coalition – a move that would later result in the religious movement declaring the government illegitimate. Rabin's government was the first in the history of Israel to rip the tenuous threads linking secularism to religiosity. Under Rabin, there could be no legitimate argument that a secular government could do God's work. Hagai Segal commented:

The upheaval of 1992 will put an end to our schizophrenic attitude towards the authorities. Until now, the government was with us and not with us, for us and against us. Once and for all it must be known who is for us and who is against us.[51]

Rabin's actions were seen as a war against religious Zionism, and the Zionists were prepared to fight.

Over the next few years, the religious settlers joined with Likud to destroy Yitzhak Rabin's political will. A campaign was launched to harass Rabin and thwart his efforts at land for peace at every turn. This campaign ended with a religious settler assassinating the Prime Minister.

But more surprisingly, only seven months after Rabin's assassination by a member of the religious-settlers movement, Likud leader and settlement advocate Benjamin Netanyahu was appointed Prime Minister. Netanyahu did not remain in office for very long, but his successful election after Rabin's assassination is indicative of the persistent symbiotic relationship between the Israeli state and the settlers movement. In the decade and a half since Rabin's assassination, thousands of Israelis have successfully settled in the West Bank.

Conclusions

In the American and Egyptian cases explored earlier in this book, the states underwent measurable secularization processes in the twenty-first century. Out of this, religious organizations grew up in opposition. The state of Israel paints a slightly different picture. Perhaps owing to the time period in which the state was created, secularization was already a valiant player in the political process. As a result, it did not increase after the creation of the state; rather, it simply remained as a viable entity. Had Herzl been unable to persuade the religious Jews to join his cause, the state of Israel may never have been created. Or, if it was created, it may have managed to be an exceptional modern state in that it would never confront a religious opposition. But Rabbi Kook's theology hindered the viability of either option by creating a parallel sphere for religion alongside secularization in the state-creation and development process.

This parallelism was maintained for two primary reasons. First, Kook's theology provided space for secularists in the redemptive process, whereas in the U.S. abortion movement and the Egyptian push for Sharia law, two competing sides were immediately at odds with one another. A gain for one inevitably meant a loss for the other. Kook's theology ensured that a gain for secularism could also be seen as a gain for religion. Second, the security interests for the state of Israel have been consistently at the center of Israeli policy. Because of the circumstances of its creation and its location in the midst of Arab states, Israel had coalesced around a value structure of physical security. The religious settlements were initially recognized to enhance that security. Thus, just as a gain for secularism could be a gain for religion, territorial gains for the religious could be seen as security gains for the secular state.

But why did this arrangement barely falter when Begin first accepted peace with Egypt? And why was it not destroyed when Yitzhak Rabin did attempt to go toe-to-toe with the religious movement? Why have no organizations committed to religiously motivated violence emerged in Israel despite such high stakes and the continued loss of land? In the next chapter we will see that the symbiotic relationship between the religious-settlers movement and the Israeli state has prevented sustained radicalized rhetoric, secretive organizational structures and ideological frames making violence a religious duty.

9 Settling the case for violence

The future of religious violence in Israel

Certainly the largest, arguably the most influential, and indisputably the most well-known sector of the religious-settlers movement, Gush Emunim presents a fascinating case to explore when considering the impact of rhetoric on the political arena. Although Gush Emunim never formally divided into different organizations within the same movement, its members clearly divided themselves into ideological, rhetorical and practical camps when proposing actions in the political process. And the same principle that was seen in both the American and Egyptian cases can be seen in the case of Gush Emunim as well. This is particularly interesting because Gush Emunim remained a single organization but still benefitted, and then later suffered from, its impact on the political sphere in which it operated.

Forming a rhetorical base

As mentioned in the previous chapter, Gush Emunim was an eventual outgrowth of the Mercaz Harav yeshiva established by Rabbi Avraham Kook in 1924. Kook was a key player in the development of religious Zionism, thanks to his interpretation of redemption as a process that can be implemented through key historical events. Rabbi Kook merged members of the Jewish Orthodoxy with members of the secular Zionist movement by suggesting that the creation of the state of Israel was a holy undertaking, whether those advocating its establishment knew it or not. This theology paved the way for a working relationship between the religious Jews and the secular Zionists for several decades, despite the consistent unresolved contradictions that plagued the motivations for both movements.

But, in the late 1960s, Mercaz Harav and the theology it promulgated was in danger of fading into obscurity. While the religious and secularist ideologies were not necessarily more at odds than any time before, the political establishment seemed unlikely to pursue the expansion of state borders regardless of the motivation. Rabbi Yehuda Kook (the son of Rav. Avraham Kook) was inspired to bemoan this state of affairs before many of his students in 1967. Thus it was considered a delightfully satisfying outcome when, three weeks later, the 1967 war occurred and Israel found itself with 28,000 square miles of new territory, occupied in an astonishing and conclusive military victory.

The 1967 war re-ignited the compatibility of the religious and secular camps. Then Prime Minister Golda Meir initially rejected US attempts toward brokering peace between Israel and Egypt because she considered the increased territory a secure buffer zone that enhanced the security of the state. While the religious Zionists supported annexing the land gained in war for other reasons, the shared interests brought the ideology of the religious Zionists a renewed place of political interest. Because Rabbi Kook and his students had anticipated the eventual accumulation of more territory, Mercaz Harav and its scholars were propelled to the center of national consciousness.

Their position at the center was cemented six years later following the 1973 war. The ceasefire for the war stipulated the return of much of Sinai to Egypt. Israelis who had bought into the security arguments in favor of annexation were at a loss to explain what appeared to be a devastating political capitulation. Rabbi Kook and his followers were well-prepared to step into the breach.

Kook and his students diagnosed the 1973 war as God's displeasure with the Meir coalition government. Meir, the Kookists believed, had sinned when she entertained the possibility of Egyptian appeasement in returning Sinai: "It is a signal that we have not done our part within the framework of the overall scheme in which there is an active role for mankind."[1] They prescribed cutting out the cancerous Meir government in new parliamentary elections and imbibing the theology of the land as redemption that characterized the Mercaz Harav yeshiva. Gush Emunim was created to lead in this effort. Gush Emunim members are well-educated individuals with a firm understanding of why they do what they do. In interviews, members consistently reference the themes of "national regeneration, the metaphysical meaning of ordinary events, the building of the Third Temple, and messianic redemption."[2]

While Gush Emunim was founded on the Kookist theology that secular intentions could bring about holy outcomes, this theology was predicated on the understanding that eventually the secularists would realize the sacredness of their undertakings and actively pursue redemption for its own sake. But the 1973 war was a reminder to the Kookists that, just as redemption could be furthered by secularists, so also could it be hindered. It was this realization that made a formal organization committed to education and settlement critical.

The organization characterized itself as fulfilling a leadership role in a society desperate for spiritual guidance.[3] To this end, Gush Emunim endeavored to transform the national dialogue regarding settlements and territory from one about political strategy to one about religious covenants. A foundational principle of Gush Emunim theology is that every piece of the Land of Israel is holy. As a result, no land is available for political negotiations. To return even the smallest or most insignificant land in exchange for any political concessions is to threaten to abrogate the covenant God formed with Abraham thousands of years earlier.[4] Indeed, those who would suggest that the Jewish rule of one section of Israel is more important than any other are dangerous individuals who miss the purpose of the Jewish state. In the early years of its existence, Gush Emunim rhetoric painted Israel as a near-living being that could not be torn apart.

Influential religious Zionist Haim Druckman employed this personification tactic in a memorable speech in the Knesset following Israel's withdrawal from portions of Sinai:

> Who does not feel the shock that has gripped every settlement in the Land of Israel, every family on the land, every true pioneer? Who has not heard their cries, the cry of the Land, over the sons that are about to be separated from her? The uprooting of settlements in the Land of Israel is the severing of a limb from a living body. These settlements are the essence of our existence and flesh of our flesh. We shall not accept the amputation of living flesh.[5]

The rhetoric of Israel's chief Rabbinate in 1979 affirmed this stance: "According to our holy Torah and unequivocal and decisive *halakhic* rulings, there exists a severe prohibition to pass to foreigners the ownership of any piece of the Land of Israel since it was made sacred by Abraham's covenant."[6] Gush Emunim founder Hanan Porat puts the same idea in its political context:

> Israel's national connection to the Land of Israel is unique among the nations – it is radically different from the ties that bind the French, English, Russian and Chinese peoples to their lands.... For us the Land of Israel is a land of destiny, a chosen land, not just an existentially defined homeland.[7]

It should be noted that the boundaries of the Land of Israel are not unanimously agreed upon, even within subsections of Gush Emunim. And yet, not a single leader of Gush Emunim has ever indicated any willingness to give up any land as a political strategy. This is interesting for several reasons. First, it demonstrates the ability within Gush Emunim toward plurality on some levels. The religious-settlers movement has demonstrated an aptitude for Schaeffer-esque co-belligerence time and again. When Gush Emunim initially broke onto the political scene, they aligned themselves with the secular Land of Israel movement, they forged paths of political access in both the Labor and Likud parties, and they required no ideological conditions for membership of the organization.

However, it is not clear whether this penchant for pluralism is the result of a genuine tolerance of alternative perspectives or an oversight fostered by a vague ideology that makes specific distinctions impossible. Kook was oblique on the day-to-day implementations of his religious ideology, and this enabled the theology to be interpreted in a variety of ways.[8] In fact, Gush Emunim has never published an official declaration specifying the organization's principles or aims. Instead, the group has relied on extensive networks and media exposure to present a program literally shaped by "facts on the ground."

Shortly after the Yom Kippur War, Gush Emunim published what Aran calls an "amateurish position paper" and this serves as the most comprehensive written declaration to date. The document defines Gush Emunim's aim as:

To bring about a great awakening of the Jewish People towards full implementation of the Zionist vision, realizing that this vision originates in Israel's Jewish heritage and that its objective is the full redemption of Israel and
of the entire world.[9]

Later on in the document, they identify their principles of action:

a   Education and publicity (a link with Torah and Jewish ethics, love of the
    Jewish People and the Land of Israel; Zionist consciousness and the vision
    of redemption; national missions and fulfillment)
b   Love of Israel
c   Jewish immigration to Israel
d   Settlement throughout the Land of Israel
e   An assertive foreign and security policy.[10]

In pursuit of these goals, Gush Emunim established educational programs to
inform the public about their policy positions. At the same time, the organization
undertook a strategic plan to increase the number of settlements in the occupied
territories. In an interesting rhetorical shift that mirrors what the emerging al
Jama'a al Islamiyya did to the socialist movement, Gush Emunim hijacked the
secular Zionist pioneer rhetoric to promote their settlements. Just as Ben-Gurion
and other early Zionists had publicized the brave and independent spirits that
would forge the new state of Israel, following the 1973 war, Gush Emunim
called for courageous individuals to do what the more cowardly government
could not by settling in new territories.

Gush Emunim brought publicity to the religious-settlers movement by invit-
ing thousands of sympathizers to march with them through sections of occupied
territory. In 1974, Operation Go Around was launched and 2000 Gush Emumin
sympathizers hiked through parts of the West Bank that Gush Emunim activists
considered crucial settlement territory. Two years later a similar activity generated more than 20,000 participants.[11]

Gush Emunim's influence in social and political circles is evident by the
shifts in terminology that had occurred within only a few years of the group's
existence. Over time, both supporters and opponents of the religious-settlers
movement alike have come to refer to "Judea" and "Samaria" instead of the less-
inflammatory designation "the West Bank."[12] This is due, at least in part, to
Gush Emunim's relentless media efforts. The organization has been remarkably
persistent about publicizing their events and availing themselves to the media.

Beyond changing the terminology used in reference to the settlements, the
infiltration of Gush Emunim's rhetoric is apparent in the success of the Likud
Party in the 1977 elections. Not only did members of the Likud Party pepper
speeches with more religious phraseology, but upon his election, Begin wore a
skull cap and visited the home of Rabbi Kook to receive his blessing.[13] Only a
few days later, Begin dramatically promised the settlers "many more Elon
Morehs."

Whether Begin truly believed the theology he was endorsing is neither clear nor particularly relevant. His election and pandering to the religious vote demonstrates that Gush Emunim had captivated the electorate to such an extent that the secular party that had dominated elections since the creation of the state was in the minority for the first time in history. In light of their political conquest, Gush Emunim members were horrified when Begin began peace talks with Egypt.

In the early years, the words used to condemn actions of the government invoked cowardly, rather than criminal, characteristics of leadership. Even Rabbi Meir Kahane, who formed the extreme right-wing Facist Kach Party, regaled the Begin government with accusations of weakness, not criminality. He said:

> The heart of the Begin tragedy is that a man who was a symbol for half a century of Jewish pride and strength surrendered Jewish rights, sovereignty and land out of a fear of Gentile pressure. It is in a word "Hillul Hashem" the humiliation and desecration of the name of God by substituting fear of the finite Gentile for the Jewish faith in the God of creation and history.[14]

While Kahane's statement clearly indicated his absence of respect toward the Begin government and its territorial capitulation, compared to the rhetorical firestorm that preceded Yitzhak Rabin's assassination years later, the statement by Kahane is relatively mild. It does, however, have some characteristics of the rhetoric that would be invoked during Rabin's administration. For example, Kahane identifies Begin's decision to trade land for security as an act of spinelessness. This inversely conveys that to resist such a temptation is an act of courage.

It wasn't until the discovery of the Jewish Underground, and the revelation that it was comprised of leaders in Gush Emunim that there existed within the organization specifically, and the movement more generally, a capability for and a willingness to engage in premeditated murder. Until this time, Gush Emunim supporters had employed aggressive and illegal methods of protest, but none of the leaders had ever condoned violence.[15] In fact Gush Emunim had actively endeavored to use rhetoric that the public could hear and understand:

> Rather than speaking the truth at all costs, most Gush spokesmen and strategists emphasize the need to "say only that which can be heard" by the public at large. The primary task, in their eyes is an ideological education that must be performed gently over a long period of time.[16]

But the Jewish Underground sect of Gush Emunim rejected the mild rhetoric that the rest of the group employed, believing that a slow march to redemption ran the risk of being thwarted by secularists in the government. The attempt to blow up the Dome of the Rock was not undertaken to overthrow the Israeli government, but rather to strengthen its position on the path to redemption. In fact, in justifying their efforts, Menachem Livni – a chief conspirator in the Dome of the Rock plot – stated, "We reject in disgust the desire to bring us to trial like criminals. We are no worse than Yitzhak Shamir, Menachem Begin, and their colleagues who went forth to defend their homeland in the 1930s and 1940s."[17] Supporters of the Underground ran with this argument, contending that the acts were self-defense. Some went further to suggest that the violence against Arabs was actually obligatory in order to preserve Israel's honor.[18]

The judges in the case of the Temple Mount conspiracy were apparently inclined to agree with Livni and the others and handed out light sentences. When the prosecution protested these sentences, high-ranking members of Likud, including Deputy Prime Minister Yitzhak Shamir, condemned the prosecution as being out of touch with national sentiment. Attempts were made in the Knesset to pass an amnesty law that would relieve the prisoners of even their light sentences.[19] The longest that any member of the Jewish Underground served in prison was six years and six months. Nearly all were pardoned by the Israeli government within the six-year time period.[20]

Within Gush Emunim, the reaction to the Underground was mixed. Some, including Yoel Bin-Nun, were disgusted by the actions of the violent members. He stressed that harming Arabs indiscriminately not only undermined the legitimacy of the state of Israel, but was counter-productive to the establishment of Jewish sovereignty in the territories.[21] But, in reaction to those at Mercaz Harav that condemned the act, 16 rabbis circulated a national petition favoring clemency for the Underground.[22]

It was the discovery of the Jewish Underground and its judicial aftermath that revealed the strength and consequence of Gush Emunim's influence in society. Studies of the organization published after the mid-1980s demonstrated a growing awareness of the significance of the group. A 1986 article written by Ehud Sprinzak characterizes Gush Emunim as an "invisible kingdom which is gradually acquiring the character of a state within a state."[23] Displaying insightful prescience, Sprinzak also wrote in 1986 that "Gush Emunim, it is clear, has introduced into Israel's public life a radical model of thinking, and a comprehensive and absolutist belief system capable of generating intense aspirations with the potential of extreme consequences."[24]

Aran notes that "before the intifada erupted in 1987, it appeared that Gush Emunim had nearly achieved its objectives. By spring of 1990, Gush Emunim appeared further than ever from its objectives."[25] In the 15 years since its creation, Gush Emunim had dramatically changed the political arena in which it operated, to the point that the organization had clear paths of access to high-powered positions of government influence. When the intifada broke out in 1987, Gush Emunim turned its attention away from influencing government policy toward a program of vigilante justice against uprisings in and around the settlements. But, far from subduing the Palestinian violence, it worsened the situation.

By 1992, many Israelis had had enough, and Yitzhak Rabin was elected to form a new coalition government. Not only was Rabin's coalition the first since 1977 to not include any Gush Emunim sympathizers, but his coalition was dependent on the support of the bloc of the Democratic Arab Party. Moreover,

Rabin revealed that he was willing to negotiate with the PLO, provided they recognized Israel's right to exist and renounced the use of terrorism.

In reaction to this change in the political scene, the religious-settlers movement stepped up their rhetoric significantly. Energy was expended to verbally attack Rabin personally, rather than just the policies he was pursuing. Rabbi Yoel Bin-Nun (the same Gush Emunim leader who had condemned the Jewish Underground's activities) recounts the decision that was made to direct a campaign of abuse specifically against the Prime Minister. He said, "The aim was to bring Rabin down by abuse.... The idea was to break Rabin, those around him, his legitimacy, his image."[26]

Gush Emunim settler Elyakim Ha'etzni highlighted parallels between Rabin's actions and those undertaken by Germany in World War II:

> Those loyal to the Greater Land of Israel have a right to declare a government that gives up territory as an illegal one, just as de Gaulle declared the Vichy government illegal.... We will treat the signing of the Oslo agreements as collaboration with the Nazis was treated in France.,th>... This is an act of treason and it is inevitable that the day will come that Rabin is tried just as Petain was.[27]

Founding Gush Emunim member Meir Indor produced posters that depicted Rabin wearing a *keffieh* and called him a liar, and Indor was the first Gush Emunim member to carry a placard labeling Rabin a traitor.[28] It was a short jump from calling Rabin a traitor to designating his treason in Rabbinical terms. And soon the inflammatory concepts of *moser* and *rodef* emerged at the forefront of opposition consciousness. The use of the word *moser* (which refers to "a Jew suspected of providing the Gentiles with information about Jews or with illegally giving them Jewish property"[29]) and *rodef* ("a person about to commit or facilitate the commitment of murder"[30]) opened a new thread in the opposition dialogue because the two terms refer to circumstances in which it is appropriate, even obligatory, for a Jew to kill another Jew. Rabbi Shlomo Aviner recognized the danger in using the two terms and urged his colleagues to stop using them "for fear of fatal consequences."[31]

In fact, Aviner's prophecy came to pass. Yigal Amir made clear that the rulings regarding *din rodef* and *din moser* influenced his willingness to act:

> Once it is a ruling, there is no longer a problem of morality. If I were involved now in the biblical conquest of the land, and as said in Joshua, I would have had to kill babies and children. I would have done so regardless of the problem of morality. Once it is a ruling, I do not have a problem with it.[32]

After Rabin's assassination, the religious-settlers movement was starkly divided in regards to the act. Rabbi Yoel Bin-Nun once again remonstrated his colleagues for their incitement, and clearly held them responsible for what had occurred. He scathingly called the rabbis who had issued the *din rodef* ruling "Jewish Hezbollah." He called for the rabbis who had issued the ruling to step down from their posts, but his suggestion was met with scorn and fury. One participant accused Bin-Nun of having blood on his hands, if any of them did, because he too had attended rallies in which Rabin had been called a traitor and a murder.[33]

Several conclusions can be drawn from the use of rhetoric in this case. First, unlike the movements in Egypt and the United States, the lines in Israel have not been clearly drawn – neither between the violent and non-violent opposition participants, nor between the religious movement and the state. This has had both positive and negative consequences. The religious-settlers movement, and its most influential organizations Gush Emunim and later the Yesha Council, have unquestionably been remiss in restricting the rhetoric used by affiliates of and participants in their organization. And in the case of Yitzhak Rabin's assassination, the ramifications were fatal. But in the case of the Dome of the Rock plot, the Jewish Underground actually forwent the political violence they had planned because of their continued interactions with rabbinical authorities. Such frank contact would not have been possible had Gush Emunim not also been participating in a national dialogue using a very different set of rhetoric. Because the settlers had been so effective in using encompassing rhetoric to secure a spot in the national dialogue, they had the access to prevent the Dome of the Rock attack from happening.

What then of the assassination of Yitzhak Rabin? The religious settlers believed that they had succeeded in securing the Land of Israel, and thereby protected the redemptive process. When Rabin was elected and the Oslo Accords undertaken, the encompassing rhetoric did not illustrate the danger of what the activists believed was happening. They sought far-stronger language to rouse national consciousness, but instead found their movement ridiculed and belittled by Rabin and his government. For the first time since 1977, a government was in power that could form a coalition without securing the support of anyone from the religious-settlement movement, and Rabin was threatening to give away the land on which they lived, and which they believe secured their redemption.

Structure

The largely encompassing nature of the rhetoric of the religious-settlers movement resulted in movement members having consistent access to the political process and this had an impact on the structure of the organization.

Like the Muslim Brotherhood and the Christian Coalition, Gush Emunim's influence was felt very quickly in Israeli politics. Yet, Gush Emunim required less from its followers than any of the cases yet studied. In fact, no formal system of membership was ever established. Activists became such by undertaking the activities promoted by the group's leadership – not by first being a recognized participant of the group. Activists were not responsible for regular fees, consistent participation, or even theological agreement. Gush Emunim was an organization characterized by a willingness to draw support and extend influence into all sectors of Israeli society and politics. And it was an organization that exalted the pioneering and adventurous spirit. Yet, most of the committed activists of Gush Emunim and the religious-settlers movement came from strong Orthodox backgrounds and were educated in yeshivot, which are identified as "by [their] very nature ... devoted to learning and analysis of religiously sanctified texts [and therefore] demand unquestioning compliance with authority."[34]

How did Gush Emunim come to develop such an incongruous structure? This section will show that it developed in response to the political context in which it was operating – a context significantly influenced by the rhetoric of the organization.

Gush Emunim began as a small band of followers of Rabbi Yehuda Kook. Kook's father founded Mercaz Harav, which the younger Kook took over at his father's passing. Kook's theology was taught to several generations of students at the yeshiva between the time of its founding in 1924 and the watershed moment of the 1967 war.

While in the celebratory spirit that characterized 1967–1973, the Labor-led coalition government did not necessarily embrace the theological argument being made by Kook and his followers, neither did their security interests conflict with this theology. Consequently, the Kookists confidently assumed that the path to redemption was irreversible and that they did not need to formally assist its progress.

But as Egypt tenaciously campaigned for Sinai's return through the War of Attrition, the Israeli government, led by Golda Meir, began to see the land as currency that could be traded for international support and security. When the organization first began, the group was united by ideology far more than structure. But within a year, four departments were established: political, financial, settlement and information, with efforts made to establish branches all over Israel.[35] Because the group never made membership a participation requirement, clear indications about the size of Gush Emunim do not exist. In the early years, the organization split its energies between land marches and actual settlements. While the settlement activity was initially conducted by hard-core supporters who were willing to endure the very difficult climate and political conditions inherent in their actions, march participants could (and did) come from any sector of Israeli society. Gush Emunim propaganda sought religious and non-religious participants, supporters of Likud and Labor, and educated or illiterate. Gush Emunim was quick to capitalize on the broad and extensive support they could garner in their marches, and used it to indicate their political reach. In so doing the group embodied the intentions of the elder Rabbi Kook. Avraham Yitzhak Kook endeavored to "expand religious influence to every aspect of individual and social life – thereby providing religious meaning even to the process of modernization itself."[36] Gush Emunim was committed to educating the public about the religious meaning they saw in the modernization process. Committed activists spoke in schools, held information meetings and invited interested individuals of all stripes to participate in religious-settlement-sponsored activities:

"They did not keep to themselves in a society apart, but entered into mainstream society as agents provocateurs who sought to change culture and the body politic."[37]

At this point, one could erroneously conclude that the structure and purpose of Gush Emunim was very much like that of the Muslim Brothers. And this is true, to a limited extent. But there are also significant differences. The Muslim Brotherhood has a clearly established structure of membership. Gush Emunim has no equivalent. The Muslim Brotherhood has an elected leadership circle that represents and guides its members. Gush Emunim was criticized in the mid-1970s because, although "membership" as such was totally open, leadership was limited to a selected few that often did not reflect or represent the interests of the larger group. Changes were eventually made to address this, but it highlights the hybrid nature of the organization.

When the Camp David Accords were signed with Egypt, Gush Emunim faced a crisis. Some members (including Yehuda Etzion, who would go on to form the Jewish Underground) argued that the failure of the religious-settlers movement to prevent the concession of Sinai was spawned by the organization's encompassing nature and concurrent acceptance of the sluggish methods of the state. Others argued it was precisely the opposite. This camp suggested that Sinai's loss was a result of the settlers being too isolated from the society around them. To remedy this, they urged further efforts toward education and increased their calls for patience:

> To prevent the repeat of Yamit in Judea and Samaria, much larger numbers of Jews had to be persuaded to settle in the territories than could be mobilized from the ranks of Gush Emunim itself, and a great deal more emphasis had to be placed on effective political organization and ideological and cultural outreach within Israeli society as a whole.[38]

The result was the creation of three new sectors of the religious-settlers movement including Yesha (the political/municipal arm), Amana (the settlement arm), and Hatehiya (a new political party).[39]

The Yesha Council, formed to legitimize the settlers movement in political circles, eventually succeeded Gush Emunim as the primary religious voice of the settlers movement. Yesha serves as an umbrella organization representing the Jewish interests of the settlers movement. When it was first created, the Yesha Council was composed of a 12-person secretariat and six different committees.[40] At the time it was established, there were no geographic requirements for the election of the members of the secretariat. This allowed Gush Emunim to ensure its influence within the burgeoning organization. But as its influence in the municipal councils became more formalized, the structure shifted to be composed of the mayors from 25 settlements and ten community leaders.[41] Yesha is derived from the acronym for the Hebrew names for the territories of Judea, Samaria and Gaza. The Yesha Council formally lobbies for the interests of the settlers in the corridors of the government.

The Yesha Council was composed largely of small groups of religious activists, tasked with mobilizing protest activities and protesters. Karpin and Friedman describe the Yesha Council as "an organizational octopus with small groups of dedicated activists reaching out to hundreds of sympathizers according to specialized lists."[42] Particularly in the months leading up to the assassination of Yitzhak Rabin, the Yesha Council demonstrated an impressive aptitude for mobilizing thousands of religious settlers very quickly. The treasurer of the Yesha Council, Efraim Cohanim, explained that the organization was able to assemble huge groups of protesters because it oversaw religious schools, neighborhoods and settlements.[43] In this respect, the organization mirrors the mobilization capacity of the Christian Coalition. And, as was true in the Christian case, through the Yesha Council, the settlers movement gained influential access to the political process by demonstrating the strength and reach of their network ties.

Amana came to represent the "feet" of the religious-settlers movement. Where the Yesha Council strove to improve the conditions of those living in the settlements, Amana was intended to build the settlements for Yesha to represent. The organization reached out to Jews all over the world and encouraged them to settle in the occupied territories. Amana eased settlers' transitions into the new areas by helping them to plug into existing community resources or form new resources where none were available. Amana coordinated who would live where, seeking to "match families with similar geographic and social characteristics to form a founding group of residents."[44] They coordinated efforts to literally build communities from the ground up, by constructing homes, developing educational and health facilities, securing funding, and constantly seeking the education of community members about the religious and political significance of their communities: "The end product is a kind of hybrid of a village and a suburb."[45]

By the mid-1980s the religious-settlers movement boasted a "highly variegated social and institutional system, including a state-supported settlement organization, regional and municipal councils and independent economic corporations."[46] Gush Emunim expert Gideon Aran indicated that at this time in the organization's history, "Sometimes it is difficult to distinguish between state affairs and Gush Emunim affairs. Even their rhetoric has begun to sound familiar."[47]

The shift in organizational structure had both positive and negative consequences for the movement as a whole. Amana, as an official settlement organization, had access to government funds directed toward legal settlements. The group used these funds to initiate 35 new settlements between 1977 and 1982 (in contrast to the five permanent settlements that were established by Gush Emunim between 1974 and 1977).[48]

But in some sense the organizations were *too* successful. When the settlements had been composed of fervently religious individuals suffering intense opposition, there was little danger of forgetting the raison d'etre of the movement. But thanks to Amana and the Yesha's success in gaining wide support in security and funding, the communities became comfortable, even affluent, places to live. Settlers did not want to risk their material comfort to protest the government's resistance to further settlements.

Moreover, to reach such a level of success, the organization had adopted far less radical rhetoric in order to appeal to a wider support base and maintain their access to corridors of power. The result was that the leaders of the movement were no longer those who could captivate followers with a strong ideological appeal, but those who knew how to produce results in a bureaucratic system. As Yishai explains, "Gush fervor had been replaced by bureaucratic institutionalization."[49]

Religious settlers who had supported Gush Emunim for its original and daring approach to territorial acquisition began to worry that the settlers movement had been lost in the state it was created to oppose. The problem was that, while Gush Emunim had been successful in forcing settlements, the activists recognized that the state still viewed these as security benefits – not holy for their own sake. Thus, while the movement may have succeeded in its physical aims, it had failed in its ideological appeal. This put the movement in a dangerous position: a government that was not ideologically committed to the preservation of all of Israel's territory could not be trusted to not give parts of it up should the opportunity be presented; but, at the same time, movement supporters could look around themselves and measure success, and therefore were unwilling to endanger that success by pushing for greater ideological intensity.

This dissatisfaction with the bureaucratization of the organization manifested itself in a dramatic way that is a remarkable testament to the power of organizational structure.

The Jewish Underground first met as a group in 1978 and was composed largely of leaders of Gush Emunim. Yeshua Ben-Shoshan and Yehuda Etzion spearheaded the organization and provided its ideological inspiration. They believed that God was so displeased by the failure of Israelis to see His hand in the redemptive process that He decided to slow the process by allowing the Camp David Accords to take place.[50] The men believed that the Dome of the Rock, located on the Temple Mount, was the symbol of Israel's sin and capitulation. Thus they felt God was calling them to blow it up. The destruction of the Dome of the Rock would also serve to thwart the effects of the Camp David Accords, as the Arab reaction was sure to be powerful.[51]

The first meeting was attended by eight men, although over time the group grew to include at least 20 people.[52] The demographics of the Underground were literally indistinguishable from Gush Emunim at large:

> The people of the Jewish terror group did not arise from the murky margins of their community, but in fact came from the best families of settler society and the heart of the believing establishment. They emerged from the preferred and well-funded settlements, from elite yeshivas and from select units in the army.[53]

These individuals met in secret usually about once a week. They discussed the logistical plans and moral implications for the plot. They studied the Temple

Mount in great detail in order to determine the best way to blow up the Dome of the Rock.

The plot to destroy the Temple Mount never came to fruition. Members of the Underground point to a single cause for the failure of the plot: they could not secure rabbinical approval for their plan. This is interesting for several reasons. While the group did engage in several violent attacks against Arabs between 1980 and 1984, the Temple Mount plot was the only time the group explored using violence for political purposes. The distinction is not made in an effort to condone the other incidences of terror for which the group was responsible. Rather, it is to separate out violence inspired by a need for revenge from violence used to influence the state. The members of the Underground have been clear in interviews since the event that the Mayors bombing, the Islamic College attacks and even the bus terror plots were in direct response to actions undertaken by Arabs against Israeli citizens. The plot to destroy the Dome of the Rock, on the other hand, was intended to facilitate the redemptive process by changing the political context. While the revenge-inspired terror acts may or may not have received Rabbinical sanction (accounts differ on this), it is certain that the Jewish Underground sought Rabbinical approval for the Temple Mount plot and were rejected.[54]

Although the Jewish Underground operated secretly, in the cell-type structure that is now common to terror organizations, it maintained its ties with religious authorities outside the cells. This was possible because Gush Emunim had garnered such political and social support for its cause that, until the terror attacks were carried out, the Israeli authorities had no reason to fear the potential for radicalism in the organization. Thus, although secrecy was important, it did not result in the isolation (ideological or physical) of Underground members. Ultimately, it was the Underground's ties with the more moderate sections of Gush Emunim that led the plot for religiously motivated political violence to be rejected by the Underground.

The political environment leading up to Rabin's assassination was quite different. Rabin was hostile to the religious settlers and had no qualms about showing it. The movement was represented in the opposition against Rabin through the Yesha Council, but decried their loss of direct access to the decision-making processes. Yigal Amir says he did not specifically approach any rabbis to receive sanction for his plan, but other accounts suggest that he approached them, but was rebuffed because of the controversial nature of his inquiry.[55] Amir has said in interviews since the assassination that he did not need a face-to-face authorization for his acts, because he had heard rabbis in the settlers movement calling Rabin *din rodef*, and he knew that meant that Rabin needed to be killed.

The Yesha Council specifically, and the settlers movement at large, quickly condemned Rabin's assassination after it had occurred and immediately absolved themselves of any responsibility for incitement. Efforts to determine whether any religious leaders in the movement had authorized Rabin's assassination came to naught. And yet, in many circles of the movement, Amir is regaled as a hero. Surveys conducted in 1996 showed that 25 percent of students in religious high schools would not condemn Rabin's assassination.[56]

Framing the consequences

The rhetorical and structural ambiguity of organizations within the religious-settlers movement have prevented the shift in the ideological framework that we saw in the American and Egyptian cases from occurring. The movement has not broken into clearly distinguishable violent and non-violent organizations because the current rhetoric and structures that dominate the movement allow for both to exist simultaneously. Those activists that have employed (or advocated the employment of) violence have done so cloaked in the ideological frame of executors of justice. They congratulate themselves as heroes in a movement frequently too cowardly to do the right thing. But, at the same time, these activists remain in the movement and demonstrate that they are still influenced by leaders in its hierarchy.

A primary part of the disjunction that developed in the religious-settlers movement is traceable to dual aims of the group: settlement and redemption. To the inner circle of Gush Emunim and graduates of Mercaz Harav, these two aims were irreversibly intertwined because settling the land was actually the fulfillment of redemption. In writing about the purpose of the movement, Hanan Porat specifies the group's religious function:

> The purpose is to bring about a grand movement of reawakening within the people of Israel in order to fulfill the Zionist vision in its entirety, with the recognition that the origins of the visions are rooted in Israel's tradition and in the foundation of Judaism and its goal – the full redemption of the people of Israel and the rest of the world.[57]

In the same document, Porat lists "settlement of the Land of Israel" as one of the foundational methods for achieving this end. Part of what made Rabbi Kook's theology so original was that it could be manifested in clear and measurable ways. As Lustick explains:

> While he [Yehuda Kook] lived, Gush Emunim drew from him authorization for its belief that redemption was the crucial challenge facing Israel and the Jewish people and that the challenge could be met by practical political accomplishments – most importantly establishment of Israeli sovereignty over territories ruled until 1967 by Israel's Arab neighbors.[58]

As Kook himself elaborated:

> True redemption is revealed in the progress of the settlement of the land, the revival of Israel in its land and in the continuing renewal of this settlement by the gathering of exiles in the possession of the land in our public devotion to its holiness.[59]

But to the greater movement and society at large, the connection was not always clear. Indeed, the tension that would plague the movement, and later its offshoots, almost always generated from activists promoting one over the other. Moreover, support for the movement was often offered by a government interested in co-opting the political solution without giving credence to its religious motivation.

The Elder Rabbi Kook believed that the Jewish state was holy – and that anyone contributing to its establishment and maintenance was, therefore, also holy. As his son explained, "we are living in the middle of redemption. The Kingdom of Israel is being rebuilt. The entire Israeli army is Holy. It symbolizes the rule of the people on its land."[60] Aran explains that according to Gush Emunim ideology, "whether the Zionists realize it or accept it, religion is Zionistic and Zionism is religious.... Zionists are saints despite themselves."[61] The consequence of this ideology was that its adherents did not believe they were using doctrine to interpret events, but rather they were using events to interpret doctrine. Kook was very clear that God used historical events to illuminate His plan. Humanity's job was to interpret these events.

Kook believed that God had instilled in every Jew a super-natural ability to conduct this interpretation. He explains:

> The distinctive excellence of the Jewish people consists in the presence of the "divine sensitivity at the core of its being" which permits Jews, as individuals and as a collectivity to experience and express divine illumination in pure, non idolatrous form.[62]

This ideological frame justifies an encompassing platform of political action. In this way, it is reminiscent of the Christian Coalition's efforts to reduce the dissonance between a secular and religious worldview. Just as Robertson assured his supporters that they were acting in the interest of the 94 percent of voters that believe in God, Gush Emunim was justifying political participation by highlighting the intrinsic holiness of all Israelis. Just as the Coalition did not force its supporters to act in confrontation with social mores, Gush Emunim characterized secular mores as unknowingly holy and thereby authorized activists to operate without dissonance among them.

But Gush Emunim differed from the Coalition in a fundamental way. The Christian Coalition never indicated that the salvation of its members or the nation was at stake in their political fight. In contrast, Gush Emunim made it clear from the beginning that redemption was on the line. This, too, produced a bifurcated response. Gush Emunim justified their political action by framing the state of Israel as a state in need of redemption, and the Jewish people a people in need of salvation. The Land was the means of attaining it and Gush Emunim was a benevolent leader illuminating the way.

The government did not have to acknowledge the holiness of their actions, it only had to allow them to take place. So, according to the framework created by Gush Emunim, the government was legitimate, even sacred, regardless of its motivations or structure of belief. But when the Israeli state threatened to cast the settlers off the occupied lands, two different frames emerged.

The first emphasized the continuing process of redemption and looked at the government's actions as an indicator that Gush Emunim had not educated society sufficiently yet. Redemption was inevitable, but perhaps not imminent. This frame emphasized the responsibilities of Gush Emunim and the settlers. They could continue to settle the land, to resist efforts to relocate them, and in so doing create facts on the ground that could allow the secularists see the redemptive process occurring around them. Violence was dangerous because it threatened to hinder Gush Emunim's ministry to the public. As a Mercaz Harav student explained, "There is room under special circumstances for illegal acts, but only on the condition that they do not arouse the hostility of the public and do not involve violence or deviation from morality."[63]

But the second frame focused more on the villains in redemption's story. A line of thinking began to emerge that suggested there were true versus untrue Jews. Instead of Kook's frame, which allowed unbelieving Jews to be a part of the redemptive process, this emerging frame potentially cast believing Jews into villainous roles if they dared question the intensity of the movement. When the government began to dabble in the exchange of land for peace, activists developed a frame that called the legitimacy of the government into question.

This framework emphasized the biblical justification of authority. When the Jews first petitioned God for a king, He acquiesced and selected His choice from among the people. Saul lost favor with God, and was eventually replaced by David who was known as a man after God's own heart. The subsequent monarchal history was a series of kings whose authority was bound in their efforts to be obedient to God. In the present state of Israel, the division of the land was a clear act of disobedience, and thus threatened the legitimacy of any government that would attempt it.

While Gush Emunim supporters were theoretically in favor of democratic government, the division of land could render such a government totally illegitimate. The authority of a democratic government is contingent on that government representing the will of God as laid out in the Torah.

This frame developed gradually, in large part because of the embeddedness of the religious settlers in the political process. When Begin was the leader engaged in peace talks, the settlers had direct access to him and his government. Any sentiments regarding the illegitimacy of the government had to incorporate the movement itself. Accordingly, Underground leader Yehuda Etzion justified what he planned to do by framing himself as simply a more dedicated and devoted Jew:

> The expurgation of the Temple Mount will prepare the hearts for the understanding and further advancing of our full redemption.... And since the state of affairs was not corrected by the government, but rather backed by it, the task had to be fulfilled by the most devoted and most dedicated. [64]

After two years of planning, Etzion finally realized no rabbi would sanction his plan. He abandoned plans to blow up the mosque, saying that he had realized the public was not yet ready to receive the understanding he sought to impart.[65]

But the period leading up to Yitzhak Rabin's assassination was characterized by a very different political climate. Rabin did not rely on any religious-settler groups for legitimacy. Whereas the first efforts toward peace agreements had only generated ripples of a frame denouncing the legitimacy of the government, Rabin's efforts were characterized not only as sin, but as an aggressive attack against God's agenda for the state.

It was therefore not much of a reach to extend the frame that characterized the Rabin government as illegitimate according to *halakhic* standards, but to use those same standards to prescribe how to deal with it. Accusations of *din rodef* and *din moser* transformed the discussion about what to do about the Rabin government from a discussion about what religious Jews had the right to do, into one about what they had the responsibility to do.

That leaders of the religious-settlers movement denied culpability in Rabin's assassination indicates that the ideological framework promoting violence as a responsibility has not yet become permanent. Three things influence this ambiguous status. First, the settlers have been very successful in transforming the arena in which they operate. They have made inroads in transforming the political rhetoric and infiltrating the political structure to such an extent that fully embracing violence would result in political loss, not gain. Second, the Israeli state has perpetuated a nebulous relationship with the movement, in large part because the movement still offers the state security and legitimacy benefits that outweigh ideological and administrative headaches that come from operating in tandem with the movement. The final factor is a composite of the first two. Despite increasing intensity and frequency of confrontations between the religious settlers and the Israeli state, both sides are still willing to maximize the compatibility of mutual aims despite opposing motivations.

Is Israel an example, then, of a state that has successfully avoided religiously motivated political violence (for the most part) by carefully holding open the political window of opportunity? The answer is "yes and no." While the religious-settlers movement is exceptional for its history of restraint (with a few notable exceptions), it has been restrained because it has been operating in a state that has not fully subscribed to the allure of secularization as of yet. While in Egypt and the United States secularization edged out religion, in Israel the two have been able to operate in concert. For much of Israel's history, the state saw land as security. But as the international arena has changed, land has increasingly been seen by the government to be a currency of peace. Begin tempered the religious backlash of this understanding by catering to religious interests in other areas. Rabin made no such effort, but a split between the violent and non-violent sectors of the movement was forestalled by the election of settlement supporter Nettanyahu seven months later.

The issue came to a head once again when Ariel Sharon decided to relinquish sovereign control of Gaza to Palestinians in 2005. Rabbis in the Yesha Council ruled that Israeli soldiers had the religious right to refuse to obey orders to evacuate settlers from Gaza. But other members of the Council were equally vocal in condemning the rulings.[66] And this time more rabbis were quick to thwart the emergence of inflammatory rhetoric. This was likely because Sharon was careful to recognize the concerns of the settlers. On the eve of the pullout, he stated:

> The settlement blocs will continue to exist.... I will not negotiate on the subject of Jerusalem. The blocs will remain territorially linked to the state of Israel. At the same time, there will be no return of 1948 Palestinian refugees to Israel.[67]

Sharon had long been allied with the movement in the past, and the events following his decision (his stroke and the election of Hamas in Gaza) undermined the finality of what he did.

The election of Hamas, the subsequent violence between Palestinian factions, and the persistence of rocket-fire launched from Gaza enabled the religious-settlers movement to regain its political footing without forcing a permanent divorce between violent and non-violent supporters. There have been consistent voices within the movement condemning the use of violence, but until the state demonstrates itself to be irreversibly at odds with the religious aims of the organization (and this will likely center around the issues of Jerusalem and West Bank settlements) it is unlikely that a formal separation will occur.

But the ambiguity can't continue for much longer. In the past, peace with any Arab state could be congratulated as progress by the international community and many within Israel. But peace with the remaining Arab hold-outs is likely to be contingent on the resolution of the Palestinian issue, and the use of land as currency will be paramount in these discussions. Sixty years of compatibility will face a crucible in the near future. Based on the American and Egyptian cases, Israel may yet have to confront the emergence of organizations committed to religious violence against the Israeli state in the years to come.

Conclusion

> There is a holy, mistaken zeal in politics, as well as in religion.
> By persuading others, we convince ourselves.
>
> (Junius)

While living in Egypt, I was regularly struck by the ubiquitous presence of armed policemen on the streets of Cairo. I noticed that the policemen in white uniforms were indifferent to my presence, while those who wore black leered and hissed at me when I walked by them. In the course of one of the interviews with the Brotherhood, the topic of the Cairene police force came up, and I mentioned my experience to the Brother. He smiled and told me that the armed policemen are divided between those in the elite Egyptian Army (not usually patrolling the streets), those who act as the Western-equivalent of policemen (those wearing white), and the riot police (those wearing black). He said that when a group of new recruits is being sorted into the three divisions, the following occurs:

> The officer in charge asks who among the recruits can read – and those individuals are put in the Egyptian Army. Those who cannot read are given the role of traffic cops. The remaining individuals are those who did not understand the question and are commissioned as riot police.

The Brotherhood member was being facetious, but at the same time, he said that my experience with the riot police was not unusual, nor was it significant compared to most. He said that the Egyptian regime depends on the riot police to follow orders without questioning them so that they will have no qualms doling out the harsh repressive measures called for by the regime.

If the riot police were more intelligent, they would not be able to act with the moral impunity they do against those the regime deems a threat. If they understood the motivations of those they were repressing, or the distinctions between the Brotherhood and the more violent organizations, they might struggle mightily against what they had been ordered to do.

The Brotherhood member who made the statement told me that he has often tried to reason with the riot police when they use force to end peaceful demonstrations instigated by the Brotherhood. He implores them to see the wrong in what they are doing and to see the humanity in those they would harm.

In the course of my research for this book, I have become impressed by the relevance of this statement to the study of religiously motivated political violence. We saw in the first three chapters that as religious organizations perceive their window of political opportunity to close, religious movements develop. As the social and political structures come to reflect more secular values, religious organizations see an increasing threat to their ability to interact with and influence the political system. The result is polarization between proponents of religion and secularism, but also among religious supporters themselves.

Often, to engage otherwise ambivalent citizens, religious leaders trumpet the decline of religion and emphasize the danger of the declining influence of religious values. But, as we saw in Chapter 4, this often occurs to ill effect. After all, those moderate voices may walk away from the shrill cry for reform entirely, leaving a remnant of extremists. This serves to exacerbate the divide of influence that prompted the religious concern in the first place, while simultaneously justifying the secular derision of the religious extremists.

If we are going to tackle the problem of religiously motivated political violence, we must be prepared to do what the Egyptian riot police do not – look carefully for differences between the violent and the non-violent organizations, in an effort to quell one and enhance the other. Even more importantly, we must recognize that the responsibility for precision must be shared by all players in this potentially deadly game.

Religious leaders must be careful in the battle-cries they sound. For example, Ralph Reed attributed the downfall of the Christian Coalition in the late 1990s to the extent of the organization's success earlier in the decade. Once George W. Bush was elected to office, conservative judges had been appointed to important judicial seats, and as a conservative contract had been made with America, many moderate Christian voters that had been mobilized to fight against secularization retreated from the arena, applauding a job well done. But rather than follow the exodus out of the arena, many leaders are sounding their *shofars* just as loudly as before.

Only a week ago,[1] I heard a voice on a conservative Christian radio station announce that if I didn't call my Congressman immediately, the ACLU might be successful in canceling Christmas. Having just put up my Christmas tree, I decided to look into the situation. A subsequent web search revealed a few local court cases about which holiday items could be displayed in public places, but nothing that was remarkably different than what has been going on for the last few decades. The point is not that religious leaders should not be concerned about efforts (local or otherwise) to undermine one of the most significant holidays of their faith. Rather, the point is that the deliberate use of inflammatory and exaggerated language has consequences beyond the preservation of national holiday celebrations. This was seen in Chapter 5 with an examination of four cases.

There is a verse in the Bible that says, "Faith is the substance of things hoped for, the measure of things unseen."[2] This places a significant burden of responsibility on religious leaders that endeavor to enter politics. In secular politics, individuals can measure their observations of candidates and policy against the scale of their interests. When action defies expectation, a tie can be easily severed. When a leader presents him or herself as representative of a religious faith, ties are based not only on actions and observations, but on a measure of faith.

Abandonment of a cause gone sour can be painted as equivalent to an absence of faith. It is for this reason that the ideological framework of religious organizations is so effective in constraining and motivating action. When the frame emphasizes not only the urgency of the cause, but the sin of inaction, decisions must be made not only against the measurement of observations, but on the scale of things not seen. The framework cannot be compared to an external system of values, as the source of the framework and values is the same. A rejection of a political cause carries the weight of a rejection of God.

Religion is powerful not because it makes this type of frame inevitable, but because it makes it far more possible. Religious leaders must bear this in mind as they form their rhetoric and articulate their doctrine. Leaders have every right – indeed, every responsibility if they believe their doctrine is true – to champion their cause and promote their agenda. But they have great responsibility to be precise in understanding the difference between a political adversary and a moral enemy. When this distinction is glossed over because of a need for a political rallying cry, they will lose their ability to be heard by any who do not agree with them and will consequently find their prophesies about the exclusionary political sphere to be self-fulfilling.

Further, as demonstrated in Chapter 6, the structure of an organization is no longer a clear indicator of its actions. As we saw in Chapter 7, the right frame can establish ideological ties as strong as physical ones. With this information, religious leaders cannot rightly argue that they do not cause anyone to act with their fiery words. The change in the political and social institutions has made leaderless resistance a genuine threat, and moral encouragement is as effective in this structure as physical reinforcement ever was in hierarchies.

But responsibility for precision does not end with the religious. When political leaders are not careful to distinguish between violent and non-violent organizations, preferring to categorize them in the same "religious-extremist" camp, they also serve to increase one while destroying the other. This book contends this is because ubiquitous repression demonstrates a diminishing influence of religious values in the political sphere, and increases the isolation between opposition and the state.

If this is indeed the case, then it becomes imperative for states to recognize that all religious organizations are not created equal. If effort is made to reward constructive, religiously motivated political activity, that level of isolation will decrease. While this may not satisfy those already embedded in the ideology and use of violence, it will have an impact on those still deliberating. The alternative is to force even organizations not governed by a violent ideological framework to mimic the secretive and isolated structures of those that are – thereby increasing their own likelihood toward violent behavior. Further, ubiquitous repression exacerbates the perceived bridge between the sacred and the secular, and reinforces the frame that says they are inevitably and constantly at war.

We saw in Chapters 8 and 9 that the emergence of organizations promoting the use of violence is a process. And, in Israel, we've seen that the process is not unstoppable. Israel differs from Egypt and the United States in that the separation between political and religious spheres of influence has not become permanent. As a result, the religious-settlers movement has maintained political access, and this has positively forestalled the formal establishment of organizations promoting the use of political violence. But we also saw that this arrangement is likely to be threatened as the Israeli government struggles to find peace with the Palestinians. It will be incumbent on future Israeli leaders to recognize religious factions as they formalize – and to reward those committed to not using violence with continued access to the political sphere.

In the course of this book, I have tried to show that, although violence is not an inevitable outcome of religion, religion has the capacity to inspire political violence. When religious organizations are pushed to the fringe of political society, their opportunities for access (and future abilities to gain access) decrease. This intensifies the justification of their cause, and ultimately isolates them even from each other. Organizations compensate by developing frames that address their moral isolation. When organizations successfully transfer the responsibility of justification from those who use violence to those who do not, we see a frame at work that firmly unites members despite structural differences.

This book was not written with the intention of condemning religious activists, nor of justifying their behavior. Rather, it was undertaken in an effort to emphasize the continuing presence of religion in the political sphere and the importance of better understanding that presence. In the continuing debate about the presence of Christianity in American politics, both sides often remark that the founders of the United States did not endeavor to separate religion and politics for the sake of the state, but for the sake of the Church. Proponents of this viewpoint contend that religion will be sullied by politics, and thus should remain in a separate sphere. It is not my intention to argue for or against the separation of Church and state, but it would do all sides well to recognize the significance of this argument. Religion is a commitment to the supernatural, while politics is a fight over interests. When religion is brought into politics, there is potential for the supernatural justification of a political agenda, and neither religion nor politics can remain unscathed.

This book has endeavored to demonstrate that religion and violence are not irrevocably linked, but neither are they inevitably at odds. When one's moral code and political interests come from the same source, any behavior has the capacity to be justified, as the furtherance of one's political interest can be seen to be a value in and of itself. When there is a separation between the source of one's political agenda and one's moral code, there is a tension when one begins to supersede the other. But when political action is religiously motivated, it is easier to believe that both the moral code and the political agenda have been designated by God, and thus if suspending one is necessary to further the other, the action is not only justified but sanctioned. When this frame is not repeatedly challenged by a structure which forces regular meaningful interaction with some dissonant perspective, violence becomes not only justified, but necessary.

One of the last interviews I did in Cairo was with a man who had helped to found al Jama'a al Islamiyya, had left it to join the Brotherhood, and then left the Brotherhood in the late 1990s to form the politically moderate Party, al Waset (literally – "The Center"). While we were talking in his office, his assistant's phone rang. The leader shook his head and moaned that "we will never convince the religious parties to listen to us if the ringers on our phones are set to play Beyonce!" The assistant laughed a little, and asked the leader what song he recommended instead. The leader punched a button on his phone and music from the soundtrack of *The Godfather* began to play. The leader grinned and said, "This way, we can convince the regime we are not averse to popular culture, but remind the extremists we are not afraid of violence when necessary."

The man was joking, of course, but his point was interesting all the same. He recognized the subtlety in the dance between religion and politics and the importance of nuance in understanding. Our responsibility can be no less.

Notes

Introduction

1 Juergensmeyer (2000).
2 Smelser (1962), Oberschall (1973), Tilly (1978), McCarthy and Zald (1987), Klandermans et al. (1988), Morris and Mueller (1992), Jenkins and Klandermans (eds.) (1995), McAdam et al. (1996), Aminzade et al. (2001), McAdam et al. (2001).
3 Clarke (1987). Gusfield (1966).
4 Called "moral reform movements," religious protest has been explained to be centered around the Status Anxiety theory and the Cultural Defense theory, both of which have pivotal assumptions about the motivations of the individuals involved in protest.
5 Sivan (1985), Lewis (2002), Pipes (2002), McTernan (2003).
6 McTernan (2003).
7 Tamney and Johnson (1988), Bolce and de Maio (1999).
8 "The Muslim Brethren" has been translated a myriad of ways over the course of its existence. There is some controversy involved in the selection of the appropriate translation (see El-Ghobashy 2005 for a complete explanation). For the duration of this book, the organization will be discussed using primarily the term "the Muslim Brethren." In some cases the term will be used interchangeably with "the Society" or "the Brotherhood or Al Ikhwan Al Muslimun"
9 Blanchard and Prewitt (1993).
10 Rosefsky-Wickham (2002).
11 For a particularly thorough articulation of these issues, see Clark (2006). Clark explains that research in the Middle East is limited by the authoritarian government structure, and the resulting pervasive presence of secret police and suspicion. The result is that many projects involving Middle East research are designed to balance methodological perfection and feasibility. Mine is no exception.

1 Changing political landscapes

1 National Consortium for the Study of Terrorism and Responses to Terrorism (2007).
2 Juergensmeyer (2000), Sivan (1985), Lewis (2002).
3 Spencer (1862).
4 Marx (1843).
5 Durkheim (1915).
6 Freud (1957).
7 Weber (1965).
8 Berger (1967).
9 Wilson (1982).
10 Lenski (1963).
11 Smelser (1962).

12 Dahl (1967).
13 Kornhauser (1959).
14 Gamson (1975), Jenkins and Perrow (1977), McAdam (1982), Schattschneider (1960).
15 Oberschall (1973), Halebsky (1976).
16 Kingdon (1984), pp. 173, 177.
17 Tarrow (1998).
18 Whittier (1995).
19 Jacobs (1970).
20 Smith (2001).
21 I am not arguing that violence is an effective means of achieving one's goals, or that the Weatherman organization was solely responsible for the social and political changes that occurred in the 1970s. The effectiveness of movements (and how to measure this) is fodder for another study. The point is simply that we do see changes in social fabric and institutional structure in response to social movements, and these changes become part of a new institution for new movements to mobilize against.
22 Esposito (1980), Burgat, (1993), Dekmejian (1995), Faksh (1997).
23 Norris and Inglehart (2004).
24 Williams (1994).
25 Ismail (2001).
26 Ibrahim (1980), Dekmejian (1995).
27 Cuneo (1989), Blanchard and Prewitt (1993), Blanchard (1994).
28 Cuneo (1989).
29 Munson (2001).
30 UNICEF (n.d.).
31 Munson (2001).
32 Denoeux (1993).
33 Arjomand (1984).
34 Jefferis (2006d).
35 Reed (1996).
36 Wilcox and Sigelman (2001).
37 Green *et al.* (1993).
38 Djupe and Grant (2001).
39 Bolce and de Maio (1999).
40 Tamney and Johnson (1988).
41 Ibid.
42 Green, Guth *et al.* (1993).
43 Djupe and Grant (2001).
44 Tamney and Johnson (1988).
45 Girard (1977), Schwartz (1997), Juergensmeyer (2000).
46 See, for example, Girard (1977), Schwartz (1997), Juergensmeyer (2000).

2 Abortion of values or the value of abortion?

1 Brooks (2000).
2 Ibid.
3 Ferree (1974), Mason *et al.* (1976), Schreiber (1978), McBroom (1986), Tallichet and Willits (1986), Mason and Lu (1988), Smith (1990), Loftus (2001).
4 Strickler and Danigelis (2002).
5 King *et al.* (1977).
6 Tilly (1992).
7 Glenn and Weaver (1979).
8 Brooks (2000).
9 Dejowski (1992), Loftus (2001).

10 Nye (1993).
11 Anon. (1975).
12 Ibid.
13 Granberg and Granberg (1980).
14 Hout and Fischer (2002).
15 Ibid.
16 Wilson (1982).
17 Durkheim (1915).
18 Aldridge (2000), p. 68.
19 Wilson (1994).
20 Carter (2000).
21 MacArthur (2001), Davis (2006).
22 Gurr (1970).
23 Hout and Fischer (2002).
24 Tilly is quoted in Tilly (1978), Cavanaugh (1986).
25 Tilly (1978).
26 Gusfield (1966), Blanchard (1994).
27 Petchetsky (1984).
28 Blanchard (1994), p. 40.
29 Ibid., p. 39.
30 Cuneo (1989), p. 85.
31 Blanchard (1994), p. 40.
32 Ibid., p. 41.
33 Ibid., p. 41.
34 Luker (1984).
35 Cavanaugh (1986).
36 Means (1970), Means (1971), Hart (1974).
37 Cavanaugh (1986).
38 Ibid. It is worth noting that the bold effect of Cavanaugh's claim was slightly muted when, sentences later, but with seemingly no awareness of the contradiction it created, Cavanaugh references a 1588 Effraenatam condemning abortion as homicide (1986, p. 267).
39 Ibid.
40 Blanchard (1994), p. 266.
41 Cavanaugh (1986).
42 Craig and O'Brien (1993).
43 Olasky (1995).
44 Ibid.
45 Blanchard (1994).
46 Ibid.
47 Cavanaugh cites Mohr (1978) on this point.
48 Craig and O'Brien (1993).
49 Cavanaugh (1986).
50 Sauer (1974).
51 Ibid.
52 Blanchard (1994).
53 Craig and O'Brien (1993).
54 Risen and Thomas (1998).
55 Ibid.
56 Ibid., p. 17.
57 Ibid.
58 Ibid., p. 48.
59 Ginsberg (1998), Risen and Thomas (1998), Solinger (1998).
60 Craig and O'Brien (1993), p. 58.

61 Schaeffer (1980), p. 24.
62 Schaeffer and Koop (1978), p. 20.
63 Ibid.
64 Schaeffer (1980), p. 120.
65 Schaeffer and Koop (1978), p. 16.
66 Ibid., p. 194.
67 Schaeffer (1976), p. 195.
68 Schaeffer and Koop (1978), p. 195.
69 Schaeffer (1985), p. 14.
70 Faux (1990), p. 134.
71 Terry (1988), p. 42.
72 McKeegan (1992), Craig and O'Brien (1993), Risen and Thomas (1998).
73 Risen and Thomas (1998).
74 See McKeegan (1992). McKeegan argues that abortion was little more than just good
    strategy in the hands of the political right. She notes that the traditional Republican
    base had been whittled away to less than 30 percent by the end of Nixon's presidency.
    But between George Wallace supporters and social conservatives, there was a full
    one-fifth of the electorate ideologically up for grabs. Abortion had the potential to
    lose 4 percent of the 30 percent of the traditional Republican base, but it could also
    bring in an additional 8 percent from social conservatives. This left a net gain of 4
    percent, and Weyrich and others were determined to get it.
75 Risen and Thomas (1998).
76 McKeegan (1992), p. 33.
77 Craig and O'Brien (1993), p. 36.
78 Risen and Thomas (1998).
79 Ibid.
80 Robertson (1989), p. 102.
81 On one occasion, Robertson prayed for a BAC1–11 jet for the CBN ministry. A year
    later, the organization was able to acquire one well below market price. More dramat-
    ically, in 1985, a hurricane was on track to hit the coast of Virginia. Robertson went
    on television and called his viewers to pray to divert the path of the storm. He later
    broadcast a staff meeting called for the same purpose. Finally, praying alone, Robert-
    son states that he was assured by God that the hurricane would not hit the area.
    Despite this, Robertson recounts that the storm continued on its path toward Virginia.
    Plagued by doubt, Robertson prayed, "Father, if I can't move a storm, how can I move
    a nation? Father I am laying a fleece out before you. If this storm hits our area, I am
    out of the presidential race completely." Hours later, prior to hitting the Virginia
    coast, the hurricane turned east and vented its rage 45 miles out to sea. Consequently,
    Robertson decided to run for president.
82 Pastor *et al.* (1999).
83 *Army of God Manual* – see author for copy.
84 Aaronson (2004).
85 Clarkson (1993).
86 Blanchard and Prewitt (1993), Baird-Windle and Bader (2001).
87 Blanchard and Prewitt (1993).
88 Baird-Windle and Bader (2001).

3 Allah's place in Egyptian politics

1 Gomma (1983).
2 Davis (1984).
3 Jefferis (2007a).
4 Jefferis (2006d).
5 Vatikiotis (1983).

6 Safran (1961).
7 The following description of the difference between Islam and Christianity summarizes a presentation arranged by one of the Egyptian Muslim Brothers, specifically for the author (Jefferis interview with El Kobri, 2006). The summary is not intended to suggest that this is the only interpretation of Islam or Christianity. As noted in the introduction of this book, the author has no intention of identifying "true Islam" or "true Christianity." Rather she only wishes to accurately represent the perceptions of each religion generated through the extensive investigation of primary and secondary sources.
8 This book will focus exclusively on the development of Sunni Islam, as this is the form that has dominated Egyptian politics.
9 Safran (1961), p. 14.
10 Warburg and Kupferschimdt (1983), p. 34.
11 Safran (1961).
12 Mitchell (1993).
13 Khadduri (1970).
14 Lia (1998).
15 Mitchell (1993), p. 8.
16 Lia (1998).
17 Khadduri (1970).
18 Mitchell (1993).
19 Ibid., p. 60.
20 Ibid.
21 Ibid.
22 Cooper (1982).
23 Mitchell (1993).
24 Ibid.
25 Ibid., p. 109.
26 Quoted in Crabbs (1975), p. 393.
27 Ibid.
28 Cooper (1982).
29 Vatikiotis (1987).
30 Kepel (1985).
31 Ibid., Fahmy (2005).
32 Kepel (1985).
33 Cooper (1982), p. 71.
34 Yadlin (1983), p. 162.
35 Ibid., p. 161.
36 Ibid., p. 173.
37 Hudaiby is quoted in Gomma (1983), p. 151.

4 A discussion of rhetoric

1 Girard (1977), Juergensmeyer (1992).
2 Schwartz (1997), p. 5, p. 17.
3 According to Gabriel, *naskh* is based on the fact that the Qur'an was written over a 22-year period of revelation to Muhammad. As there are many verses in apparent contradiction with each other, scholars developed the idea of *naskh* to support the belief that the later passages superseded earlier ones.
4 Gabriel (2002).
5 Green and Guth (1988).
6 Ibid., p. 154.
7 Pastor *et al.* (1999) 61(2): 423–444.
8 Green and Guth (1988) 50(1): 150–165.
9 Pastor, Stone, *et al.* (1999) 61(2): 423–444.

10 Jefferis (2006h).
11 American Atheists (2000).
12 www.mipt.org.
13 Brockhoeft (1994).
14 Rahnema (1994), p. 167.
15 Qutb (1964), p. 46.
16 Kepel (1985), p. 61.
17 Abed-Kotob (1995).
18 Ibrahim (1980) 12(4): 423–453.
19 Abed-Kotob (1995) 27(3).
20 Ibid.
21 Ansari (1984).
22 Hafez and Wiktorowicz (2004).
23 The second variable Hafez and Wiktorowicz identify as important (pre-emptive repression) is not relevant to either of the cases at hand. In the case of the Muslim Brothers, the organization had developed a significant network of support before the regime even noticed its existence. Al Jama'a al Islamiyya was endorsed and supported by the regime when it initially began to take root in Egyptian universities.

5 The consequence of rhetoric

1 Robertson (1989), p. 31.
2 Isaiah 1:5.
3 Jefferis (2006h).
4 Ibid.
5 American Atheists (2000).
6 Jefferis (2006h).
7 Bennett (1996).
8 Birnbaum (1995).
9 Easton (2000).
10 Ibid., p. 217.
11 Interestingly, Reed's flexibility in the form of his message is biblically based. Reed quotes the apostle Paul in his book *Active Faith*, saying "I have become all things to all people that I may by all means win some."
12 Easton (2000), p. 257.
13 Of course, Reed was not always successful in his choice of semantics. Early on in the life of the Coalition, Reed seemed to consider war analogies to be the best representations of his purpose, saying things like "I want to be invisible. I paint my face and travel at night. You don't know it's over until you're in a body bag. You don't know until election night" (Boston 2001); and later, "It's like guerilla warfare. If you reveal your location, all it does is allow your opponent to improve his artillery bearings. It is better to move quietly, with stealth, under the cover of night" (Boston 2001). Many Coalition opponents, and even some supporters, were troubled by the violent allusions Reed was drawing, seeing them as unbefitting a Christian message. And then, less than a year later, Reed himself began encouraging supporters to avoid using these violent metaphors, and he began replacing them in his own speeches with allusions to sports instead (Boston 2001).
14 The manual is not available on the Army of God website, and when asked, members coyly deny authorship. The author of this book secured a copy from a non-profit pro-choice organization in Boston, MA. The manual has never been officially published, and thus has no helpful citation information.
15 Baird-Windle and Bader (2001).
16 *Army of God Manual.*
17 This assertion is common among Army members. Most share a history of involve-

ment in non-violent anti-abortion organizations before their "graduation" to Army methods. Most, including Shannon, cited a desire to do more for the babies after reading or encountering Army rhetoric.

18 Shannon (n.d.).
19 Bower (1996).
20 Ibid.
21 Shannon (n.d.).
22 Bower (1996).
23 Hill (2003).
24 Ibid.
25 Ibid.
26 Anon. (2003).
27 Aaronson (2004).
28 Bray (2003a).
29 Jefferis (2007b).
30 Psalm 24:10–12.
31 Bray (1988).
32 www.armyofgod.com.
33 Bob Lokey is a dramatic exception. When asked in an interview about the role of grace in the lives of those involved with abortion generally, and women who have had abortions specifically, Lokey said that abortion is so grievous a sin that salvation is no longer offered to that woman. Lokey claims to "have that directly from the Lord God Almighty" (Jefferis 2007d). However, most other Army of God members emphasize that even the sin of abortion can be justified by Jesus' saving grace.
34 Jefferis (2007d).
35 Ibid.
36 Jefferis (2007b).
37 Brockhoeft (1994).
38 Ibid.
39 Ibid.
40 Griffin (n.d.).
41 Brockhoeft (1994).
42 Spingola (n.d.).
43 al-Zayat (2004).
44 See, for example, Pipes (2004).
45 Khadduri (1970).
46 Al-Banna (n.d.).
47 Khadduri (1970).
48 Rahnema (1994), p. 134.
49 Al-Banna (1978).
50 Sullivan and Abed-Kotob (1999).
51 Jefferis (2006d).
52 Ibid.
53 Jefferis (2006b).
54 Altman (2006).
55 Jefferis (2006c).
56 Jefferis (2006e).
57 Sullivan and Abed-Kotob (1999), p. 52.
58 Ibid.
59 Rubin (1990).
60 Sullivan and Abed-Kotob (1999).
61 Ramadan (1991), p. 177.
62 Multiple Brotherhood leaders have argued that if the state were to better incorporate the Brotherhood into the political system, the organization would be bettered

equipped to limit the establishment of these violent offshoots. Sullivan and Abed-Kotob (1999) summarize the argument of Ahmad Hasanayn: "Violence at the hands of individual Islamists erupts not because of organizational doctrine, but because of the inability of the Brotherhood to control its followers." This line of reasoning will be pursued in greater detail at the end of this chapter, and in Chapter 6.

63 Kepel (1985).
64 Ibid., p. 133.
65 Ibid., p. 135.
66 Ibid.
67 Beinin and Stork (eds.) (1997).
68 Jefferis (2006b).
69 Ibid.
70 Kepel (1985).
71 Mady (2004).
72 Al-Banna (n.d.).
73 Rahman (1989). This charter is summarized and translated in Sullivan and Abed-Kotob (1999), pp. 84–86.
74 Rahman (1989), Sullivan and Abed-Kotob (1999), p. 84.
75 Sullivan and Abed-Kotob (1999).
76 Ibid., p. 85.
77 Anon. (1997).
78 Ibid.
79 Sullivan and Abed-Kotob (1999), p. 85.
80 Ibid.
81 Anon. (1997).
82 Ibid.
83 Mubarak (1996), p. 322.
84 Ibid.
85 Sullivan and Abed-Kotob (1999), p. 60.
86 Ibid., p. 62.
87 Ibid., p. 61.
88 Jefferis (2006g).
89 Jefferis (2006f).
90 Kepel (1985).
91 Sullivan and Abed-Kotob (1999).
92 Jefferis (2006g).
93 Kepel (1985).
94 Ibid.
95 Al-Rahman later served as the leader of al-Jama'a. He moved to the United States and was arrested in relation to the World Trade Center bombings in 1993. He continues to act as one of the leaders of the organization. While he had temporarily supported a call for non-violence, he revoked it later, and still calls for violent actions against various targets.
96 Kepel (1985).
97 Hafez and Wiktorowicz (2004).
98 Abdo (2000).
99 Hafez (2003).
100 Abdo (2000), p. 21.
101 Ibid.
102 Hafez (2003).
103 Hafez uses these events to make a fascinating argument regarding the use of violence. He contends that it is because the regime acted so vehemently against al-Jama'at, and were so indiscriminate in their repression of members, supporters and even distant affiliates of the organization, that future acts of violence were under-

taken. He argues that when violence from the regime is indiscriminate, social move-ments will be much more likely to use violence in response. This book takes that explanation one step further, arguing that this occurs because organizations perceive themselves as being pushed further to the fringe of society, exacerbating the issues that put them there in the first place.

104 Mubarak (1996), p. 321.
105 Hafez (2003).
106 Ibid.
107 Mubarak (1996), p. 318.
108 Napoli (1998).
109 Halawi (1999).
110 Clearly, there is still much not known about al Jama'a al Islamiyya. As this book was being written, several members imprisoned after Sadat's assassination were released, and before that some of the organization's leaders renounced violence. While living in Cairo, this author attempted to get in touch with members of the organization, but was warned off by numerous intermediary contacts. The author was able to meet with one member, but only very briefly, and despite the questions asked, he provided no new information about the organization. This is likely because the arrangement between the government and the formerly imprisoned members is so new – few members are willing to risk their freedom by talking to someone not authorized by the government – and the government is not interested in undermining their position as a solid partner in the "war on terror." Hopefully, such an impasse will not last forever (indeed, some journalists have been able to get access), as al Jama'a al Islamiyya could offer far greater insight into the development and suste-nance of violent organizations.
111 Jefferis (2006e).
112 Jefferis (2006c).

6 The power of structure

1 Milgram (1974).
2 Zimbardo (2007).
3 All participants had been subject to a battery of personality tests. The 24 participants were selected based on their apparent normal physical and mental health. The guards who displayed such abusive behavior demonstrated no measurable personality differ-ences from the prisoners prior to the start of the experiment.
4 Darley (1992).
5 Ibid.
6 Quoted in Darley (1992), p. 209.
7 Darley (1992).
8 Milgram (1974), p. 62.
9 Ibid.
10 Darley (1992).
11 Bittner (1963).
12 Schattschneider (1960), p. 35.
13 Oberschall (1978).
14 Tilly (1978).
15 McCarthy and Zald (1987).
16 Oberschall (1968), Oberschall (1973), Gamson (1975), Oberschall (1978), Tilly (1978).
17 Nice (1988).
18 Tilly (1978).
19 Gamson (1992); quoted in Oberschall (1993), p. 28.
20 Oberschall (1993).

21 When Beam refers to traitors, he means government officers or others committed to prohibiting the works of the organization.
22 Beam (1992).
23 Ibid.
24 Ibid.
25 Gerlach (2001), p. 303.
26 Ibid.
27 Studies of Islamic terrorist organizations support this hypothesis. Young men with no means of providing for themselves, much less their families, turn to organizations that can meet their physical needs. There are accounts of interviews with terrorists, in which the terrorists explain their introduction to their organization based on that organization's ability to feed them.
28 Stern (2003), p. 165.
29 Shannon (n.d.), Brockhoeft (1994), Jordi (2006), Jefferis (2007b), Jefferis (2007d).
30 Aronson (1992), Hinton (1996).
31 Pennsylvania Christian Coalition (1992).
32 Jefferis (2006a).
33 The amendment would "prevent abortion opponents from declaring bankruptcy to avoid paying fines imposed after violent protests at abortion clinics" (Shenon 2002). However, a Christian Coalition-issued press release indicates a different understanding of the amendment's significance: "The patently unfair amendment, not germane to a bankruptcy reform bill, would discriminate against one class of Americans: peaceful Pro-Life demonstrators. Supporters of the amendment said it was aimed at supposed violence at abortion mills, a red herring argument" (U.S. Newswire 2005).
34 The primary lobbying group in favor of bankruptcy reform was the Coalition for Responsible Bankruptcy Laws, an organization founded by Visa, MasterCard and the American Bankers Association, among others. Ford Motor Co., General Motors and Daimler Chrysler are also members of the organization (Bailey 2002).
35 Jefferis (2006a).
36 Pennsylvania Christian Coalition (1992).
37 Ibid.
38 Mitchell (1993).
39 Ibid.
40 Jefferis (2007a). While the author obtained this information in an interview, it is also available in the bylaws of the Ikhwan, found in Abdalla al-Nafisi's (1989) work, *Al Haraka al-Islamiyya ra'ya Mustaqbaliyya*, pp. 401–416. It can also be found in a summarized form at www.ikhwanweb.com.
41 Ibid.
42 Ibid.
43 Mitchell (1993).
44 Al-Ikhwan al-Muslimin (2007).
45 Ibid.
46 Ibid.
47 Ibid.
48 Jefferis (2006e).
49 This report was provided to the author by a member of the Egyptian government on the condition that it could be read and quoted by the author, but not cited or redistributed.
50 Jefferis (2006e).
51 Ibrahim Hudaiby is the great-grandson of the general guide of the Brotherhood following the death of Hassan al-Banna. Ibrahim is active in the present Brotherhood.
52 Jefferis (2006d).
53 Quoted in Stern (2003).

54 *Army of God Manual.* See author for copy.
55 Jordi (2006).
56 Shannon (2007).
57 Ibid.
58 *Army of God Manual.*
59 Ibid., p. 16.
60 Ibid., p. 51.
61 *Army of God Manual.*
62 Jefferis (2006f).
63 Jefferis (2006g).
64 Ibid.
65 Hafez (2003).
66 Ibid.
67 Prior to this time, the group employed violence but did not have a separate branch for this purpose.
68 Hafez (2003).
69 Gauch (1993).

7 The impact of ideological frames

 1 Eckstein (1980).
 2 Gurr (1970).
 3 Russell (1974), Paige (1975).
 4 Nelson (1979).
 5 Bowen and Gurr (1968), pp. 20–24.
 6 Norris and Inglehart (2004).
 7 Said (1980).
 8 Schwedler (2001).
 9 McVeigh and Sikkink (2001).
10 Euben (1999).
11 Bittner (1963).
12 Bray (2003b).
13 Ibid.
14 Bray (2003a).
15 Husseini (2001).
16 Parsa (2000).
17 Quoted in Weedon (1987), p. 108.
18 Benford and Snow (1988).
19 Ibid.
20 Entman (1993).
21 Robertson (1986).
22 Bittner (1963).
23 Aronson (1992).
24 Hinton (1996).
25 Stephen Jordi might beg to differ from a semantics perspective. He disagrees that the actions he has undertaken for his cause are violent at all. He says that "Violence is defined as unnecessary force. This is a common and unwholesome mistake. Murder, unjust killing is violent. Capital punishment, killing the murderer, is not violence – it is justice. I advocate justice" (in a letter to the author, 2006). But even in his refusal to consider his actions as violence, Jordi maintains the shift in frame we are discussing. Because those who would not advocate justice – indeed, those who would thwart justice – are those in the wrong: which is the same frame as is advocated by the rest of the Army.
26 Hill (2003).

27　Shannon (n.d.).
28　Risen and Thomas (1998), p. 83.
29　Brockhoeft (1994).
30　Spitz is quoted in Stern (2003), p. 152.
31　www.christiangallary.com.
32　The *Nuremburg Files* is a list of abortion providers and affiliates (clinic personnel, judges and politicians on record as supporting abortion, etc.). The list provided as much information as Horsely and O'Toole could get about the individuals, and when any of the individuals was killed by an anti-abortionist, their name is left on the list, with a line drawn through it. Those only wounded are left on in grey typeface.
33　Levin and Pinkerson (2000).
34　Benford and Snow (2000), pp. 611–639.
35　Bray (n.d.).
36　Ibid.
37　Brockhoeft (1994).
38　Ibid.
39　Hill (2003).
40　Ibid.
41　Hill references the *Westminster Larger Catechism* Q99.4, saying in reference to the sixth commandment (Thou shalt not kill) "that as, where a duty is commanded, the contrary sin is forbidden; and where a sin is forbidden, the contrary duty is commanded…" Hill goes on to conclude, "The sin forbidden in the sixth commandment is murder; one of the contrary duties is the prevention of murder."
42　Hill (2003).
43　Brockhoeft (1994).
44　Ibid. www.armyofgod.com/Brock2.html.
45　Thomas Jefferson (1776) *Declaration of Independence*.
46　Hill (2003).
47　In July 1994, *the Ethics and Religious Liberty Commission of the Southern Baptist Convention* issued "The Nashville Statement of Conscience: Why the Killing of Abortion Doctors is Wrong." In the statement, the authors state:

> United States civil law is structured to recognize the broader mandate of government to use force and the threat of force, judiciously and carefully to deter and punish evil and protect the innocent from any wrongdoing. The government protects its citizenry from domestic wrong-doers through the law enforcement and criminal justice systems. Private citizens are rightly barred from authorizing themselves to perform these functions.

48　This is in reference to the biblical passage Mark 9:43: "And if thy hand offend thee, cut it off: it is better for thee to enter into life maimed, than having two hands to go into hell, into the fire that never shall be quenched."
49　Hill (2003).
50　Brockhoeft (1994).
51　Jefferis (2007c).
52　Brockhoeft (1994).
53　Hill (2003).
54　Ibid.
55　Schwartz (1997).
56　Rahnema (1994).
57　Qutb (1964), p. 46.
58　Hudaiby (1997).
59　Qutb (1964), p. 11.
60　Al Baqarah 256; quoted in Hudaiby (1997).
61　Qutb (1964), p. 46.

62 Sullivan and Abed-Kotob (1999).
63 Al-Banna (n.d.).
64 Qutb (1964), p. 48.
65 Ibid., p. 59.
66 Ibid., p. 60.
67 Ibid., p. 61.
68 Ibid., Esposito (1983).
69 Hudaiby (1997).
70 Qutb (1964), p. 63.
71 Jansen (1986), pp. 160–161.
72 Ibid., p. 165.
73 Ibid., p. 193.
74 Ibid., p. 199.
75 Ibid., p. 168.
76 Ibid., p. 170.
77 Kepel (1985).
78 Mubarak (1996), p. 317.
79 Hafez and Wiktorowicz (2004), p. 75.

8 Breaking new ground: the religious-settlers movement in Israel

1 Sprinzak (1991), p. 11.
2 Bickerton and Klausner (2007).
3 Lipsky (2008).
4 Bein (1934); quoted in Lipsky (2008), p. 13.
5 Herzl (1904), p. xix.
6 Ibid., pp. 28–29.
7 Ibid., pp. 89–90.
8 Heilman (1992).
9 Ibid., p. 15.
10 Ibid.
11 Karpin and Friedman (1998), p. 35.
12 Kaplan (1992).
13 Ibid.
14 Ravitzky (1994), p. 304.
15 Friedman (1994), p. 4.
16 Kaplan (1992), p. 153.
17 Friedman and Sivan (1990).
18 Don-Yehiya (1994).
19 Ibid.
20 Quoted in Friedman (1992), p. 17.
21 Sprinzak (1991).
22 Ibid.
23 Ibid.
24 Quoted in Friedman (1992), p. xxx (of introduction).
25 Reznik (2002).
26 Ben-Gurion; quoted in Quigley (2005), p. 98.
27 Ibid., p. 99.
28 Kook; quoted in Sprinzak (1991).
29 Ibid., p. 44.
30 Ibid., p. 44.
31 Aran (1991), p. 273.
32 Friedman (1992).
33 Quoted in Aran (1991), p. 268.

34 Quoted in Don-Yehiya (1994), p. 271.
35 Quoted in Zertal and Eldar (2007), p. 17.
36 Ibid., p. 19.
37 Ibid.
38 Friedman and Sivan (1990).
39 Quoted in Friedman (1992), p. 18.
40 Aran (1991), p. 1.
41 Don-Yehiya (1994), p. 276.
42 Sprinzak (1991), p. 104.
43 In response to Sprinzak (1986), p. 37.
44 Quoted in Friedman (1992), p. 32.
45 Aran (1991), p. 280.
46 Zertal and Eldar (2007).
47 Ibid.
48 Sprinzak (1999).
49 Zertal and Eldar (2007).
50 Ibid.
51 Ibid., p. 131.

9 Settling the case for violence: the future of religious violence in Israel

1 Aran (1991), 1, p. 277.
2 Sprinzak (1986), p. 6.
3 Aran (1991), 1.
4 Sprinzak (1986).
5 Quoted in Lustick (1988), p. 85.
6 Quoted in Sprinzak (1986), p. 7.
7 Quoted in Lustick (1988), p. 84.
8 Sprinzak (1986), p. 6.
9 Aran (1991), 1, p. 290.
10 Ibid., p. 290.
11 Sprinzak (1981).
12 Aran (1991), 1.
13 Ibid.
14 Sprinzak (1991), p. 82.
15 Sprinzak (1986).
16 Lustick (1988), p. 117.
17 Quoted in Zertal and Eldar (2007), p. 89.
18 Don-Yehiya (1994).
19 Zertal and Eldar (2007).
20 Ibid.
21 Don-Yehiya (1994).
22 Newman and Hermann (1992).
23 Sprinzak (1986), p. 10.
24 Ibid., Sprinzak (1986).
25 Aran (1991), 1, p. 288.
26 Karpin and Friedman (1998), pp. 66, 68.
27 Ibid., p. 69.
28 Ibid.
29 Sprinzak (1999), p. 253.
30 Ibid., p. 254.
31 Ibid., p. 256.
32 Ibid., p. 280.

33 Karpin and Friedman (1998).
34 Don-Yehiya (1994).
35 Yishai (1987).
36 Don-Yehiya (1994), p. 267.
37 Kaplan (1992), p. 188.
38 Lustick (1988), p. 62.
39 Yishai (1987).
40 Ibid.
41 www.ynet.co.il/english/articles/0,7340,L-3020756,00.html.
42 Karpin and Friedman (1998).
43 Ibid.
44 www.amana.co.il/Index.asp?CategoryID=101&ArticleID=166.
45 Aran (1991), 1, p. 283.
46 Sprinzak (1986).
47 Aran (1991), 1, p. 283.
48 Yishai (1987).
49 Ibid., p. 123.
50 Sprinzak (1991).
51 Friedman (1986).
52 Interviews with Etzion reveal 20 people were to have participated in the attacks (see Sprinzak 1986), while other accounts put the number closer to three-dozen (see Karpin and Friedman 1998).
53 Zertal and Eldar (2007), p. 76.
54 Sprinzak (1986).
55 Karpin and Friedman (1998).
56 Ibid.
57 Hanan Porat; quoted in Sprinzak (1991), p. 66.
58 Lustick (1988), p. 37.
59 Rabbi Kook; quoted in Friedman and Sivan (1990), p. 18.
60 Zvi Yehuda Kook; quoted in Sprinzak (1991), p. 46.
61 Aran (1990), p. 162.
62 Rabbi Avraham Yitzhak Kook; quoted in Lustick (1988), p. 30.
63 Quoted in Don-Yehiya (1994), p. 279.
64 Quoted in Sprinzak (1986).
65 Sprinzak (1999).
66 Erlanger (2004).
67 Erlanger (2005).

Conclusion

1 Early December 2007.
2 Hebrews 11:1 (NIV Version).

Bibliography

Anon. (1975). "US Civil Rights Commission: Any Abortion Amendment Unconstitutional: Repeal Existing Anti-Abortion Laws." *Family Planning Perspectives* **7**(3): 116–117.

Holy Bible: New International Version, Tyndale House Publishers.

Anon. (1997). "The Islamic State in Egypt is Approaching." *Nida'ul Islam*, April–May.

Anon. (2003). "Excerpts from Condemned Abortion Doctor Killer Paul Hill." Associated Press. Online, available at: http://www.fadp.org/news/TampaBayOnline-20030903.htm.

Aaronson, T. (2004). "Bombs for Babies. Stephen Jordi planned to blow up abortion clinics. Does that make him a terrorist?" *News Times*, 15 July.

Abdo, G. (2000). *No God But God: Egypt and the Triumph of Islam*. New York, Oxford University Press.

Abed-Kotob, S. (1995). "The Accomodationists Speak: Goals and Strategies of the Muslim Brotherhood of Egypt." *International Journal of Middle East Studies* **27**(3): 321–339.

Abu al-Sa'ud, Mahmud (1989). *The Islamic Movement: Future Vision and Papers on Self Criticism (Al Haraka al-Islamiyya ra'ya Mustaqbaliyya)*. Cairo: Madbuli Library.

Al-Banna, H. (n.d.) "To What Do We Invite Humanity?" *Ikhwan Web*. Online, available at: http://www.ikhwanweb.com/Article.asp?ID=804&SectionID=104.

Al-Banna, H. (1978). *Five Tracts of Hassan al-Banna (1906–1949): A Selection from the Majmu'at Rasa'il al-Imam al-Shahid Hasan al-Banna*. Berkeley, University of California Press.

Al-Ikhwan al-Muslimin, a.-I. (2007). Muslim Brotherhood: Structure and Spread. *Ikhwan Web*. Online, available at: www.ikhwanweb.net/Article.asp?ID=817&LevelID=2&SectionID=116 (last accessed June 14, 2008).

al-Zayat, M. (2004). *The Road to Al-Qaeda: the Story of Bin Laden's Right-Hand Man*. London, Pluto Press.

Aldridge, A. (2000). *Religion in the Contemporary World: a Sociological Introduction*. Cambridge, Polity Press.

Altman, I. E. (2006). "Current Trends in the Ideology of the Egyptian Muslim Brotherhood." *Current Trends in Islamist Ideology* 4.

Aminzade, R. R., J. A. Goldstone, D. McAdam and E. J. Perry (2001). *Silence and Voice in the Study of Contentious Politics*. Cambridge, Cambridge University Press.

Ansari, Hamied N. (1984). "The Islamic Militants in Egyptian Politics." *International Journal of Middle East Studies* 16(1) (March): 123–144.

Aran, G. (1990). "Redemption as a Catastrophe: the Gospel of Gush Emunim," in M. Friedman and E. Sivan (eds.), *Religious Radicalism and Politics in the Middle East*." New York, State University of New York, pp. 157–176.

Aran, G. (1991). "Jewish Zionist Fundamentalism: the Bloc of the Faithful in Israel," in R. S. Appleby and M. E. Marty (eds.), *Fundamentalisms Observed*. Chicago, University of Chicago Press, pp. 265–344.

Arjomand, S. (1984). *From Nationalism to Revolutionary Islam*. New York, Macmillan.

Aronson, E. (1992). "The Return of the Repressed: Dissonance Theory Makes a Comeback." *Psychological Inquiry* 3(4): 303–311.

American Atheists (2000). "Robertson Again Calls for Christian Revolt over Supreme Court Prayer, Abortion Rulings." *Flashline*, American Atheists.

Bailey, H. (2002). *Going For Broke: Lobbying and the Bankruptcy Bill*. Washington, D.C., The Center for Responsive Politics.

Baird-Windle, P. and E. J. Bader (2001). *Targets of Hatred: Anti-Abortion Terrorism*. New York, Palgrave.

Beam, L. (1992). "Leaderless Resistance." *The Seditionist* **12**. Online, available at: http://www.louisbeam.com/leaderless.htm.

Bein, A. (1934). *Theodor Herzl*. Philadelphia, Jewish Publication Society of America Tranlation published in 1941; trans. by Maurice Samuel.

Beinin, J. and J. Stork (eds.) (1997). *Political Islam: Essays from Middle East Report*. Berkeley, University of California Press.

Benford, R. D. and D. A. Snow (1988). "Ideology, Frame Resonance, and Participant Mobilization," in B. Klandermans, H. Kriesi and S. Tarrow (eds.), *From Structure to Action: Comparing Movement Participation across Cultures, International Social Movement Research*. Greenwich, JAI Press.

Benford, R. D. and D. A. Snow (2000). "Framing Processes and Social Movements: an Overview and Assessment." *Annual Review of Sociology* 611–639.

Bennett, J. (1996). "Leader of Christian Coalition Denies Shifting on Abortion." *New York Times*, May 5.

Berger, P. (1967). *The Sacred Canopy*. New York, Doubleday.

Bickerton, I. and C. Klausner (2007). *A History of the Arab Israeli Conflict*. Upper Saddle River, Pearson Prentice Hall.

Birnbaum, J. H. (1995). "The Gospel According to Ralph: Reed's Burgeoning Christian Coalition Evokes Zeal and Fear as it Mobilizes to Dominate the Political Order." *Time* 145(20): 28–36.

Bittner, E. (1963). "Radicalism and the Organization of Radical Movements." *American Sociological Review* 28(6): 928–940.

Blanchard, D. A. (1994). *The Anti-Abortion Movement and the Rise of the Religious Right*. New York, Twayne Publishers.

Blanchard, D. A. and T. J. Prewitt (1993). *Religious Violence and Abortion*. Gainsville, University Press of Florida.

Bolce, L. and G. de Maio (1999). "The Anti-Christian Fundamentalist Factor in Contemporary Politics." *The Public Opinion Quarterly* 63(4): 508–542.

Boston, Rob (2001). "Guerillas and Bodybags and Sharks ... Oh My! A Short History of Pat Robertson's Christian Coalition." *Euphorian*. Online, available at: www.mail-archive.com/ctrl@listserv.aol.com/msg83571.html.

Bowen, D. and T. R. Gurr (1968). "Deprivation, Mobility and Orientation Toward Protest of the Urban Poor." *American Behavioral Scientist* (March–April): 20–24.

Bower, A. (1996). "Soldier in The Army of God." *Albion Monitor*.

Bray, M. (n.d.) "The Restoration of Fatherhood (Or Some Fresh Ideas for Promise Keepers)." Online, available at: http://www.armyofgod.com/MikeBrayFathersRights.html.

Bray, M. (1988). *A Time to Kill: a Study Concerning the use of Force and Abortion.* Bowie, Reformation Press.

Bray, M. (2003a). "A Call for Prolife Organizations to Repentance." Online, available at: http://www.armyofgod.com/MikeBray1.html

Bray, M. (2003b). "James Kopp: Man of Peace." Online, available at: http://www.armyofgod.com/MikeBray1.html.

Brockhoeft, J. (1994). "The Brockhoeft Report." *Prayer & Action News.* Online, available at: http://www.armyofgod.com/BrockSelect.html.

Brooks, C. (2000). "Civil Rights Liberalism and the Suppression of a Republican Realignment in the United States, 1972–1996." *American Sociological Review* 65: 483–505.

Burgat, F. and W. Dowell (1993). *The Islamic Movement in North Africa.* Austin, Center for Middle Eastern Studies at the University of Texas in Austin.

Carter, S. L. (2000). *God's Name in Vain: the Wrongs and Rights of Religion in Politics.* New York, Basic Books.

Cavanaugh, M. (1986). "Secularization and the Politics of Traditionalism: the Case of the Right to Life Movement." *Sociological Forum* 1(2): 251–283.

Clark, J. (2006). "Field Research Methods in the Middle East." *PS: Political Science and Politics* 49.

Clarke, A. "Moral Protest, Status Defense, and the Anti-Abortion Campaign." *The British Journal of Sociology* 38(2): 235–253.

Clarkson, F. (1993). "Inside The Covert Coalition." *Church and State.* Online, available at: http://www.theocracywatch.org/clarkson_inside.html.

Cooper, M. (1982). *The Transformation of Egypt.* Baltimore, The Johns Hopkins University Press.

Crabbs, J. J. (1975). "Politics, History and Culture in Nasser's Egypt." *International Journal of Middle East Studies* 6(4): 386–420.

Craig, B. H. and D. M. O'Brien (1993). *Abortion and American Politics.* Chatham, Chatham House Publishers.

Cuneo, M. (1989). *Catholics Against the Church: Anti-Abortion Protest in Toronto, 1969–1985.* Toronto, University of Toronto Press.

Dahl, R. A. (1967). *Pluralist Democracy in the United States: Conflict and Consent.* Chicago, Rand McNally and Company.

Darley, J. M. (1992). "Social Organization for the Production of Evil." *Psychological Inquiry* 3(2): 199–218.

Davis, E. (1984). "Ideology, Social Class and Islamic Radicalism in Modern Egypt," in S. A. Arjomand (ed.), *From Nationalism to Revolutionary Islam.* London, Macmillan Press.

Davis, M. (2006). *More than a Purpose: an Evangelical Response to Rick Warren and the Megachurch Movement.* Enumclaw, Pleasant Word Press.

Dejowski, E. (1992). "Public Endorsement of Restrictions of Three Aspects of Free Expression by Homosexuals: Socio-Demographic and Trend Analysis 1973–1988." *Journal of Homosexuality* 23: 1–18.

Dekmejian, H. (1995). *Islam in Revolution: Fundamentalism in the Arab World.* Syracuse, Syracuse University Press.

Denoeux, G. (1993). *Urban Unrest in the Middle East: a Comparative Study of Informal Networks in Egypt, Iran and Lebanon.* Albany, SUNY Press.

Djupe, P. A. and J. T. Grant (2001). "Religious Institutions and Political Participation in America." *Journal for the Scientific Study of Religion* 40(2): 303–314.

Don-Yehiya, E. (1994). "The Book and the Sword: The Nationalist Yeshivot and Political Radicalism in Israel," in M. E. Marty and R. S. Appleby (eds.), *Accounting for Fundamentalism: The Dynamic Character of Movements.* Chicago, University of Chicago Press.

Durkheim, E. (1915). *The Elementary Forms of the Religious Life.* London, Allen and Unwin.

Easton, N. J. (2000). *Gang of Five: Leaders at the Center of the Conservative Crusade.* New York, Simon and Schuster.

Eckstein, H. (1980). "Theoretical Approaches to Explaining Collective Political Violence," in T. R. Gurr (ed.), *Handbook of Political Conflict.* New York, Free Press.

El-Ghobashy, M. (2005). "The Metamorphosis of the Egyptian Muslim Brothers." *International Journal of Middle East Studies* 37: 373–395.

Entman, R. (1993). "Framing: Toward Clarification of a Fractured Paradigm." *Journal of Communication* 43(4): 51–58.

Erlanger, S. (2004). "As Gaza Pullout Vote Nears, Tension Among Israelis Rises." *New York Times,* October 21. Online, available at: http://www.nytimes.com/2004/10/21/international/middleeast/21israel.html?fta=y.

Erlanger, S. (2005). "Sharon Criticizes Netanyahu for Quitting over Gaza Plan." *New York Times,* August 11. Online, available at: http://query.nytimes.com/gst/fullpage.htm l?res=9903E1DC143EF932A2575BC0A9639C8B63&sec=&spon=&pagewanted=all.

Esposito, J. L. (1980). *Islam and Development: Religion and Sociopolitical Change.* Syracuse, Syracuse University Press.

Esposito, J. L. (1983). *Voices of Resurgent Islam.* New York, Oxford University Press.

Euben, R. (1999). *Enemy in the Mirror: Islamic Fundamentalism and the Limits of Modern Rationalism – a Work of Comparative Political Theory.* Princeton, Princeton University Press.

Fahmy, K. (2005). "An Officer and an Ottoman Gentleman: the Similarities Between Gamal Abdel Nasser and Mohammed Ali." *Al-Ahram Weekly* 758, 1–7 September.

Faksh, M. (1997). *The Future of Islam in the Middle East: Fundamentalism in Egypt, Algeria, and Saudi Arabia.* Westport, Praeger Publishers.

Faux, M. (1990). *Crusaders: Voices from the Abortion Front.* New York, Carol Publishing Group.

Ferree, M. (1974). "A Woman for President? Changing Responses 1958–1972." *Public Opinion Quarterly* 38: 390–399.

Freud, S. (1957). *The Future of an Illusion.* London, Hogarth Press.

Friedman, M. (1994). "Habad as Messianic Fundamentalism," in M. E. Marty and R. S. Appleby (eds.), *Accounting for Fundamentalisms: the Dynamic Character of Movements.* Chicago, University of Chicago Press, pp. 328–360.

Friedman, M. and E. Sivan (1990). *Religious Radicalism and Politics in the Middle East.* New York, State University of New York Press.

Friedman, R. (1986). "Inside the Jewish Terrorist Underground." *Journal of Palestine Studies* 15(2): 190–201.

Friedman, R. (1992). *Zealots for Zion: Inside Israel's West Bank Settlement.* New York, Random House.

Gabriel, M. A. (2002). *Islam and Terrorism: What the Quran Really Teaches About Christianity, Violence, and the Goals of Islamic Jihad.* Lake Mary, Charisma House.

Gamson, W. (1975). *The Strategy of Social Protest.* Homewood, Dorsey.

Gamson, W. (1992). *Talking Politics*. Cambridge, Cambridge University Press.

Gauch, S. (1993). "Terror on the Nile." *Africa Report* 38(3): 32–35.

Gerlach, L. P. (2001). "The Structure of Social Movements: Environmental Activism and its Opponents," in D. Ronfeldt and J. Arquilla (eds.), *Networks and Netwars: The Future of Terror, Crime and Militancy*. Santa Monica: Rand Corporation.

Ginsberg, F. (1998). "Rescuing the Nation: Operation Rescue and the Rise of Anti-Abortion Militance," in R. Solinger (ed.), *Abortion Wars: a Half Century of Struggle*. Los Angeles, University of California Press.

Girard, R. (1977). *Violence and the Sacred*. London, Johns Hopkins University Press.

Glenn, N. and C. N. Weaver (1979). "Attitudes Toward Premarital, Extramarital, and Homosexual Relations in the US in the 1970s." *Journal of Sex Research* 15: 108–118.

Gomma, A. (1983). "Islamic Fundamentalism in Egypt During the 1930s and 1970s: Comparative Notes," in G. Warburg and U. Kupferschimdt (ed.), *Islam, Nationalism and Radicalism in Egypt and the Sudan*. New York, Praeger.

Granberg, D. and B. W. Granberg (1980). "Abortion Attitudes, 1965–1980: Trends and Determinants." *Family Planning Perspectives* 12(5): 250–261.

Green, J. C. and J. L. Guth (1988). "The Christian Right in the Republican Party: the Case of Pat Robertson's Supporters." *The Journal of Politics* 50(1): 150–165.

Green, J. C., J. L. Guth and K. Hill (1993). "Faith and Election: the Christian Right in Congressional Campaigns 1978–1988." *The Journal of Politics* 55(1): 80–91.

Griffin, M. (n.d.) Untitled essay. Online, available at: www.armyofgod.com/MichaelGriffin.html.

Gurr, T. (1970). *Why Men Rebel*. Princeton, Princeton University Press.

Gusfield, J. R. (1966). *Symbolic Crusade: Status Politics and the American Temperance Movement*. Urbana, University of Illinois Press.

Hafez, M. M. (2003). *Why Muslims Rebel: Repression and Resistance in the Islamic World*. Boulder, Lynne Rienner.

Hafez, M. M. and Q. Wiktorowicz (2004). "Violence as Contention in the Egyptian Islamic Movement," in Q. Wiktorowicz (ed.), *Islamic Activism: a Social Movement Theory Approach*. Bloomington, Indiana University Press.

Halawi, Jailan (1999). "Bin Laden Behind Massacre?" *Al Ahram Weekly*, 20–26 May, p. 430. Online, available at: http://weekly.ahram.org.eg/1999/430/eg21.htm

Halebsky, S. (1976). *Mass Society and Political Conflict*. New York, Cambridge University Press.

Hart, H. L. A. (1974). "Abortion Law Reform: the English Experience," in R. Perkins (ed.), *Abortion: Pro and Con*. Cambridge, Shenckman.

Heilman, S. (1992). *Defenders of the Faith: Inside Ultra-Orthodox Jewry*. Berkeley, University of California Press.

Herzl, T. (1904). *The Jewish State: an Attempt at a Modern Solution of the Jewish Question*. New York, The Maccabean Publishing Company.

Hill, P. (2003). "Mix my blood with the blood of the Unborn." Online, available at: http://www.armyofgod.com/PHillBookForward.html.

Hinton, A. (1996). "Agents of Death: Explaining the Cambodian Genocide in terms of Psychosocial Dissonance." *American Anthropologist* 98(4): 818–831.

Hout, M. and C. Fischer (2002). "Why More Americans Have No Religious Preference: Politics and Generations." *American Sociological Review* 67(2): 165–190.

Hudaiby, M. (1997). "Islam in Politics and Power." *Harvard International Review* 19(2).

Husseini, S. (2001). "Ashcroft and Anti-Abortion Extremism: Widow of Dr. Barnett Slepian and Others Question Whether Ashcroft would Protect Abortion Providers."

Institute for Public Accuracy. Washington, D.C. Online, available at: www.accuracy. org/newsrelease.php?articleId=757&type=&searchterms=Ashcroft%20and%20Anti-Abortion.

Ibrahim, S. E. (1980). "Anatomy of Egypt's Militant Islamic Groups: Methodological Notes and Preliminary Findings." *International Journal of Middle East Studies* 12(4): 423–453.

Ismail, S. (2001). "The Paradox of Islamist Politics." *Middle East Report* 221: 34–39.

Jacobs, H. (1970). *Weatherman*. Berkeley, Ramparts Press.

Jansen, J. J. G. (1986). *The Neglected Duty: the Creed of Sadat's Assassins and Islamic Resurgence in the Middle East*. New York, Macmillan Publishing Company.

Jefferis, J. (2006b). Interview with Dr. Mun'em Abul Fotouh.

Jefferis, J. (2006f). Interview with Abul Ela Maady.

Jefferis, J. (2006g). Interview with Dia'a Rashwan.

Jefferis, J. (2006c). Interview with Dr. Habib.

Jefferis, J. (2006d). Interview with Ibrahim Hudaiby.

Jefferis, J. (2006e). Interview with Islam Lotfy.

Jefferis, J. (2006a). Interview with Jim Backlin.

Jefferis, J. (2006h). Interview with Pat Robertson.

Jefferis, J. (2006i). Interview with El Kobri.

Jefferis, J. (2007a). Email from Ibrahim Hudaiby.

Jefferis, J. (2007c). Interview with Bob Lokey.

Jefferis, J. (2007d). Interview with Bob Lokey.

Jefferis, J. (2007b). Interview with Dave Leach.

Jenkins, C. J. and B. Klandermans (eds.) (1995). *The Politics of Social Protest*. Minne–apolis, University of Minnesota Press.

Jenkins, C. J. and C. Perrow (1977). "Insurgency of the Powerless: Farm Worker Movements 1946–1972." *American Sociological Review* 42: 249–268.

Jordi, S. (2006). Personal Correspondence.

Juergensmeyer, M. (1992). "Preface," in C. Candland (ed.), *The Spirit of Violence: an Interdisciplinary Bibliography of Violence*. New York, Harry Frank Guggenheim Foundation.

Juergensmeyer, M. (2000). *Terror in the Mind of God: the Global Rise of Religious Violence*. Berkeley, University of California Press.

Kaplan, L. (1992). *Fundamentalism in Comparative Perspective*. Amherst, University of Massachusetts Press.

Karpin, M. and I. Friedman (1998). *Murder in the Name of God: the Plot to Kill Yitzhak Rabin*. New York, Metropolitan Books.

Kepel, G. (1985). *Muslim Extremism in Egypt: the Prophet and the Pharaoh*. Berkeley, University of California Press.

Khadduri, M. (1970). *Political Trends in the Arab World: the Role of Ideas and Ideals in Politics*. Baltimore, Johns Hopkins Press.

Kingdon, J. (1984). *Agendas, Alternatives, and Public Policies*. Boston, Little Brown.

King, K., J. O'Balswick and I. E. Robinson (1977). "Continuing Premarital Sexual Revolution Among College Females." *Journal of Marriage and Family* 39(3): 455–459.

Klandermans, B., H. Kriesi and S. Tarrow (1988). *International Social Movements Research: From Structure to Action – Comparing Social Movement Research Across Cultures*. London, Jai Press Inc.

Kornhauser, W. (1959). *The Politics of Mass Society*. New York, Free Press.

Lenski, G. (1963). *The Religious Factor.* New York, Doubleday.

Levin, M. and D. Pinkerson (2000). *Soldiers in the Army of God.* Home Box Office television.

Lewis, B. (2002). *What Went Wrong: Western Impact and Middle Eastern Response.* Oxford, Oxford University Press.

Lia, B. (1998). *The Society of Muslim Brothers in Egypt: the Rise of an Islamic Movement 1928–1942.* Reading, Ithaca Press.

Lipsky, L. (2008). *The Jewish State.* Project Gutenberg eBook. Online, available at: http://www.gutenberg.org/files/25282/25282-8.txt.

Loftus, J. (2001). "America's Liberalization in Attitudes Toward Homosexuality, 1973–1998." *American Sociological Review* 66: 762–782.

Luker, K. (1984). *Abortion and the Politics of Motherhood.* Berkeley, University of California Press.

Lustick, I. S. (1988). *For the Land and the Lord: Jewish Fundamentalism in Israel.* New York, Council on Foreign Relations Press.

McAdam, D. (1982). *The Political Process and the Development of the Black Insurgency.* Chicago, University of Chicago Press.

McAdam, D., J. D. McCarthy and M. N. Zald (1996). *Comparative Perspectives on Social Movements.* Cambridge, Cambridge University Press.

McAdam, D., S. Tarrow and C. Tilly (2001). *Dynamics of Contention.* Cambridge, Cambridge University Press.

MacArthur, J. (2001). *Ashamed of the Gospel: When the Church Becomes Like the World.* Wheaton, Crossway Books.

McBroom, W. (1986). "Changes in Role Orientation of Women: a Study of Sex Role Traditionalism over a Five Year Period." *Journal of Family Issues* 7: 149–159.

McCarthy, J. D. and M. N. Zald (1987). *Social Movements in Organizational Society.* New Brunswick, Transaction Books.

McKeegan, M. (1992). *Abortion Politics: Mutiny in the Ranks of the Right.* New York, Free Press.

McTernan, O. (2003). *Violence in God's Name: Religion in an Age of Conflict.* Maryknoll, Orbis Books.

McVeigh, R. and D. Sikkink (2001). "God, Politics and Protest: Religious Beliefs and the Legitimation of Contentious Tactics." *Social Forces* 79(4): 1425–1458.

Mady, A.-E. e. (2004). *Violent Egyptian Islamist Groups: Historical Roots, Intellectual Foundations, and Critical Self-Appraisals.* Cairo, Al Wasat Party.

Marx, K. (1843). *Contribution to the Critique of Hegel's Philosophy of Right.* Cambridge University Press.

Mason, K. and Y.-H. Lu (1988). "Attitudes Toward Women's Familial Roles: Changes in the United States, 1977–1985." *Gender and Society* 2(1): 39–57.

Mason, K., J. Czajka and S. Arber (1976). "Change in US Women's Sex-Role Attitudes." *American Sociological Review* 41: 573–596.

Means, C. (1970). "A Historian's View," in R. Hall (ed.), *Abortion in a Changing World.* New York, Columbia University Press.

Means, C. (1971). "The Phoenix of Abortional Freedom: Is a Penumbral or 19th Amendment Right about to Arise from the Legislative Ashes of a 14th Century Common-Law Liberty?" *New York Law Forum* 17: 335–362.

Milgram, S. (1974). *Obedience to Authority.* London, Tavistock.

Mitchell, R. P. (1993). *The Society of Muslim Brothers.* New York, Oxford University Press.

Mohr, J. (1978). *Abortion in America: the Origin and Evolution of National Policy – 1899–1900*. New York, Columbia University Press.

Morris, A. D. and C. M. Mueller (1992). *Frontiers in Social Movement Theory*. New Haven, Yale University Press.

Mubarak, H. (1996). "What Does the Gama'a Islamiyya Want? An Interview with Tal'at Fu'ad Qasim," in J. Beinin and J. Stork (eds) *Political Islam: Essays from Middle East Report*. Berkeley: University of California Press.

Munson, H. J. (1986). "The Social Base of Islamic Militancy in Morocco." *Middle East Journal* 40(2): 267–284.

Munson, Z. (2001). "Islamic Mobilization: Social Movement Theory and the Egyptian Muslim Brotherhood." *The Sociological Quarterly* 42(4): 487–510.

Napoli, J. (1998). "Egyptian Government Continues to Blame West for Ills after Luxor Massacre." *Washington Report on Middle East Affairs*: 47–48.

Nelson, J. M. (1979). *Access to Power: Politics and the Urban Poor in Developing Nations*. Princeton, Princeton University Press.

Newman, D. and T. Hermann (1992). "A Comparative Study of Gush Emunim and Peace Now." *Middle Eastern Studies* 28(3): 509–530.

Nice, D. C. (1988). "Abortion Clinic Bombings as Political Violence." *American Journal of Political Science* 32(1): 178–195.

Norris, P. and R. Inglehart (2004). *Sacred and Secular: Religion and Politics Worldwide*. Cambridge, Cambridge University Press.

Nye, M. A. (1993). "Changing Support for Civil Rights: House and Senate Voting 1963–1988." *Political Research Quarterly* 46(4): 799–822.

Oberschall, A. (1968). "The Los Angeles Riot of 1965." *Social Problems* 15(3): 322–341.

Oberschall, A. (1973). *Social Conflict and Social Movements*. Englewood Cliffs, Prentice-Hall, Inc.

Oberschall, A. (1978). "Theories of Social Conflict." *Annual Review of Sociology* 4: 291–315.

Oberschall, A. (1993). *Social Movements*. New Brunswick, Transaction Books.

Olasky, M. (1995). *Abortion Rites: a Social History of Abortion in America*. Washington, D.C., Regnery Publishing Co.

Paige, J. M. (1975). *Agrarian Revolutions*. New York, Free Press.

Parsa, M. (2000). *States, Ideologies and Social Revolutions: a Comparative Analysis of Iran, Nicaragua and the Philippines*. Cambridge, Cambridge University Press.

Pastor, G. S., W. J. Stone and R. B. Rapoport (1999). "Candidate-Centered Sources of Party Change: the Case of Pat Robertson, 1988." *The Journal of Politics* 61(2): 423–444.

Pennsylvania Christian Coalition (1992). County Action Plan.

Petchetsky, R. (1984). *Abortion and Women's Choice: the State, Sexuality, and Reproductive Freedom*. New York, Longman.

Pipes, D. (2002). *Militant Islam Reaches America*. New York, W.W. Norton and Company.

Pipes, D. (2004). "Identifying Moderate Muslims." *New York Sun*, November 23. Online, available at: www.danielpipes.org/2226/identifying-moderate-muslims.

Quigley, J. (2005). *The Case for Palestine: an International Law Perspective*. Durham, Duke University Press.

Qutb, S. (1964). *Milestones (Ma'alim fi al-Tariq)*. Damascus, Dar al-Ilm.

Rahman, O. (1989). *Mithaq al-Amal al-Islami (The Charter of Islamic Action)*. Cairo.

Rahnema, A. (1994). *Pioneers of Islamic Revival*. London, Zed Books.

Ramadan, A. A. (1991). "Fundamentalist Influence in Egypt: the Strategies of the Muslim Brotherhood and the Takfir Groups," in M. E. Marty and R. S. Appleby (eds.), *Fundamentalisms and the State: Remaking Polities, Economies and Militance*. Chicago, University of Chicago Press.

Ravitzky, A. (1994). "The Contemporary Lubavitch Hasidic Movement," in M. E. Marty and R. S. Appleby (eds.), *Accounting for Fundamentalism: the Dynamic Character of Movements*. Chicago, University of Chicago Press, pp. 303–327.

Reed, R. (1996). *Active Faith: How Christians Are Changing the Soul of American Politics*. New York, Simon and Schuster.

Reznik, S. (2002). "Political Culture in Israel in the Era of Peace: the Jewish Underground and the Conscientious Objection Movement, 1979–1984." *Peace and Change* 27(3): 357–384.

Risen, J. and J. Thomas (1998). *Wrath of Angels: the American Abortion War*. New York, Basic Books.

Robertson, P. (1986). "A Presidential Bid Launched." Online, available at: www.patrobertson.com/Speeches/PresidentialBidLaunched.asp.

Robertson, P. (1989). *The Plan*. Nashville, Thomas Nelson Publishers.

Rosefsky-Wickham, C. (2002). *Mobilizing Islam: Religion, Activism and Political Change in Egypt*. New York, Columbia University Press.

Rubin, B. (1990). *Islamic Fundamentalism in Egyptian Politics*. New York, St Martin's Press.

Russell, D. E. H. (1974). *Rebellion, Revolution, and Armed Force: a Comparative Study of Fifteen Countries with Special Emphasis on Cuba and South Africa*. New York, Academic Press.

Safran, N. (1961). *Egypt in Search of Political Community: an Analysis of the Intellectual and Political Evolution of Egypt, 1804–1952*. Cambridge, Harvard University Press.

Said, E. (1980). "Islam Through Western Eyes." *The Nation*, April 26. Online, available at: www.thenation.com/doc/19800426/19800426said.

Sauer, R. (1974). "Attitudes Toward Abortion in America: 1800–1973." *Population Studies* 28(1): 53–67.

Schaeffer, F. (1976). *How Then Should We Live? The Rise and Decline of Western Thought and Culture*. Old Tappan, Fleming H. Revell Company.

Schaeffer, F. (1980). *A Christian Manifesto*. Wheaton, Crossway Books.

Schaeffer, F. (1985). "Foreword," in J. Scheidler (ed.), *Closed: 99 Ways to Stop Abortion*. Westchester, Crossway Books.

Schaeffer, F. and E. C. Koop (1978). *Whatever Happened to the Human Race?* Old Tappan, Fleming H. Revell Company.

Schattschneider, E. E. (1960). *The Semi-Sovereign People*. New York, Holt, Rinehart and Winston.

Schreiber, E. (1978). "Education and Change in American Opinions on a Woman for President." *Public Opinion Quarterly* 42: 171–182.

Schwartz, R. M. (1997). *The Curse of Cain: the Violent Legacy of Monotheism*. Chicago, University of Chicago Press.

Schwedler, J. (2001). "Islamic Identity: Myth, Menace or Mobilizer?" *SAIS Review* 21(2): 1–17.

Shannon, S. (n.d.) *Join the Army (Or How to Destroy a Killing Center if You're Just an Old Grandma Who Can't Even Get the Fire Started in her Fireplace)*. Army of God.

Shannon, S. (n.d.) *Toward the Use of Force*. Army of God. Online, available at: www.armyofgod.com/ShelleyForce.html.

Sivan, E. (1985). *Radical Islam, Medieval Theology and Modern Politics*. New Haven, Yale University Press.

Smelser, N. J. (1962). *Theory of Collective Behavior*. New York, Free Press.

Smith, D. (2001). "No Regrets for a Love of Explosives: in a Memoir of Sorts, a War Protester Talks of Life with the Weathermen. *New York Times*, September 11. Online, available at: www.nytimes.com/2001/09/11/books/no-regrets-for-love-explosives-memoir-sorts-war-protester-talks-life-with.html.

Smith, T. W. (1990). "Liberal and Conservative Trends in the United States since WWII." *Public Opinion Quarterly* 54: 479–507.

Solinger, R. (1998). *Abortion Wars: a Half Century of Struggle*. Los Angeles, University of California Press.

Spencer, H. (1862). *First Principles*. Online, available at: http://socserv2.socsci.mcmaster.ca/~econ/ugcm/3ll3/spencer/firprin.html.

Spingola, C. (n.d.) "Thanks be to God and the Christian Terrorist: A Commentary." Online, available at: www.armyofgod.com/ChuckSpingola.html.

Sprinzak, E. (1981). "Gush Emunim: The Tip of the Iceberg." *The Jerusalem Quarterly* 21. online, available at: www.geocities.com/alabasters_archive/gush_iceberg.html.

Sprinzak, E. (1986). *Fundamentalism, Terrorism and Democracy*. Washington, D.C., The Wilson Center.

Sprinzak, E. (1986). *Gush Emunim: The Politics of Zionist Fundamentalism in Israel*. The American Jewish Committee: Institute of Human Relations.

Sprinzak, E. (1991). *The Ascendance of Israel's Radical Right*. Oxford, Oxford University Press.

Sprinzak, E. (1999). *Brother Against Brother: Violence and Extremism in Israeli Politics from Atalena to the Rabin Assasination*. New York, Free Press.

Stern, J. (2003). *Terror in the Name of God: Why Religious Militants Kill*. New York, HarperCollins.

Strickler, J. and N. Danigelis (2002). "Changing Frameworks in Attitudes Toward Abortion." *Sociological Forum* 17(2): 187–201.

Sullivan, D. and S. Abed-Kotob (1999). *Islam in Contemporary Egypt: Civil Society vs. the State*. London, Lynne Rienner Publishers.

Tallichet, S. and F. Willits (1986). "Gender Role Attitude Change of Young Women: Influential Factors from a Panel Study." *Social Psychology Quarterly* 49: 219–227.

Tamney, J. and S. Johnson (1988). "Explaining Support for the Moral Majority." *Sociological Forum* 3(2): 234–255.

Tarrow, S. (1998). *Power in Movement*. Cambridge, Cambridge University Press.

National Consortium for the Study of Terrorism and Responses to Terrorism (2007). *Global Terrorism Database*. US Department of Homeland Security (at University of Maryland).

Terry, R. (1988). *Operation Rescue*. New York, Randall Terry.

Tilly, C. (1978). *From Mobilization to Revolution*. Reading, Addison-Wesley Publishing Company.

Tilly, C. (1992). War and the International System, 1900–1992. CSSC Working Paper.

UNICEF (n.d.) "At a Glance, Egypt." Online, available at: www.unicef.org/infobycountry/egypt.html.

Vatikiotis, P. J. (1983). "Religion and State," in G. Warburg and U. Kupferschimdt (eds.), *Islam, Nationalism, and Radicalism in Egypt and the Sudan*. New York, Praeger.

Vatikiotis, P. J. (1987). *Islam and the State*. London, Croom Helm.

Warburg, G. and U. Kupferschimdt (1983). *Islam, Nationalism, and Radicalism in Egypt and the Sudan*. New York, Praeger Publishers.

Weber, M. (1965). *The Sociology of Religion*. London, Methuen.

Weedon, C. (1987). *Feminist Practice and Poststructuralist Theory*. Oxford, Basil Blackwell.

Whittier, N. (1995). *Feminist Generation: The Persistence of the Radical Women's Movement*. Philadelphia, Temple Books.

Wilcox, C. and L. Sigelman (2001). "Political Mobilization in the Pews: Religious Contacting and Electoral Turnout." *Social Science Quarterly* 82(3): 524–535.

Williams, R. (1994). "Movement Dynamics and Social Change: Transforming Fundamentalist Ideology and Organizations," in M. E. Marty and R. S. Appleby (eds), *Accounting for Fundamentalisms: The Dynamic Character of Movements*. Chicago, University of Chicago Press, vol. 4, pp. 785–834.

Wilson, B. (1982). *Religion in Sociological Perspective*. Oxford, Oxford University Press.

Wilson, T. C. (1994). "Trends in Tolerance Toward Rightist and Leftist Groups, 1976–1988: Effects of Attitude Change and Cohort Succession." *The Public Opinion Quarterly* 58(4): 539–556.

Yadlin, R. (1983). "Militant Islam in Egypt: Some Sociocultural Aspects," in G. Warburg and U. Kupferschimdt (eds.), *Islam, Nationalism, and Radicalism in Egypt and the Sudan*. New York, Praeger.

Yishai, Y. (1987). *Land or Peace: Whither Israel?* Palo Alto, Hoover Institution Press.

Zertal, I. and A. Eldar (2007). *Lords of the Land: the War over Israel's Settlements in the Occupied Territories 1967–2007*. New York, Nation Books.

Zimbardo, P. (2007). *The Lucifer Effect: Understanding How Good People Turn Evil*. New York, Random House.

Index